Everything and Nothing

Everything and Nothing

Markus Gabriel

Graham Priest

polity

Copyright © Markus Gabriel and Graham Priest 2022

The right of Markus Gabriel and Graham Priest to be identified as Authors of this Work has been asserted in accordance with the UK Copyright, Designs and Patents Act 1988.

First published in 2022 by Polity Press

Polity Press
65 Bridge Street
Cambridge CB2 1UR, UK

Polity Press
111 River Street
Hoboken, NJ 07030, USA

All rights reserved. Except for the quotation of short passages for the purpose of criticism and review, no part of this publication may be reproduced, stored in a retrieval system or transmitted, in any form or by any means, electronic, mechanical, photocopying, recording or otherwise, without the prior permission of the publisher.

ISBN-13: 978-1-5095-3746-4
ISBN-13: 978-1-5095-3747-1 (pb)

A catalogue record for this book is available from the British Library.

Library of Congress Control Number: 2022934661

Typeset in 10.5 on 12pt Sabon LT Pro
by Cheshire Typesetting Ltd, Cuddington, Cheshire
Printed and bound in Great Britain by TJ Books Ltd, Padstow, Cornwall

The publisher has used its best endeavours to ensure that the URLs for external websites referred to in this book are correct and active at the time of going to press. However, the publisher has no responsibility for the websites and can make no guarantee that a site will remain live or that the content is or will remain appropriate.

Every effort has been made to trace all copyright holders, but if any have been overlooked the publisher will be pleased to include any necessary credits in any subsequent reprint or edition.

For further information on Polity, visit our website:
politybooks.com

Contents

Preface		vi
Introduction *Laureano Ralón*		1

I Essays
1. Everything and Nothing *Graham Priest* — 19
2. Is There Such a Thing as Everything? *Markus Gabriel* — 39
3. Some Thoughts on Everything *Graham Priest* — 69
4. Some Thoughts on "Some Thoughts on Everything" (Which Are Not about Everything) *Markus Gabriel* — 83

II Bonn Discussions *Markus Gabriel and Graham Priest*
5. Existence — 99
6. Intentionality — 110
7. Non-Wellfoundedness — 120
8. Everything, Nonsense, and Wittgenstein — 128
9. Nothingness — 138

III Postscript *Gregory S. Moss*
10. Transcending Everything — 153

References and Bibliography — 190
Index — 198

Preface

This book had its origin when Markus Gabriel (MG) invited Graham Priest (GP) to give the Ernst Robert Curtius Lecture at the University of Bonn in November 2017. The recording of the lecture found its way onto the internet.[1] Laureano Ralón saw it and suggested that it might form the beginning of a discussion between us on the matters raised, which could be turned into a book. He kindly offered to be involved in the realization of the project. This book is the result.

The Introduction is by Laureano. Chapter 1 is the written-up version of the original lecture. Chapters 2, 3, and 4, written respectively by MG, GP, and MG, continue the discussion. These form Part I of the book. Philosophical discussions are often most productive when pursued face to face. So, in August 2021, GP visited MG in Bonn, where we spent a week together in order to explore further the dialectical space of matters. Part II comprises edited versions of the discussions that took place. Finally, we thought that an essay by Gregory Moss might be an appropriate capping stone for the discussion, since he is familiar with both our works but has his own take on matters. Happily, he agreed to write such an essay, and this forms Part III of the book.

Laureano and Greg both have distinctive views on the matters of the book, and the fact that we include them here does not necessarily imply that we agree with them. Indeed, it will probably be clear that in places we do not. However, we welcome their perspectives on matters and are grateful to them for the roles they have played in bringing this book into existence. As will be even more clear, we do not always reach agreement with each other, but such is philosophy; and it has been a pleasure for each of us to engage with the thought of the other.

We thank Philipp Bohlen, Alexander Englander, and Jan Voosholz for their tremendous help during the editing process and for their

---

[1] www.youtube.com/watch?v=66enDcUQUK0&t=2s.

inputs to our discussions. Moreover, MG thanks his team (in addition to the ones already mentioned: Charlotte Gauvry, Laura Michler, Joline Kretschmer and Jens Rometsch) for their philosophical contributions to the detailed debates we had about MG's chapters during the writing process. Laura Michler and Joline Kretschmer also helped with the editing process of those chapters. We owe thanks to the University of Bonn, in particular to the International Centre for Philosophy for supporting this project with funding for the Curtius lecture as well as for GP's visit in August 2021. This would not have been possible without the help of MG's assistant, Annette Feder, who made sure that our meetings could safely take place under the complicated conditions of an ongoing pandemic.

Last but not least, we would like to thank John Thompson from Polity Press for his enthusiasm for this project and his ongoing support.

Markus Gabriel, Bonn,
Graham Priest, New York,
January 2022

Introduction
Laureano Ralón

This volume gathers together writings by two of the most ingenious living philosophers of our time. Markus Gabriel and Graham Priest need no introduction, but the circumstances that brought them together and, by implication, my own involvement in this project need to be made explicit. I came up with the basic idea and format of this book after watching Priest's Robert Curtius Lecture of Excellence on the subject of "everything and nothing," delivered at the University of Bonn's International Center of Philosophy in the fall of 2017. At the time, I had just completed the required coursework for my PhD and was travelling through Europe as an exchange student, attending as many advanced graduate seminars as I could in ontology and metaphysics. These were being taught by a new generation of realist and materialist philosophers (Quentin Meillassoux, Maurizio Ferraris and Graham Harman, among others), all of whom were widely regarded as challenging the anti-realist, phenomenological and postmodern heritage of twentieth-century continental philosophy – an orthodoxy that has been referred to as a "well-entrenched mixture of phenomenological subjectivism, post-Foucaultian systematic genealogical skepticism and late-Derridean exasperated textualism."[1] It was during that trip that I met Gabriel in person at a talk he gave at the University of Paris (Panthéon-Sorbonne), where he discussed what is arguably his most systematic book, *Fields of Sense: A New Realist Ontology*.[2] As for Priest, I discovered his groundbreaking work in logic and metaphysics shortly afterwards, when I was trying to figure out the meaning of Meillassoux's "contradictory entity," an enigmatic concept he introduces in *After Finitude: An Essay on the Necessity of Contingency*. Meillassoux writes:

> As contradictory, this entity is always-already whatever it is not. Thus, the introduction of a contradictory entity into being would result in the

---
[1] Gironi (2018), p. 12.
[2] Gabriel (2015a).

implosion of the very idea of determination – of being such and such, of being this rather than that. Such an entity would be tantamount to a "black hole of differences", into which all alterity would be irremediably swallowed up, since the being-other of this entity would be obliged, simply by virtue of being other than it, *not* to be other than it.[3]

What was this entity which was said to be every single thing *and* nothing in particular, an illogical *something* that seemed to defy ontological classification? And how was it different from Priest's own account of nothing(ness), which he likewise defined as a paradoxical yet not completely illogical entity – both an object and the absence of all objects?

In 2018, I had a chance to interview Priest for the website www.figureground.org, motivated by these and other questions concerning his novel take on such fundamental issues as everything, nothing, the nature of objects, and their mereological sum or fusion via "gluons" – a metaphysical entity I had never heard of before, but which seemed to play an indispensable role in his ontological system. In addition to discussing different aspects of his work and thought, we addressed contemporary developments in so-called continental realism,[4] zooming in on Markus Gabriel's fields-of-sense ontology. Off the record, we also touched on the meaning of Meillassoux's contradictory entity, with Priest making the important observation that Meillassoux never actually endorses the possibility of a contradictory object in *After Finitude*. Indeed, he does quite the opposite: for the French philosopher, a truly contradictory entity is inconceivable in the context of his ontological materialism, which embraces radical contingency while affirming the principle of identity in order to differentiate his own take on speculation from earlier approaches that took the form of differential process ontologies. This is why Meillassoux also writes that,

> Accordingly, real contradiction can in no way be identified with the thesis of universal becoming, for in becoming, things must be this, *then* other than this; they are, *then* they are not. This does not involve *any* contradiction, since the entity is never simultaneously this and its opposite, existent and non-existent. A really illogical entity consists rather in the systematic destruction of the minimal conditions for all becoming – it suppresses the dimension of alterity required for the deployment of any process whatsoever, liquidating it in the formless being which must always already be what it is not.[5]

---

[3] Meillassoux (2008), p. 70.
[4] Ennis (2011).
[5] Meillassoux (2008), p. 70.

Strictly speaking, Meillassoux's contradictory entity is not an object but a limit concept introduced from a negative heuristic to set the limits of his speculative enterprise, which, as I understand it, should be interpreted not as a form of materialism but as a study of modality.[6] By contrast, Priest's conception of nothing(ness) as a paradoxical entity which is simultaneously an object *and* the absence of all objects is presented as a *true contradiction* and as the *ground of reality*. In other words, the ground of reality for Priest is neither a super-chaotic and hyper-contingent Great Outdoors (Meillassoux), nor a primordial flux of vital becoming (Bergson), nor an aesthetic realm of intensive processes (Whitehead), virtual multiplicities or larval subjects (Deleuze). Instead, the ground of reality is nothing(ness) understood as a truly contradictory entity – an entity which does not exist because it is not embedded in the spatio-temporal and causal nexus but nevertheless possesses a reality of its own: *the reality that makes it what it is*. If, with the notion of hyper-chaos, Meillassoux sought to differentiate his philosophy not only from the above-mentioned Heideggerian/Derridean orthodoxy but also from its more affirmative and crypto-vitalistic alternative (the kind of relational/dynamic metaphysics introduced by Bergson and Whitehead and perfected by Deleuze and Latour), in Priest we find a "persistence of the negative"[7] that returns him anew to the Kant–Hegel–Heidegger axis that earlier analytic philosophers – following in the footsteps of Moore and Russell – had rejected at the turn of the twentieth century. More importantly for our purposes, Priest's emphasis on nothing(ness) brings him in close proximity to the New Realism of Gabriel, which, unlike other forms of continental realism, is heavily influenced by German idealism and Husserlian/Heideggerian phenomenology.

Although Gabriel and Priest had already exchanged views informally on the subject of everything and nothing, the Figure/Ground interview served as an important catalyst for the present book. One of the most compelling aspects of the Figure/Ground repository is that it is more than a mere aggregate of interviews. In fact, the collection is more like a sum or fusion in the technical sense utilized by Priest, with each entry referring to other entries to form a network that exhibits a certain diachronicity. Interestingly enough, during our conversation Priest expressed the need for further dialogue across the continental-analytic divide, confessing to be surprised that the continental realism with which Gabriel and Meillassoux are associated rarely alludes to

---

[6] Sachs (2018).
[7] Noys (2010).

the fact that so-called analytic philosophers reacted against this anti-realism much earlier. This was a provocative remark, to which we should add that the name itself – "New Realism" – was borrowed more or less consciously from a very specific Anglo-American development. In "A Brief History of New Realism," Maurizio Ferraris – the other founding member of twenty-first-century New Realism – traces the origins of the turn to six American philosophers who, back in the 1910s, called themselves the "New Realists," namely, Walter Taylor Marvin, Ralph Barton Perry, Edward Gleason Spaulding, Edwin Bissel Holt, William Pepperell Montague, and Walter Boughton Pitkin:

> These names are unlikely to ring a bell to the reader – which speaks for the little success of the movement. New Realism had no Bertrand Russell nor any Wittgenstein or Moore. In the successive phase of "critical realism", it had Lovejoy, Santayana, and Sellars (Roy Wood, father of the more famous Wilfrid Sellars), but the philosophical mainstream went along with analytic philosophy, which seemed to envisage a stronger break and more interesting new approaches.[8]

A few comments about this passage are in order. First, the New Realists of the early twentieth century were not doing analytic or scientific metaphysics but, rather, philosophy of perception; they were arguing with British Idealists such as T. H. Green, F. H. Bradley, and Bernard Bosanquet about whether the content of perceptual episodes was confined to the mind. Second, Ferraris's conclusion that the New Realists became extinct with the advent of the linguistic turn is a little too hasty. Although it is true that, on some narratives, New Realism was abandoned because it embraced a very demanding version of perceptual realism (one requiring that hallucinations and illusions be just as real as veridical perceptions), we should not forget that the New Realists did strongly influence the ecological psychology of J. J. Gibson, who in turn influenced Hubert Dreyfus's highly influential reading of Heidegger. From there to Harman's object-oriented philosophy there are but a few steps. As for the "interesting new approaches" alluded to by Ferraris, in the Figure/Ground interview Priest himself identified a strong theme of realism in analytic philosophy throughout the twentieth century. The resurgence of realism in analytic metaphysics that Priest refers to is most likely the realism in the 1970s of Kripke, David Lewis, and David Armstrong, who in a way were rejecting the anti-realism of Carnap, Quine, and Nelson Goodman.

[8] Ferraris (2016), p. 593.

Beyond this trajectory, however, there is an "undercurrent" in analytic philosophy, somewhat occluded from view by the empiricist surface of analytic philosophy, which Robert Brandom associates with a "Neo-Kantian tradition" comprising David Lewis, Rudolf Carnap, Wilfrid Sellars, and John McDowell. As Brandom sees it, the narrative of the history of analytic philosophy initiated by Moore and Russell, according to which the movement was given its characteristic defining shape as a recoil from Hegel (a certain Hegel – one seen through the lenses of the British Idealism), necessitated a concomitant rejection of Kant, since these thinkers "understood enough about the Kantian basis of Hegel's thought to know that a *bolus bolus* rejection of Hegel required a diagnosis of the idealist rot as having set in already with Kant."[9] Now, for Brandom, this narrative picks out but one current in the analytic river; it does not reflect the whole story, and I tend to agree with him. Although Priest's background is in logic, he can be said to join Sellars, Brandom, and McDowell in the rediscovery of Kant and Hegel that took place in analytic philosophy during the second half of the twentieth century,[10] and I cannot emphasize strongly enough that this is one aspect of his philosophical orientation – together with his interest in oriental thought – that renders the conversation with Gabriel and the new German philosophy so fruitful. For, unlike Meillassoux, Harman, and Ferraris, Gabriel does not think that we need to combat Kantian correlationism in order to combat anthropocentrism and embrace a realist conception of sense. The complementarity of sentience and sapience, sensibility and understanding, is ineliminable for both Gabriel and Priest, even though they both try to overcome traditional (Aristotelian) and modern (Kantian) metaphysics and salvage the role of philosophical speculation by exploring what lies beyond the limits of human cognition. It is this basic tacit agreement that the Kantian revolution constitutes a point of no return for philosophy that makes it possible for them to converse and disagree in meaningful and constructive ways.

Later in the Figure/Ground interview, Priest had a chance to address Gabriel directly:

What's your take on Markus Gabriel's fields-of-sense ontology?
I'm very sympathetic to the idea that everything is what it is by being in a network (field, if you like) in which it relates to other things. That's very similar to Markus' view, I think – though I am coming at it from Mahayana Buddhist views concerning emptiness. There is

[9] Brandom (2015), p. 34.
[10] Redding (2007).

one important difference between us here, though. Markus takes these fields to be local: there are many relatively autonomous fields. I think that in the last instance there is one single field. This is essentially the Chinese Huayan Buddhist version of the Indian view. (All these things are explained in Part 3 of my book *One* (OUP, 2014).) Another difference between us is that Markus holds that there is no world, i.e., no sum of everything. I think there is: it is simply the mereological whole comprising all objects (as I explained in the Bonn lecture). Essentially, Markus infers his view (though not explicitly) from the claim that the proper parthood relation cannot be antisymmetric. I think it can be.[11]

At stake is the difference between a radical ontological pluralism (Gabriel's position) that is completely disconnected from the dualistic Parmenidean heritage systematized by Plato and Aristotle – a universe where there is technically neither everything nor nothing(ness) but an ever expanding in-between consisting of objects appearing in fields nested in other fields in an infinite regress of sense – *and* a pluralistic monism (Priest's position) in which objects fuse together with other objects to create ever larger mereological sums that top out at the mega-object "everything," which paradoxically can be part of itself due to a *principle of symmetry*. I will do my best to unpack these two positions in just a moment, but first I should say a little more about how this project came into being.

Given the passage I have just quoted, the next logical step after the Priest interview (which to date remains one of the most widely read Figure/Ground entries) was to approach Gabriel and invite him to respond in the spirit of good conversation. Gabriel accepted right away. However, I immediately realized that an in-depth discussion about such fundamental metaphysical categories as everything and nothing(ness) deserved a more comprehensive back-and-forth than the Figure/Ground environment could afford. Against my better judgment, the sensible alternative was to revert to the gold standard and propose a collaborative volume taking the form of a polemic in which the two philosophers would have a chance to exchange their views and address/criticize their respective ontological commitments at some length. To my surprise, our protagonists welcomed the idea enthusiastically, and in no time we had signed a contract with Polity Press, which now delivers a fine edition aptly titled *Everything and Nothing*.

Having an original idea in philosophy is the closest we get to a miracle. Over the past few decades, Gabriel and Priest have made

---

[11] For my interview with Priest, see www.figureground.org.

ground-breaking contributions to a field that is in urgent need of rejuvenation. I believe they managed to do so by strategically situating themselves within a zone of indiscernibility where the borders separating the problematic analytic-continental divide in philosophy tend to soften. "It is agreeable to imagine a future in which the tiresome 'analytic-continental split' is looked back upon as an unfortunate, temporary breakdown of communication," writes Richard Rorty[12] in his introduction to Wilfrid Sellars's *Empiricism and the Philosophy of Mind*. Like Sellars, Rorty, Brandom, and McDowell, Priest is part of a new generation of analytic philosophers that is well read in the work of Kant, Hegel, Heidegger, and the Pragmatist tradition. Similarly, Gabriel is part of a new generation of continental philosophers that is not afraid to engage with their analytic counterparts, aware that both sides of the split share common German roots in the work of Husserl and Frege. If the labels "post-analytic" and "post-continental" mean anything, they serve to emphasize the disposition of philosophers who, like Gabriel and Priest, are willing to meet each other halfway to realize Rorty's vision. However, unlike Rorty and like Sellars, Gabriel and Priest recognize that metaphysics always returns; that any attempt to eliminate its meta-conceptual resources is destined to fail. Although metaphysics had a tough time in the twentieth century, with virtually everybody on both sides of the Atlantic – from phenomenology through pragmatism and logical empiricism to postmodernism – agreeing that it was a lost cause, metaphysics (a certain metaphysics, at least) is now back in fashion. For the consummation of metaphysics, both traditional and modern, does not imply the absolute end of metaphysics. *Something* must take its place as we leave it behind, and, in Gabriel and Priest, we find creative attempts to explore what lies beyond the limits of human thought but always conscious that the main Kantian conquests cannot be relinquished. Above all, metaphysics is ontology and epistemology, for, otherwise, how do we *know* that what we say exists *truly* exists? Ray Brassier expresses this problematic best when he writes:

> Ontology is an attempt to answer the question "What is there?" But this cannot be answered by listing names of entities, for example, "table," "chair," "tree," "Cyprus," "Dante," and "Aeroflot." "Table," "chair," and "tree" are common nouns – that is, names for types of objects. "Cyprus," "Dante," and "Aeroflot" are proper nouns – that is, names for particular objects. Listing nouns, whether names of types

[12] Rorty (1997), p. 12.

or names of particulars, is uninformative because it offers us names without explaining what a name is or how it is related to its nominatum. If ontology is to take the measure of Kant's critique of dogmatic metaphysics, it cannot remain content with conjuring yet another more or less arbitrary account of what there is; it must explain how we *know* what there is.[13]

Although I said at the outset that Gabriel and Priest needed no introduction, I believe the main challenge for readers of a book like this is to determine where exactly each thinker stands on the various issues beings discussed, especially as philosophical lines are constantly being redrawn in the new century and historical metaphysics is slowly being replaced by *something* else. In what follows, I provide some basic pointers to orientate the reader, and I will do so by situating the exchange between Gabriel and Priest against the background of recent developments in continental philosophy.

The first hypothesis that I would like to suggest is that, when our protagonists refer to everything and nothing(ness), they do so with an eye on what lies between these two poles: mainly objects but also facts, fields of sense, gluons, and so on. It is important not to lose sight of this "in-between" because all along there is a sense in which everything (the most general metaphysical category) and nothing (the most empty metaphysical category) connect on some level. And, if they do connect, it is partly because both thinkers follow Heidegger in conceiving of *nothing* as *something* that is more interesting than just *nothingness* understood as the ineffable, the absolute absence of objects, or what we get when we remove all things and are left with nothing. In modern Western philosophy the concept of nothingness is typically associated with Hegel, although I should point out that, in the Transcendental Analytic, Kant offers an interesting and little discussed "table of nothing," in which he makes a valiant effort to think through the intricacies of nothingness. Kant begins by observing that his discussion of the concept "nothing," though "not in itself especially indispensable, nevertheless may seem requisite for the completeness of the system."[14] He then constructs a fourfold table of nothing where the notion takes the form of 1) an empty concept without an object (*ens rationis*), 2) an empty object of a concept (*nihil privativium*), 3) an empty object without a concept (*nihil negativium*), and 4) an empty intuition without an object (*ens imaginarium*). Kant writes:

---

[13] Brassier (2013), p. 102.
[14] Kant (1998), A290.

One sees that the thought-entity (No. 1) is distinguished from the non-entity (No. 4) by the fact that the former may not be counted among the possibilities because it is a mere invention (although not self-contradictory), whereas the latter is opposed to possibility because even its concept cancels itself out. Both, however, are empty concepts. The nihil privatium (No. 2) and the ens imaginarium (No. 3), on the contrary, are empty *data* for concepts. If light were not given to the senses, then one would also not be able to represent darkness, and if extended beings were not perceived, one would not be able to represent space. Negation as well as the mere form of intuition are, without something real, not objects.[15]

An in-depth discussion of Kant's table of nothing is well beyond the scope of this introduction. What is important to note, for our purposes, is that both Gabriel and Priest are much more liberal and democratic than Kant was in terms of the kinds of entities that can be *bona fide* objects (unicorns, Peter Pan, Sherlock Holmes, etc.). Whereas Kant applies the category of nothing to a series of intangible, impossible, and imaginary entities such as shadows, squared circles, and so on, for Gabriel and Priest these are perfectly good objects insofar as they can appear in specific fields of sense or else be the correlates of an intentional state. In a way, Kant not only degrades certain objects (such as shadows) by turning them into nothingness; he also degrades "nothing" by inadvertently turning it into *something*.

Fundamentally, the problem with Kant's table of nothing is that it approaches the issue by way of marginal objects, things that in his view are not part of possible experience, since only objects of sensibility – phenomenal appearances that are encountered in space and time and can be subsumed under empirical concepts and general categories – technically exist for him. Of course, Gabriel would oppose this on the grounds that it suffices for an object to appear in a field of sense in order for it to exist, and Priest would oppose it by stating that there *are* non-existing objects which are perfectly good objects, even though they do not exist insofar as they lack causal efficacy.

Unlike Kant and Hegel, Priest follows in the footsteps of Heidegger and asks whether the nothing can be conceived in a way that is neither nothingness nor an impossible object. Is there a nothing *qua* object in addition the ineffable nothingness? This is a question that Priest – and to some extent also Gabriel – is willing to entertain, although both come at it from slightly different angles as result of their respective

---

[15] Kant (1998), B349.

ontological commitments. For Gabriel, the nothing is a limit concept much in the same way as Meillassoux's contradictory entity is a limit concept. We catch a glimpse of the "nothing" as distinct from nothingness when we try to think about the "world" *qua* mega-object or all-encompassing totality, which does not and cannot exist. For the world to exist it would have to constitute itself as the field of sense of all fields of senses, which is impossible in a truly pluralistic universe disconnected from the Parmenidean axis. For Priest, on the other hand, the mega-object everything is an object like any other, albeit one as paradoxical as the object "nothing" insofar as everything can be a proper part of itself.

The second hypothesis that I would like to suggest is a little more controversial, namely, that Gabriel and Priest not only try to rethink metaphysics in a post-metaphysical context; they also provide important resources for to rethink *flat ontology* in the aftermath of the realist/speculative turn in post-continental philosophy. I acknowledge that the idea is not entirely original since, in a chapter provocatively titled "How Flat Can Ontology Be?," Gabriel had already addressed the principle of flat ontology at some length, claiming that "what DeLanda describes is rather a flat metaphysics than a flat ontology."[16] Briefly, the term "flat ontology" was popularized in the new century by Manuel DeLanda and Graham Harman as a basic tenet of their respective ontological systems. In assemblage theory and object-oriented philosophy, the term became synonymous with a non-hierarchical, horizontal and unilateral ontology without epistemology, part of a more general move to combat the asymmetry of anthropocentrism by rejecting the epistemic correlation associated with Kantian transcendentalism. In DeLanda's pioneering attempt to devise a naturalized assemblage theory, the parts of a whole (what he sometimes calls the "material" and "symbolic components" of the assemblage) are said to interact with each other through *relations of exteriority* which, unlike relations of interiority, are said to be *obligatorily contingent* rather than *logically necessary*. As such, these relations articulate or express a more fundamental solidarity among things that in a way serves to invert the tired postmodern "motto" that the whole is larger than the sum of its parts – or what DeLanda calls the "organismic metaphor."[17] One consequence of this is that the parts are regarded as greater than the whole, since every individual component is not exhausted by the place it occupies in that whole but withdraws or withholds a surplus in reserve like the potentialities of an untapped oil field.

---

[16] Gabriel (2015a), p. 9.
[17] DeLanda (2006), p. 8.

The important thing to note is that, in the context of this anti-anthropocentric move, objects are conceived no longer as intentional objects or objects-for-consciousness, the correlations of intentional states, but as *objects-for-themselves*, autonomous units that are irreducible upward to their relations with other objects (overmining) and downward to their most fundamental components and micro-processes (undermining). If phenomenology attempts to explain the mind in terms of the mind itself – that is, without any scientistic attempts to reduce consciousness to its material neurological base or microphysical brain processes – then Harman's own version of flat ontology – his object-oriented radicalization of Heideggerian phenomenology – constitutes an attempt to explain objects as being just themselves in a world without human spectators. Suddenly, there were "objects everywhere,"[18] and every single thing in the universe, both human and inhuman, was considered to be an object at the most fundamental (ontological) level. Unlike idealist and constructivist subject-oriented philosophies, object-oriented ontology was said to be not only *flat* but also *democratic* since, again, every single thing in the universe was reconceived as an object and all objects were meant to be equally objects. Objects *qua* objects were capable of interacting and communicating among themselves at the ontological level through basic (neither cognitive nor causal) mechanisms that did not necessitate the conceptual resources of the human understanding; nor were they determined by the physical micro-processes we associate with nature. Objects-for-themselves – by virtue of being objects and nothing more – created networks and assemblages that replicated themselves while simultaneously and paradoxically withdrawing into themselves to become generative mechanisms, a kind of executant or infra-reality responsible for what took place in the realm of experience, namely, the emanation of caricatures or sensual façades (which has more to do with the objectivation of phenomena than with the subjectivation of appearances by a human subject).

These early expressions of continental realism were extremely controversial and caught on only in specialized fields and sub-fields such as architecture, media studies, and literary criticism. Within philosophy proper, however, they were subject to harsh criticism. Although Gabriel's field of sense ontology emerged against the background of the speculative turn associated with Meillassoux, Harman, DeLanda, and Ferraris – and to this day Gabriel defends a realist conception of sense, claiming among other things that existence *qua* "appearing is

[18] Žižek (2016).

fairly inhuman"[19] – his own version of "New Realism" does not constitute a dogmatic regress to a substantialist or unilateral ontology; nor does his philosophy propose a thoroughly revisionist process metaphysics such as that of Whitehead or Deleuze. To be sure, Gabriel's ontology is flat not because it rejects epistemology in favor of a more originary domain that is neither the logical space of reasons, nor the natural space of causes, nor the phenomenological space of motivations. After all, he is well aware that metaphysics is both ontology and epistemology even as he tries to defend a realist conception of sense. Instead, a close look at his *metametaphysics* reveals that, in addition to objects appearing in fields of sense, there are facts and a global sense of the situation. Hence, a basic epistemic dimension is contemplated by Gabriel, albeit one that has been unmoored from the human subject. To exist is to appear in a field of sense under a certain mode of presentation or arrangement, which is not strictly or exclusively phenomenological, for numbers and other abstract entities can appear without this implying a phenomenal appearance tied to human sensibility, just as subatomic "particles" can appear in (be detected by) particle accelerators without strictly speaking displaying a phenomenal component consisting of secondary qualities akin to human sensory consciousness. In essence, Gabriel's metametaphysics is flat not because it rejects epistemology to propose a world without spectators but because it refuses to partition the universe into a manifest image and a scientific image of humanity in the world – each with their respective ontologies corresponding roughly to perceptual and theoretical knowledge. For Gabriel, fields of sense are found all across the universe and permeate all levels of reality, with human consciousness offering but a more complex type. Thus, for Gabriel,

> An ontology is *flat* as opposed to *hierarchical* if it unifies all objects insofar as they exist. A flat ontology claims that all objects are equal insofar as they are objects or that all fields of sense are equal insofar as they are fields of sense. In other words, flat ontology resists the idea of a governing principle that unifies all objects.[20]

Instead of object–object relations articulated by permanently unobservable and undetectable metaphysical mechanisms such as *emanation*, *allure*, and *sincerity*, Gabriel's neutral realism claims that the universal glue that makes things hang together is *sense*. And sense is for Gabriel roughly what "gluons" are for Priest. These are the in-between, the universal cement that holds objects and fields and facts

---

[19] Gabriel (2015a), p. 166.
[20] Gabriel (2015a), p. 9.

together. Yet, unlike facts, sense and gluons are part of the structure of the real, as opposed to the formal structures of our thought about the real.

At first sight, to claim that to exist is to appear in a field of sense structured by facts and a global sense of the situation, or to say that to exist is to be an object or a mereological sum of objects fused together by gluons, does not appear to say much. However, that is the price we pay when we do metaphysics. After all, we are concerned with objects in general, not with the specific objects of the specialized sciences. As such, a metaphysical system must be a theory of absolutely everything, and the challenge for the philosopher is to remain consistent throughout such formidable endeavor. For all his originality and inventiveness, Harman's object-oriented philosophy fails to be consistent.[21] His quadruple object scheme – a kind of roadmap to the universe that is supposed to tell us how *all* objects without exception must behave – fails to contemplate how absolutely everything in the universe truly functions. For instance, there are "things" at the subatomic level of reality which are not technically objects and do not behave as such even if we call them "objects" for efficiency's sake. *Pace* Whitehead, the universe is neither atomistic nor anthropomorphic, and the middle-sized dry goods that Harman takes as the starting point of his ontology (tables, chairs, armies, etc.) are but a perspective on the universe – a very anthropocentric perspective.

Gabriel and Priest, on the other hand, can speak consistently about objects because, in their view, objects are not metaphysical entities that withdraw or subsist beyond all access and relational contact (cognitive and causal). As we saw earlier, they both recognize that Kant's Copernican revolution sets a point of no return for philosophy, a basic standard for rationality. The transcendental dimension and the epistemic correlation are ineliminable because to perceive something is to perceive something *as* something: a free and reflexive move from the object of representation to the representation of the object. Moreover, as Kant taught us, we can speak meaningfully only about what we encounter in space and time, whereas talk about things in themselves, withdrawn real objects, or subsisting entities presupposes an *aperspectival perspective* – an impossible position. Even Priest, who is quite fond of paradoxes and brought about a revolution in logic by claiming that there are true contradictions and non-existing objects, would not go so far as to toy with dogmatic metaphysics in this way. The kind of paradoxes that he entertains are circumscribed by his logical and ontological commitments, in

[21] Wolfendale (2014).

particular, by the fact that an object is above all an epistemic category: everything we can think of, talk about, refer to, quantify over, and is the correlate of an intentional state. Notice that his definition remains well within the bounds of the Copernican revolution, since, for Kant, let us remember, an object was neither a substance nor a noumenon but an empty form – the sum of the meta-conceptual categories of the understanding.

For Gabriel, on the other hand, neither Harman's nor Priest's definition of the object will do, since to be an object is something which fundamentally precedes the subjectivation of appearances by the human mind. To be an object is above all to appear in a field of sense governed by facts and a global sense of the situation, and none of this is in principle a strictly human activity. Objects can appear in consciousness as correlates of intentional states, but they can also appear in other fields of sense which are not particularly human. This position seems to enlarge the category of object, which is understood no longer as being something that tends to correlate with human subjects but, rather, as a more originary stepping forth governed by sense. The difference, however, is subtle, since Priest technically does not object to the idea that objects are always already part of a background, with nothing(ness) being the ultimate ground of reality. More generally, the two philosophers endorse a realist conception of objects, since objects are not mental representations. Nevertheless, unlike Harman, both Gabriel and Priest offer *relational* definitions of objects to affirm their realism. An object is not in the mind but becomes something meaningful when we think/talk about it, quantify over it, and so on. Similarly, an object can function as a field of sense, but it becomes a proper object when it appears in one.

One final difference between our protagonists that is worth pointing out as I bring this introduction to a close is that Gabriel's ontology can be said to be more *affirmative* than Priest's. Although Gabriel never refers to the ontogenetic processes whereby objects become objects (e.g., Whitehead/Deleuze), sticking to a more strictly phenomenological definition of existence *qua* appearing, his radically pluralistic universe is one in which there is always something new, with fields proliferating without end in an infinite regress of sense. We are always confronted with *something*, which is why nothing(ness) does not carry the same weight for him as it does for Priest. Whereas nothing, for Gabriel, is a limit concept, *something* we catch a glimpse of when we try to think about the world, for Priest, nothing can be *something*, and in this sense at least his philosophy can be said to be more Heideggerian than Gabriel's. This brings us back to the idea of a zone of indiscernibility: there is a becoming analytic in Gabriel and a becoming continental in Priest that renders the divide more obsolete than ever before, opening up the door for new and unprecedented ways of doing philosophy in a century where historical metaphysics is being replaced by *something* yet to be determined.

Part I
Essays

I

Everything and Nothing

Graham Priest

1.1 Introduction

Everything – the totality (in some sense of totality) of all things – and nothing(ness) – the absence of all things – are strange objects. They certainly court paradox in various ways. And many philosophers, whether for this reason or for some other, reject them as objects at all. Or, to put it in a way that is not question-begging: they take the words "everything" and "nothing" either not to be in the category of names or, if they are, not to refer to anything.

In this chapter I will argue that everything and nothing are indeed bona fide objects – though, at least in the case of nothing, this does deliver paradox.

The first part of this chapter is devoted to a discussion of appropriate background matters. We will need to look at the question of what objects are, at matters mereological, and at the words "everything" and "nothing" themselves. After that, we will look at everything, and at some of the reasons that have been advanced against it. I will then turn to the much more contentious issue of nothing. I will argue that it is indeed a paradoxical object – both an object and not, both ineffable and not – but one which, in a sense to be made clear, is the ground of reality.[1]

1.2 Background

1.2.1 Objects

First, then, what is an object? An object is the kind of thing that one can name, be the subject of predication, be quantified over, be the object of an intentional mental state. Thus, Australia is an object,

---

[1] This is an expanded version of the Ernst Robert Curtius Lecture, given at the University of Bonn, November 2017.

since one can refer to it by the name "Australia." It is an object, since one can say "Australia has six states," so predicating "has six states" of it. It is an object, since one can quantify over *it*, as in saying that some continents (such as Australia) are entirely in the southern hemisphere. And Australia is an object, since one can think about it, wish one were *there*, and so on.

In what follows, it will be useful to have some appropriate symbolism. Let me use Gx for "x is an object" ("G" is for *Gegenstand*). Gx can be defined in a very simple way:

- $Gx := \mathfrak{S}y \; y = x$

To be an object is simply for there to be something which is identical to it or, more simply, to be something.

A word on notation. I follow the convention of Priest (2016) here and use $\mathfrak{A}$ and $\mathfrak{S}$ for the universal and particular quantifiers, respectively. $\mathfrak{A}$ is read *all*. $\mathfrak{S}$ is read *some*. It is not to be read as *some existent* or *there exists*. The reason for this will soon become clear.

Now, given that $x = x$ is a logical truth, so are $\mathfrak{S}y \; y = x$ and $\mathfrak{A}x\mathfrak{S}y \; y = x$. That is $\mathfrak{A}xGx$: everything is an object – or, given the standard relation between the universal and the particular quantifiers, $\neg\mathfrak{S}x \neg Gx$: nothing is not an object. No surprises here.

Next, note that some objects do not exist: Sherlock Holmes, Zeus, Vulcan (the sub-Mercurial planet whose existence was postulated in the late nineteenth century to explain the precession of Mercury's perihelion). Clearly, these can all be named; I have just named them. One can predicate things of them: Sherlock Holmes is a fictional detective (or even: Sherlock Holmes does not exist). One can quantify over them "Some objects that occur in works of fiction actually existed" (e.g., Napoleon); some did not (e.g., Sherlock Holmes); some things do not exist (e.g., Vulcan). They can be the objects of intentional states: the Homeric Greeks worshipped Zeus; anyone who reads Conan Doyle's stories thinks about Sherlock Holmes. By all the criteria of objecthood, then, some objects are non-existent. This is a view which may be called, following the late Richard Sylvan, *noneism*.

Given noneism, if one wants to attribute existence to an object, one may employ a one-place predicate, "x exists"; Ex, which *pace* the way that Kant is usually (mis)interpreted, is a perfectly good one-place predicate. In particular, if one wants to say that there exists something that satisfies the condition $A(x)$, one can say $\mathfrak{S}x(Ex \land A(x))$.[2]

---

[2] Noneism is discussed and defended at length in Priest (2016).

Note also that, given this notion of objecthood, if n is any meaningful noun phrase, it refers, since there are grammatical (and true) sentences of the form "I am thinking of n", "n is self-identical", etc.).

1.2.2 Mereology

The next preliminary topic is that of mereology. This is the study of the relationship between parts and wholes. In contemporary philosophy, the study of this was introduced by Edmund Husserl and, as a formal theory, by the Polish logician Stanisław Leśnewski. It is now a well-studied part of formal logic.[3]

Many things have parts. Books have chapters; symphonies have movements; people have arms and legs (etc.); (some) countries have states. We would not normally think of the whole as a part of itself, but it does no harm to do so, as a sort of limit case – an improper part. Parts that are not the whole – or the empty part, which is usually ignored in standard mereology; I will come back to this – may be called *proper parts*. So let us write $x < y$ for "x is proper part of y.". We may then define "x is a (non-null) part of y" as $x \leq y$, where:

- $x \leq y := x < y \lor x = y$

Next, we need the notion of an overlap. When does one object overlap another? When they have a part (maybe the whole itself) in common. Thus, the time of the Western Roman Empire and the first millennium have a part in common (the time from 0 CE until the collapse of the empire). Turkey and Europe overlap, since they have a part in common (the part of Turkey in the Balkans). And Great Britain and England overlap, since they have a part in common, viz., England. So if we write "x overlaps y" as $x \bigcirc y$, this may be defined as follows:

- $x \bigcirc y := \mathfrak{S}z(z \leq x \land z \leq y)$

I note *en passant* that there is a question as to whether the identity of two objects can be defined in terms of a relationship between their parts. A standard answer is that it can be: two objects are the same if they overlap exactly the same things. This cannot hold if $<$ does not satisfy anti-symmetry. In that case we may just have to use a more generic criterion of identity, such as having all properties in common.

We must next look at the notion of a mereological *sum*, or *fusion*. The mereological sum of a bunch of objects is the whole which you

---

[3] For a survey of the subject, see Varzi (2009). Unless a separate reference is given, details of all the claims made about mereology in what follows can be found here.

get when you put those things together. Thus, the sum of my parts (my arms, my legs, etc.) is me. Australia has six states.[4] The sum of their geographical masses is the geographical mass of Australia. Beethoven's 9th Symphony has four movements; and their sum is the symphony itself.

Now, when does a bunch of things have a sum? In the examples given, it seems clear that the objects in question (my members, the states of Australia, the movements of the 9th Symphony) have a sum: the objects in question. Some philosophers hold that *every* bunch of objects has a sum. This is at least a simple view; but it has some odd consequences. Consider the objects which are my appendix, left thumb, and right eye ball. Do these have a sum? Certainly not one with a standard name. Or consider the objects which are the Buddha's left earlobe, the rings of Jupiter, and the *Ode to Joy*. Do these have a sum? A number of philosophers would say "no." To have a sum, the objects in question have to have some sort of connection, a certain integrity. They must not be a gerrymandered bunch, as are the examples above. It is remarkably difficult to say exactly what this means, but fortunately we do not have to worry about this here.[5] For, in what follows, the only sums we will meet will not be of this gerrymandered kind.

So suppose that we have a bunch of things, say the things which satisfy some condition, $A(x)$. (Thus, $A(x)$ might be: x *is a state of Australia* or x *is a movement of the 9th Symphony*.) Let us write the sum of the things satisfying $A(x)$ as $\sigma x A(x)$. When does something overlap this? Well, if something overlaps one of the states of Australia, it overlaps Australia; and if it overlaps Australia, it must overlap one of its states. So, in general, something will overlap an object just if it overlaps some part:

- $y \bigcirc \sigma x A(x)$ iff $\mathfrak{S}x(A(x) \wedge x \bigcirc y)$

Indeed, we can characterize the sum of the xs which satisfy $A(x)$ as an object, z, which satisfies this condition:

[S] $\mathfrak{A}y(y \bigcirc z$ iff $\mathfrak{S}x(A(x) \wedge x \bigcirc y))$

Before we leave mereology, there is a subtlety here that should be noted. Whatever the condition $A(x)$ is, $\sigma x A(x)$ is, in fact, a perfectly good object. It has a name, "$\sigma x A(x)$." It can be the object of an inten-

---

[4] Plus a couple of territories; but let us ignore these here.
[5] For discussion and references, see Priest (2014a) and (2014b), 6.8. I note that there are also some philosophers who hold that no bunch of things has a sum – mereological nihilists. I think that this view can be safely ignored here.

tional state. Thus, you can think about it, wonder whether it exists, etc. So the debate about whether or not some things have a sum is not about this.

Some things have the properties they are characterized as having. Thus, if we define an object as one which is a federal capital city and in Australia, this is indeed both a federal capital city and in Australia: it is Canberra. But if we characterize an object as one which is existent and is a goblin, it is not true that this thing is existent and a goblin, since no goblins exist. What is at issue here for a noneist is simply whether a sum does indeed satisfy its characterizing condition, [S]. If the things in question are not gerrymandered, it does. If they are, the point is moot, as noted. However, as also noted, this will not be an issue in what follows.

1.2.3 *Quantifiers and Noun Phrases*

Next, let us turn to the words "everything" and "nothing" themselves. These, and similar "every-" and "no-" words, can be quantifiers. Thus:

- He put everything in the fridge

means:

- $\mathfrak{A}x$(he put x in the fridge)

and:

- There is nothing in the fridge

means:

- For no x (x is in the fridge)

that is:

- $\neg \mathfrak{S}x(x$ is in the fridge)

However, they can also be noun phrases. Thus, suppose that someone is in the midst a crowd. One might say:

- She found herself in the middle of everyone.

This most certainly does not mean:

- $\mathfrak{A}x$(she found herself in the middle of x)

That is, for every person in the crowd she found herself is the middle of that person. It means that she found herself in the middle of the mass of people. That is what "everyone" refers to in this context.

Or, again, consider:

- If everything were something, *it* would be a very strange object.

The "something" is a quantifier, but the "everything" is not, since the "it" refers back to it.

Similarly, when it is claimed that:

- God created the world out of nothing

this most certainly does not mean:

- For no x (God created the world out of x)

since it entails that God created the world, which the latter does not; it would be true if God did not create the world at all. What it means is that there was nothingness, and then (poof!) there was the world. Nothingness is what "nothing" refers to in this context. Again, one might say:

- Hegel and Heidegger wrote about nothing, but they said different things about it.

This does not mean that Hegel and Heidegger never wrote. It means that they wrote about something, namely nothingness (and that they said different things about *it*).

I note that some philosophers have claimed that the word *nothing* can be used only as a quantifier. Thus, Carnap, in a critique of Heidegger, says:[6]

> The construction of sentence (1) ["We seek the Nothing"][7] is simply based on the mistake of employing the word "nothing" as a noun, because in ordinary language it is customary to use it in this form in order to construct negative existential statements.

Carnap is just wrong about this. "Nothing" can be a noun phrase, as we have just seen. And Heidegger is well aware that the word is ambiguous. Thus, in *The Metaphysical Foundations of Logic*, he says:[8]

> "Thinking about nothing" is ambiguous. First of all it can mean "not to think." But logic as the science of thinking obviously never deals with not thinking. Secondly, it can mean "to think nothingness," which

---

[6] Carnap ([1932] 1959), pp. 70f.
[7] This translation already makes the sentence sound strange. A better translation is simply: we seek nothing(ness). German capitalizes all nouns and places a definite article before abstract nouns, where English often has none.
[8] Heidegger (1992), p. 3.

nonetheless means to think "something." In thinking of nothingness, or in the endeavor to think "it," I am thoughtfully related to nothingness, and this is what thinking is about.

Of course, the fact that "nothing" is ambiguous makes for the possibility of amusing puns, as when Lewis Carroll's Alice in *Through the Looking Glass* meets the White King, and he admires her good eyesight when she says that she can see no one on the road.[9]

One more thing about "every-" and "no-" words. When used as quantifiers, these normally have a bounded scope, the bound being determined by the context. Thus suppose that someone has been shopping. When they get home, we might say:

- They put everything in the fridge.

We don't mean that they put literally *everything* in the fridge (the sun, Heidegger, the number π) – just those things that they had bought. Similarly, if they are hungry, they might go to be fridge, only to be disappointed, since:

- There was nothing in the fridge.

Again, we do not mean that there was absolutely *nothing* in the fridge. There was air, bacteria, and maybe a plastic bag. We mean that there was nothing which was edible.

However, we *can* use "every-" and "no-" words with completely unlimited scope. Thus we might say, implausibly:

- Everything can be made the subject of scientific investigation

and mean literally *everything*: the sun, the number π, Heidegger, morality, beauty. Similarly, if I say:

- After you die, you will experience nothing

I mean, quite literally, absolutely nothing at all.

Finally, a world of notation. I will use **e** for the noun phrase *everything*, where the *every* in question has the widest possible scope. It is the object which includes every thing, in a completely unrestricted sense. Similarly, I will use **n** for the noun phrase *nothing*, where the *no* in question has the widest possible scope. It is the object which includes no things, in a completely unrestricted sense.

---

[9] For an erudite and very amusing essay on nothingness, see Heath (1967).

1.3 Everything

So much for the preliminary material. Now let us turn to the first of the two objects in our sights: everything, e. This has a very simple mereological definition:

- e := $\sigma x G x$

e is the mereological sum of all objects – that is, all things. This is certainly no gerrymandered bunch of things, so worries about e satisfying its defining condition do not arise.[10]

Now, there are a number of philosophers who have rejected the object e. One of these is Alain Badiou. In *Being and Event*,[11] he argues that there is no such thing, on the ground that there is no universal set.[12] Now, it is true that there is no universal set in Zermelo–Fraenkel set theory (ZF), which is the orthodox set theory of our day. But there are certainly different set theories in which there is such a set, such as Quine's NF and paraconsistent naive set theories. Moreover, even many orthodox set theorists who deny the existence of a set of all things take there to be such a totality: it is just not a set; it is a proper class.[13]

However, this is really beside the point, because e is not the *set* of all things: it is the *mereological fusion* of all things. A set of things is not the same as their mereological fusion; and a member of a set is not the same as a part of a mereological fusion. The easiest way to see this is to note that, if one takes some object, x, the set of which this is the only member is its singleton, $\{x\}$, an object which is distinct from x. (It has just one member, and x may have many or none. It may not even be a set.) However, if one takes the fusion of a bunch of objects of which there is only one, x, this is x itself.

e is, in fact, a perfectly standard object in mereology. The usual way of proving in ZF that there is no universal set is by showing that, if there were, it would lead to a contradiction, in the form of Russell's paradox. No such paradox besets standard mereology, simply because one can prove that it is consistent. The mereological

---

[10] I note that this leaves open the question of whether or not e is an existent object. It has parts that exist and parts that do not. But what should one say about e itself? Fortunately, the matter does not have to be resolved here.

[11] Badiou (2005).

[12] I take it that what I am calling e is what he calls "the One," a totality of absolutely everything. I note that he does allow for multiplicities in a certain sense. But neither e nor the One – if this is different – is a multiplicity. It is a unity: one single thing.

[13] On these matters, see Holmes (2017) and Priest (2006a), chs 2, 18.

universe simply has the structure of a Boolean Algebra.[14] In particular, it has a top element.

A philosopher who rejects e for much more sophisticated reasons is Markus Gabriel.[15] Gabriel argues that any object can be what it is only by being a part of what he calls a "field of sense." Thus, the opera *Madam Butterfly* can be what it is only because it is in a network of relations to music, composers, singers, audiences, and so on. And an electron can be what it is only because it is in a network of relations to subatomic particles, electrical charges, electroscopes, etc. This is a view with which I have a great deal of sympathy.[16]

Clearly an object is a proper part of its field of sense. So, if we write the field of sense of the object x as $f(x)$, then we have that $x < f(x)$. Now, suppose that there were an object e, the argument goes, then $e < f(e)$. But since $f(e)$ is an object, it must be a part of e, since everything is; indeed, it is a proper part, since it is distinct from e. Hence $f(e) < e$. Putting these two things together, we see that we have a non-well-founded sequence of proper parts:

- ... $< f(e) < e < f(e) < e < ...$

And Gabriel takes this to be impossible.

Now, first, infinitely descending chains of proper parts are quite compatible with standard mereology. Objects which allow for this have now come to be called *gunk*; but there is something special about this particular infinite chain, since it allows for looping. In particular, we have an a and b such that $a < b$ and $b < a$. This is not allowed in standard mereology, which takes anti-symmetry (if $x < y$ then it is not the case that $y < x$) as an axiom.

However, there is a perfectly good mereological theory which allows for loops of this kind. Cotnoir and Bacon give such a theory. Indeed, they show how one can be obtained by taking a standard axiomatization of mereology and simply dropping the anti-symmetry axiom.[17] And, of course, since the standard mereological theory is consistent, the theory obtained by dropping this axiom is also consistent.

There is then, of course, the question of why one should suppose that such a theory is correct; and here one should note that there are

---

[14] Possibly without a bottom element. I will come back to this.
[15] Gabriel ([2013] 2015c), ch. 3, (2015a), ch. 7. I take the following argument from the first of these.
[16] See Priest (2014b), chs 11, 12.
[17] Cotnoir and Bacon (2012), §4.1.

independent reasons as to why one might expect this kind of mereological loop to be possible.

First, there is a beautiful short story by J. L. Borges, "The Aleph."[18] In this story the narrator visits a friend who takes him to a spot in his cellar, *the aleph*, from which a person can see, spread out before them, the whole world. And, of course, in what the narrator sees spread out before him is himself viewing the aleph, in which there is the narrator viewing the aleph, and so on. We have exactly a regress of the kind in question. Of course, this is only a story, but it is a quite coherent one. So it shows that this kind of regress is conceptually possible.[19]

Next, consider, the pair of propositions a and b, which are as follows:

- $a := b$ or snow is white
- $b := a$ or grass is green

How to understand what, exactly, propositions are is a somewhat contentious matter. But there are certainly natural understandings on which the propositions c and d are parts of the proposition $c \vee d$.[20] Given such an analysis, we have the loop:

- $... < a < b < a < b < ...$

And whether or not such an analysis of propositions is right, we see, again, the conceptual possibility of this kind of regress.[21]

The sort of parthood structure involved in Gabriel's situation can be illustrated by a simple model. Let us suppose, for the sake of illustration, that there are, as well as the objects e and $f(e)$, two other objects, a and b. Then, if we write $x \to y$ to indicate that x is a proper part of y, the model can be depicted thus:

$$\begin{array}{c} f(e) \\ \uparrow\downarrow \\ e \\ \nearrow \nwarrow \\ a \quad\quad b \end{array}$$

---

[18] Borges (1971).
[19] There is a similar story in the Buddhist *Huayan Sūtra*. This concerns the Tower of Maitreya. When Sudhana enters the tower, he sees the whole cosmos before him. And part of this is the Tower of Maitreya, containing Sudhana, looking at the cosmos spread out before him, part of which ...
[20] See, e.g., Barwise and Etchemendy (1987), whose account provides for the possibility of this sort of regress. Indeed, that this is so is an integral part of their solution to the liar paradox.
[21] For other examples of the same kind, see Cotnoir and Bacon (2012).

Every object distinct from e is a proper part of it. And e, in turn, is a proper part of f(e).[22]

1.4 Everything and Intentionality

Given the possibility of this kind of mereological structure, then, Gabriel's argument against e fails. However, the situation is worse than this. It is not just that his case against e does not work. The claim that there is no such thing as e faces serious problems of its own.

We seem to say many true things about e, or the world, as Gabriel calls it, and as I will call it for this section. Gabriel himself gives a number of putative examples of such:[23] "the world is not my left hand," "the world is the world," and, indeed, for Gabriel, "the world does not exist." How is this possible if there is no such thing as the world?

Gabriel avers that, despite appearances, the noun phrase "the world" is meaningless,[24] as, then, is any statement about it. Not only does this seem implausible (we appear, after all, to understand the claims in question), but it makes Gabriel's own claim that the world does not exist meaningless.[25]

It would be better to take the name, not to be meaningless, but to have no referent.[26] The question then arises as to how to understand statements that use non-referring names.[27] One solution is to take all such sentences to be false – or, at least, neither true nor false. Perhaps one can bite the bullet here concerning "the world is self-identical," but, again, Gabriel cannot take this strategy, since his own claim is that the world does not exist. His best strategy is, in fact, to take all atomic sentences (that is, sentences without connectives, quantifiers,

---

[22] In (2015a), p. 188, Gabriel does concede that it is possible for a field of sense to be a part of itself. The problem is specifically with f(e). This concession would seem to weaken his case. What is required, if f(e)'s being a proper part of itself cannot be ruled out on general grounds, is an independent justification for the claim that f(e) is different in this regard from any other field of sense. Gabriel says (p. 189) that, if f(e) were part of itself, it would "differ from each and every single thing that is unified by it" – which would have unacceptable consequences. But this is precisely to claim that f(e) is not a proper part of itself, and so begs the question.
[23] Gabriel (2015a), p. 202ff.
[24] Gabriel (2015a), p. 203.
[25] "This chapter is the heart of the matter, and I will argue in some detail that the world does not exist" (Gabriel (2015a), p. 187.)
[26] And perhaps this is what Gabriel means. He makes no explicit distinction between sense and reference.
[27] For the various strategies that may be deployed here, see Priest (2008), 13.4.

or modal operators) to be false and then to apply the standard rules for these constructions. At least, in that way, "the world does not exist" comes out as true (since it is the negation of a false sentence).

The trouble with this strategy is that there seem to be atomic sentences about the world which *are* true – crucially, those that deploy intentional verbs (that is, verbs that record a mental state directed towards an object). Thus, you can think about the world. (You just have.) You can wonder whether it really does exist. (Perhaps you are doing so now.) I (at least) believe in it. And so on. One can even quantify over it, as in "there is something that Priest believes in that Gabriel does not" (viz., the world).

On the present strategy, it has to be maintained that, despite appearances, such claims are false. This is a hard position to sustain. Suppose that I am thinking about the world (as it seems to me). I am certainly in some cognitive state, and one that is much like the one I am in when I'm thinking of Melbourne. It's just that the target of my thought is different. One might claim that I have just misidentified the kind of state that I'm in. And it's true that we do sometimes misidentify what sort of cognitive state we are in. I might believe that I hate someone when what I really experience is love. But, even in this case, there is still an object of my intensional state. With this strategy, I cannot be in any intensional state at all – at least not one with that object – or the problem reappears.

Maybe, then, we have the cognitive state correct but we misidentify its object. It would be somewhat bizarre to hold that, when thinking of the world, I am thing of Melbourne, π, or Markus Gabriel. Perhaps the most plausible suggestion here is that I am thinking, not about the object, but about a representation of the object, such as a word, picture, or concept.[28] Objects and their representations are not the same thing. London is a city; but, whatever it is, a representation of London is not a city: it is a word, picture, thought, etc. Moreover, when I am thinking of an object, I am not thinking of its representation (unless it is the odd kind of object which is its own representation). When I think that London is in the UK, I am not having the thought that a representation of London is in the UK – which may or may not be true, depending on what the representation is. Similarly, when I am thinking about the world, I am not thinking about a representation of the world. I know full well that the world is the mereological sum of everything; it is not a representation. If representations are mereological sums at all, they are not the sum of everything. We seem to be forced, then, to conclude that intentional

---

[28] This is suggested by a remark of Gabriel (2015a), p. 202.

states that appear to be directed at the world really are directed at the world.[29]

Gabriel's attempts to avoid the obvious objection do not, hence, seem to work.

1.5 Nothing

1.5.1 That it is Contradictory

Let us now turn to our other, and much more problematic, notion: nothingness, **n**. As for **e**, there is a very simple mereological definition: **n** is the mereological sum of no things – that is, all the things that are not objects:

- **n**:= $\sigma x \neg G x$

Unlike **e**, **n** is not a standard part of mereology.[30] It is usually assumed that, for things to have a fusion, there must be some of them. However, it is hard to find a justification for such an assumption, and it would seem to be no more problematic than that there can be a set which has no members – the empty set ∅. Note, also, there can be no worry to the effect that the things to be fused in this case are gerrymandered: there aren't any. It follows that **n** satisfies its characterizing condition:[31]

- $y \bigcirc \mathbf{n}$ iff $\mathfrak{S}x(\neg Gx \wedge x \bigcirc y)$

Now, **n** is an object. One can name it: "**n**." One can predicate things of it – for example, self-identity. It can be the object of an intentional state. For example, one can think about it (you are now); one can wonder whether it exists (perhaps you are now). Heidegger, indeed, claimed in "What is Metaphysics?" that one can have a direct phenomenological experience of nothing:[32]

---

[29] On the general problems of accounts of intentional verbs which do not treat them at face value, see Priest (2016), pp. xxix–xxi.

[30] And, unlike the situation for **e**, the question of whether or not **n** is an existent object seems relatively easy to answer. If to exist is to have the ability to enter into causal interactions (as advocated in Priest (2016), pp. xxvii ff.), it does not exist. For there is nothing there which enters into a causal interaction.

[31] I note that the introduction of **n** allows one to define a more general notion of parthood, $\leq_n$, where $x \leq_n y := x = \mathbf{n} \vee x \leq y$. It might be thought that it is this more general notion that should be used in the definition of overlap. However, this would be wrong; for then, since, for any x, $\mathbf{n} \leq_n x$, every two objects would overlap. This is no more right than taking every two sets to intersect, since they both have the empty set as a subset.

[32] Heidegger (1977), pp. 102f.

Does such an attachment, in which man is brought before the nothing itself, occur in human existence?

This can and does occur, although rarely and only for a moment, in the fundamental mood of anxiety (Angst) . . .

Anxiety reveals the nothing.

However, we do not need to follow Heidegger down this path of Gothic pessimism. **n** is an object. In particular, since $\mathfrak{A}xGx$, $G\mathbf{n}$, by universal instantiation.

But **n** is (also) not an object. For it is what remains after all objects have been removed. That is, it is the absence of all objects. So $\neg G\mathbf{n}$.

This, perhaps more controversial aspect of **n** can, in fact, be proved formally and mereologically, given what we have already seen. The proof is as follows.[33] The deduction is the middle column. The left column gives the line numbers, and the right column gives the reason why that line follows from the lines before. (Those who don't care for formal proofs, can just skip this and take my word that the deduction is valid!)

1	$\neg \mathfrak{S} y \neg G y$	
2	$\mathfrak{A} x \neg x \bigcirc \mathbf{n}$	$x \bigcirc \mathbf{n} \leftrightarrow \mathfrak{S} y (\neg G y \wedge x \bigcirc y)$
3	$\neg \mathbf{n} \bigcirc \mathbf{n}$	
4	$\neg \mathfrak{S} z\, z \leq \mathbf{n}$	$\mathbf{n} \bigcirc \mathbf{n} \leftrightarrow \mathfrak{S} z (z \leq \mathbf{n} \wedge z \leq \mathbf{n})$
5	$\neg \mathbf{n} \leq \mathbf{n}$	
6	$\mathbf{n} \neq \mathbf{n}$	$\mathbf{n} \leq \mathbf{n} \leftrightarrow \mathbf{n} = \mathbf{n} \vee \mathbf{n} < \mathbf{n}$
	↙ ↘	
7	$x = \mathbf{n}$ $x \neq \mathbf{n}$	
8	$x \neq \mathbf{n}$	
	↘ ↙	
9	$\mathfrak{A} x\, x \neq \mathbf{n}$	
10	$\neg \mathfrak{S} x\, x = \mathbf{n}$	
11	$\neg G \mathbf{n}$	$G y \leftrightarrow \mathfrak{S} x\, x = y$

Line 1 was established when G was introduced. Given this, nothing satisfies the right-hand side of the biconditional on line 2, so nothing satisfies the left-hand side either. Line 3 follows by universal instantiation. Given this, the left-hand side of the biconditional on line 4 is true, as then is the right-hand side, giving line 5. The biconditional on line 6 is the definition of $\leq$, and line 5 entails that both disjuncts are false. The argument then splits at line 7. $x = \mathbf{n} \vee x \neq \mathbf{n}$. The left column assumes the left disjunct; the right assumes the right. In the left-hand

---

[33] I take this from Priest (2014a).

column, line 8 follows from line 6 by the substitutivity of identicals. In the right-hand column, this held in any case. So, in either case $x \neq \mathbf{n}$, giving us line 9. Line 10 is a simple quantifier inference, and line 11 follows from the definition of G, shown in the biconditional.[34]

Hence, $G\mathbf{n} \wedge \neg G\mathbf{n}$: **n** both is and is not an object. This is the first fact to be established about it.[35]

1.5.2 That it is Ineffable

Let us move to the second. Since **n** is the absence of everything, there is literally nothing there of which to predicate anything. One can therefore say nothing about it.[36] In "What is Metaphysics?," Heidegger has again been here before us:[37]

> What is the nothing? Our very first approach to the question has something unusual about it. In our asking we posit the nothing in advance as something that "is" such and such; we posit it as a being. But that is exactly what it is distinguished from. Interrogating the nothing – asking what, and how it, the nothing, is – turns what is interrogated into its opposite. The question deprives itself of its own object.

n, then, is ineffable. Of course, one *can* say things about it, too: I have been saying many things in this essay (as does Heidegger). So **n** is effable as well.

Indeed, if something is an object, one can say something of it – for example, that it is self-identical – so it is effable. Conversely, if something is effable, one can say something of it, and to predicate anything of it requires it to be an object. So something is effable iff it is an object. Contrapositively, something is ineffable iff it is not an object. The contradictory status of **n**'s being effable therefore follows simply from the contradictory status of its objecthood.

Indeed, **n** is in rich company here. Many philosophers have argued that certain things are not objects. In orthodox Christian philosophy, to hold that God is an object is an act of impiety (even blasphemy); Wittgenstein, in the *Tractatus*, argues that things such as the *form* of

---

[34] I note that there is a quicker argument from line 6 to line 11. By definition, $G\mathbf{n} \models \mathbf{n}, = \mathbf{n}$, and since $\neg \mathbf{n} = \mathbf{n}$, $\neg G\mathbf{n}$. But this argument is more problematic, since it appeals to the contraposibility of $\models$, which may fail in some paraconsistent logics, such as *LP*.

[35] I should point out that there are consistent theories of formal mereology with the empty fusion – for example, Bunt (1985). In this, contradiction is avoided by defining overlap differently. $x \bigcirc y$ is $\mathfrak{S}z(z \neq \mathbf{n} \wedge z \leq_n x \wedge z \leq_n y)$. This prevents **n** from being a part of itself. The account appears to be inadequate precisely because it does not do justice to the intuitively correct facts about the contradictory nature of **n**.

[36] See Priest (2014b), 13.11.

[37] Heidegger (1977), pp. 98f.

a state of affairs (or a proposition) are not objects; Heidegger holds that *being* is not an object. These philosophers all conclude that the thing in question is, strictly speaking, ineffable. In each case, absent some fast and very wobbly footwork, they are committed to its being an effable object (as well), since they talk about it.[38]

Of course, in each of these cases, the philosopher is hostage to a theory which tells us that there is this thing which is not an object; such theories are prone to be contentious and may well be rejected. The theory which assures us that **n** is not an object is far simpler than any of these. Indeed, it is hardly a theory at all – just a simple consequence of the fact that **n** is the absence of all things.

1.5.3 That it is the Ground of Reality

Ontological dependence, or, as it is often called nowadays, *grounding*, has been the subject of much discussion in the recent literature on analytic metaphysics. In truth, the notion of ontological dependence has always played an important role in metaphysics, East and West.[39] However, the recent literature has forced it and its properties onto center-stage.

There is much that should be said if the notion – or notions; arguably there is more than one – of ontological dependence is to be sorted out.[40] However, while we can ignore most of the details here, let me make a few comments. Many argue that the notion is not definable in terms of something more basic. If so, so be it. However, I think it is natural to understand dependence – at least in the sense that will be operative here – as follows. *A*'s being the case depends on *B*'s being the case just if (if *B* were not be the case *A* would not be the case).

That is, $\neg B > \neg A$, where $>$ is the counterfactual conditional.[41] (And, since dependence is factual, one had better conjoin *A* and *B*.)[42]

---

[38] These matters are discussed at greater length in Priest (2019).
[39] See Bliss and Priest (2017).
[40] For some of this, see Bliss and Trogdon (2014) and Tahko and Lowe (2015).
[41] How to understand such conditionals is somewhat moot. But see Priest (2008), ch. 5, and (2018b).
[42] There are some standard objections to a counterfactual analysis of dependence. This is not the place to discuss them in detail, but let me just note the following. It is often claimed that counterfactual conditionals with necessarily false antecedents are vacuously true, so the analysis does not give the right results. However, it is perfectly straightforward to give an analysis of such counterfactuals according to which this is not the case, using impossible worlds. (See Berto et al. (2018). See, further, Wigglesworth (2013) and (2015), from whom I take the idea that one may use impossible worlds in an analysis of ontological dependence.) Next, it may be claimed that counterfactuals have the wrong structural properties. Dependence is transitive and anti-reflexive. Counterfactual conditionals are not transitive but are reflexive. The properties of dependence are contentious,

Now, turning to the subject at hand: some things depend for being what they are on other things. Thus, being the shadow of a tree (s) depends for being what it is upon the tree (t) being a tree. If t were not a tree, s would not be the shadow of a tree. The dependence does not go the other way. If s ceased to be the shadow of a tree (say, if the sun went in), t would still be a tree.

Similarly, being the set $s = \{0, 1, 2\}$ depends for being what it is upon containing the number 0. If 0 were not a member of s, s would not be $\{0, 1, 2\}$. Again, the dependence does not go the other way. If s were not $\{0, 1, 2\}$, 0 could still be a member of it.

Next, some things depend for being what they are upon being distinct from something else. Thus, being the spouse (s) of a person (p) depends on s being distinct from p. If s were the same (person) as p, s could not be the spouse of p. The dependence does not go in the other direction. If s is not the spouse of p, it does not follow that s is p.

Similarly, being a hill (h) depends for being what it is upon being distinct from its surrounding plane (p). If h were the same (height) as p, it would not be a hill. Again, the dependence does not go the other way. If h is not a hill, it does not follow that it is p. It might be a ravine.

Now, *being something* can be said in many ways. However, there is a most fundamental one, namely being an object. It is fundamental in that being anything at all presupposes being an object. Something cannot have *any* property unless it is an object. Let us consider this most fundamental sense of being something.

Something (g) being an object depends on its being distinct from **n**. If g were the same (in ontological status) as **n**, it would not be an object, since **n** is not an object. The dependence does not go the other way. If g were not an object, it would not follow that it is identical with **n**. There may be non-objects other than **n**.[43]

Indeed, one might say that what it is to be an object is to "stand out" against the background of nothingness, in just the way that a hill is what it is because it stands out against the background of the surrounding plain. Recall that *exist* comes etymologically from the Latin

---

but, if one subscribes to those cited, one can take the counterfactual to be merely a sufficient condition for dependence; a necessary and sufficient condition is being in the transitive closure of the counterfactual relation. And one can make dependence anti-reflexive simply by defining it as $(\neg B > \neg A) \land \neg(\neg A > \neg B)$.

[43] Thus, see Priest (2014a), esp. Part 1. As noted on p. 180, though, there is a different dependence in the other direction. For something to be **n** depends on its not being g: if it were g, it would be an object, and so not **n**.

ex (out) *sistere* (made to stand), and so means literally something like *made to stand out*.[44] One could picture it thus:

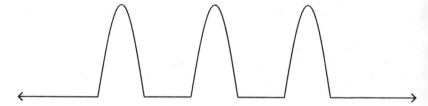

The peaks might represent hills standing out against the surrounding ground; or they might represent objects standing out against the background of **n**.

Hence, **n** is the ground of reality, in the sense that it is the ground of every object, reality being composed of objects.

Heidegger has again been here before us. In "What is Metaphysics?," we have:[45]

> The nothing is neither an object nor any being at all. The nothing comes forward neither for itself nor next to beings, to which it would, as it were, adhere. For human existence the nothing makes possible the openedness of beings as such. The nothing does not merely serve as the counterconcept of beings; rather it originally belongs to their essential unfolding as such. In the Being of beings the nihilation of the nothing occurs.

Or again, reverting to the more Gothic theme:[46]

> In the clear night of the nothing of anxiety the original openness of beings as such arises: they are beings – and not nothing. But this "and not nothing" we add in our talk is not some kind of appended clarification. Rather it makes possible in advance the revelation of beings in general. The essence of the originally nihilating nothing lies in this, that it brings Dasein for the first time before beings as such.

It should be noted that, when Heidegger talks about beings here, he is not talking about existent things: he is talking about objects, whether existent or not.[47]

---

[44] True, I do not take being an object to be the same as being an existent object; but many people do.

[45] Heidegger (1977), pp. 98f.

[46] Heidegger (1977), p. 105.

[47] Thus "everything we can talk about, everything we have in view, everything towards which we comport ourselves in any way" is a being (entity) (Heidegger (1962), p. 26). And when we say something "is" and "is *such and so*," then that something is, in such an utterance, represented as an entity (Heidegger (2000), p. 93).

If we represent *being dependent upon* as →, then we can depict the situation thus:[48]

$$g_1 \quad g_2 \quad g_3 \quad \cdots$$
$$\searrow \quad \downarrow \quad \swarrow$$
$$\mathbf{n}$$

(The "*g*"s are for *Gegenstände*.) Note that **n** is not an object and so does not depend for being what it is upon being other than nothingness.[49] Hence, there is no arrow from **n** to **n**.

Of course, things are more complex in our dialetheic landscape. For **n** *is* an object as well. So, like all objects, it does depend on **n**. So we have:

$$g_1 \quad g_2 \quad g_3 \quad \cdots$$
$$\searrow \quad \downarrow \quad \swarrow$$
$$\mathbf{n}$$
$$\circlearrowleft$$

Or, more accurately, since **n** both is and is not an object:

$$g_1 \quad g_2 \quad g_3 \quad \cdots$$
$$\searrow \quad \downarrow \quad \swarrow$$
$$\mathbf{n}$$
$$\varnothing\!\circlearrowleft$$

What we have seen, then, as promised, is that, in the sense explained, **n** is the ground of reality (all objects), including being and not being a ground of itself. (The diagram, incidentally, shows that this is a non-trivial situation. That is, not everything is true in it. It is only the relationship of **n** to itself which is contradictory.)[50]

1.6 Conclusion

What we have seen in this essay is that everything, e, and nothing, **n**, despite reservations one might have to the contrary, are quite legitimate objects which have perfectly natural mereological definitions.

---

[48] Note that this use of the arrow is quite different from my prior use of it to represent parthood.
[49] Since n=n and Gn, ¬(n = n > ¬Gn).
[50] Since Heidegger has appeared a few times in this essay, it is perhaps worth noting the following. Heidegger took being to be the ground of beings. He also identified being with nothingness. In wrestling with the problem of how to talk about being/nothingness without treating it as an object, he came to the conclusion that it both is and is not an object. See Casati and Priest (2019).

e requires us to countenance a non-well-founded mereology, though a quite consistent one. **n** is an object which is ineffable and grounds all objects. However, it is not a consistent object but a dialetheic one. It is also not an object, is not ineffable, and does and does not ground itself.

Everything is interesting; but perhaps nothing is more interesting than nothing.

2

Is There Such a Thing as Everything?

Markus Gabriel

There are electrons and elections, numbers and chairs, artworks and planets, sentences and pains, and many other things. A prominent and promising way of making sense of this apparent fact is that we can think of all these things in one fell swoop by somehow collectively putting them under the heading of "everything." Some philosophers believe that it is even inevitable that we think about everything there is to the extent to which there seems to be a linguistic, or rather logical, phenomenon of absolutely unrestricted quantification. For example, whatever there is, it surely is itself, which we can state in simple first-order logic thus: $\forall x(x = x)$. However, it is unclear how exactly the issue of unrestricted quantification is connected with the commitment to there being something like an all-encompassing object (the maximal whole of which everything, including itself, is a part) or domain of objects (the world).[1] While Priest in his chapter argues that, in addition to unrestricted quantification, there is an all-encompassing object which he calls everything (from now on "e" for short), I disagree.

There are significant philosophical, empirical, scientific and ordinary debates about which things actually belong to everything.[2] Is there a God? Are there many gods? Is there intrinsic moral value to human actions? Are there any other universes that sprung forth from the Big Bang? Are there intelligent extra-terrestrial beings? The list of entities whose membership in any putative list "everything" has been disputed for different kinds of reasons is long. It is hard to determine how long it actually is.

---

[1] For discussion see Williamson (2003) and Rayo and Uzquiano (2006).
[2] Quine famously puts this point thus: "A curious thing about the ontological problem is its simplicity. It can be put in three Anglo-Saxon monosyllables: 'What is there?' It can be answered, moreover, in a word – 'Everything' – and everyone will accept this answer as true. However, this is merely to say that there is what there is. There remains room for disagreement over cases; and so the issue has stayed alive down the centuries" (Quine (1948), p. 21).

Yet, just as it seems to be straightforward to introduce the operation of including something in a list of everything, there is an almost equally plausible line of thought which leads us into nothingness: if we can challenge the existence of some entities by way of questioning their membership status vis-à-vis everything, we can let the negative operation run amok and assume that there are absolutely none of the things we earlier assumed there were.[3]

Against this background, it seems natural to follow Priest's ingenious proposal to treat everything and nothing as objects in the sense of something we can talk and think about – albeit in purely formal terms transcending any more specific ontological commitments of theories of an empirical stripe. Priest's proposal permits us to make sense of traditional metaphysical statements about the object corresponding to the most comprehensive concept on the one hand (everything) and the object associated with the least comprehensive concept on the other hand (nothing). When we realize, for instance, that as a matter of exegesis Heidegger disagrees with Hegel on the exact way in which being and nothing are one and the same, we seem to understand that the dispute is about something. Thus, pace Carnap, there is linguistic evidence of a meaningful use of being and nothing as nouns in grammatical noun phrases.[4] Insofar as being and nothing are objects of metaphysics, Carnap's linguistic strategy of rebutting metaphysics for good is unsustainable.[5]

In this context, I have proposed an alternative attack on metaphysics insofar as we think of it as the discipline studying the architecture of absolutely everything, of reality as a whole, being, the world or whatever you want to call the maximal object of inquiry.[6] I have argued that e does not exist. My preferred term for the maximal object is "the world." According to my *no-world-view*, then, the world does not exist.[7] Priest's e is one version of conceiving of the world, namely by way of introducing the mereological fusion of all objects into a single object, e. Thus, Priest and I apparently disagree, though it would be infelicitous to claim at the outset that there is something (namely e) about whose properties we disagree.

---

[3] For a recent discussion see Buchheim (2018).
[4] Priest (2014c).
[5] See, of course, Carnap ([1932] 1959). More recently, see the Neo-Carnapian debate in contemporary metaontology which discusses the consequences of Carnap's later transition (Carnap 1950). A good overview is Blatti and Lapointe (2016).
[6] For some discussion of the variety of notions of metaphysical totality, see Gabriel (2015a), pp. 2–5.
[7] Gabriel (2015c); Gabriel (2015a), ch. 7. For associated reasons, I maintain that there is also no such thing as nothing or nothingness; see Gabriel (2020d), §3.

Is There Such a Thing as Everything? 41

In his chapter challenging the no-world-view, Priest argues that I ought to accept e within the framework of my *ontology of fields of sense* (from here on = FOS). To be sure, according to his own conception of existence, to be is to be causally efficient. Thus, within Priest's own framework, e does not exactly exist.[8] Yet, it is an object and therefore belongs to being. Given that *being* in Priest seems to be sufficiently similar to *existence* in FOS, if he is right, FOS turns out to be committed to a view which (despite some minor mereological heterodoxy) would count as metaphysical by its own lights. Priest's concept of being an object could well be sufficiently similar to my concept of existence *qua* appearing in a field of sense such that one could potentially formulate the objection that FOS entails the existence of e despite itself (while it would still remain a viable option to reject e's existence in terms of Priest's own ontology).

In what follows, I intend to counter the challenges presented by Priest. First (I), I will address his explicit objections to my claim that FOS entails that there is no such thing as e and his conclusion that I ought therefore to give up on the no-world-view.

In the second part (II) I introduce the concept of metametaphysical nihilism as a possible way of locating the no-world-view in the metametaphysical landscape. According to my proposal, the world occupies the position of nothingness, meaning that discourse about the world (metaphysics) is empty in virtue of there being no object whose architecture or structure could be investigated by the methods (if any) of metaphysics *qua* theory of absolutely everything. And so, nothingness, far from being an object, boils down to the non-existence of the world. If you like, this is yet another version of "being and nothing are one and the same": where the metaphysician thought she was in touch with a maximal object of investigation, I claim we find nothing.

2.1 Replies to Priest

In this part of my chapter, I will distinguish three objections against the no-world-view.

The first objection (I.1) maintains that there are stories, paradigmatically Jorge Luis Borges' "The Aleph", which present a "quite coherent"[9] scenario in which the world is a proper part of itself. If this

---

[8] Priest (2014b), p. xxii: "For the record, I take it that to be is to have the potential to enter into causal relations."
[9] Graham Priest, Ch. 1, p. 28.

were the case, it would substantiate the conceptual possibility of the world belonging to itself in a way explicitly ruled out by FOS.

The second objection (I.2) presents a logical version of a mereological loop which is independent of the specific setting of the example(s) from fiction.

The third and final objection (I.3) derives, on the basis of these examples, the conclusion that FOS is compatible with a slightly heterodox, yet metaphysically laden non-well-founded mereology.

2.1.1 *"The Aleph"*

Before discussing Priest's first case against the no-world-view, let me rehearse some assumptions from FOS. According to FOS, to exist is to appear in a field of sense (a fos), which we can call "the main tenet":

- (The Main Tenet): To exist is to appear in a fos.

In this context, "appearance" is a technical term designed to capture intensional membership in a fos. By "intensional membership," I refer to the idea that a given domain of objects (such as the domain of astrophysics populated by galaxies, planets, etc., or the domain of impressionistic paintings populated by works by Monet, Pissarro, etc.) is furnished.

We can think of this fact by way of the notion of a "furnishing function" that maps objects onto a domain so that the domain is isolated from some other domains.[10] For instance, while there aren't any trolls in Norway, there are trolls in Norwegian mythology. Trolls make an appearance in Norwegian mythology but not in Norway, despite the fact that Norwegian mythology appears in Norway. Thus, according to FOS, appearing is not always transitive.[11]

"Intensional membership" is a commitment to a rejection of extensionalism: it is not the case that, for all fos, two fos, fos1 and fos2, are identical iff they contain the same objects. What matters is the way in which the objects are arranged (their sense) and that way corresponds to a mode of presentation to thought where the fos in question is accessible to fallible knowers. Some senses, some modes of presentation, are isolated from fallible knowers for different kinds of reasons.[12] The reality of senses, of intensional membership in fields, exceeds the reality of what is actually known as well as the reality of what is knowable in principle for fallible, embodied knowers such as ourselves.

---

[10] See Gabriel (2018b), where I draw on Chalmers (2009).
[11] See explicitly Gabriel (2015c), pp. 81–91.
[12] See Gabriel (2020a), pp. 80, 227.

FOS has sometimes triggered the following suspicion, which I call the *Mehlich–Koch objection*.[13] If it is sufficient for something's existence to appear in a fos, and if the world appears in some fos (and be it fictional), the world exists. But this contradicts the no-world-view, meaning that either some of the (meta-)ontological assumptions of FOS or the no-world-view need to be revised.

If this were correct, FOS would be compatible with a view I have dubbed "metametaphysical fictionalism."[14] According to this view, the world does not exist simpliciter – or in virtue of being part of the "furniture of reality", as the saying goes. Yet, it exists in virtue of being imagined. Objects which are essentially imagined – i.e., which would not have existed had they not made an appearance in the context of actual exercises of the imagination – are fictional.[15] If the world essentially exists in our imagination, then, according to FOS, it exists, which would be sufficient to reject one of FOS's claims, regardless of how outlandish metametaphysical fictionalism might be for other reasons.

However, like almost any other view, FOS need not (and does not) accept that the introduction of any old word in a fragment of a natural language is sufficient to give it a coherent meaning. There is a distinction between believing that one can imagine something and one's actually imagining it. As I will argue in this part of my contribution, the world, in addition to being non-existent, is also unimaginable.

In this context, we can now take a look at Priest's first challenge.[16] For Priest argues that, by the lights of my own ontological assumptions, there is an object which has the individuating properties of what I call "the world" and which makes an appearance in a short story. Thus, it exists within the fos of the short story which means that it exists. Given that this contradicts the no-world-view, FOS seems to stand in urgent need of revision.

The actual short story Priest cites is Borges' "The Aleph." The short story was reprinted as part of *The Aleph and Other Stories*.[17] Within the short story within the collection, a narrator is introduced to an object (or, rather, pseudo-object, as I shall argue) named "the aleph,"

---

[13] Gabriel (2020d), p. 79.
[14] Gabriel (2015a), p. 259.
[15] For this account of fictional objects, see Gabriel (2020d), §§1–5. See also Gabriel (2020c).
[16] For more on this concept, see Gabriel (2020d), §10. To be sure, Priest does not want to defend metaphysical fictionalism. He uses "The Aleph" as (fairly weak) evidence of the conceptual possibility of his object e.
[17] Borges (1971).

our bone of contention. It would lead us too far afield to provide a detailed reading of the entire short story, which deals with a host of semantical and metametaphysical themes. However, some poetological reconstruction is needed in order to show that the context of the short story itself undermines any straightforward metaphysical interpretation according to which the term "the aleph" in the story is designed to refer to an aleph (albeit within the range of make-believe). My argument, then, is that there is not even a "quite coherent" way of thinking about the aleph within the frame of the short story; so it is not really the case that there is an actual aleph with the ontological status of a fictional object within the fos of "The Aleph." I then intend to generalize this point introduced in my poetological reading so that no invention of any other apparently "quite coherent" story containing a version of object e actually contains such an object.

Let's start by looking at "The Aleph" (not the aleph, of course). We, the readers, first become acquainted with a mysterious object called "the aleph" through a narrator called "Borges."[18] He tells us that he saw an aleph in a basement in a house in Buenos Aires. In light of the characterizing descriptions of this peculiar object, Priest is quite right in assuming that this object might "correspond" to his object e. If the aleph existed (and be it in someone's imagination), it would correspond to the world as conceived by FOS. For the aleph is an object in which it is possible to observe absolutely every object *uno eodemque actu* – including the aleph itself observed by the observer of the aleph.

A fictional character by the name of Carlos Daneri introduces the narrator to the object by telling him that it "is one of the points in space that contains all other points."[19] Daneri maintains that there is "a world down there [había un mundo en el sótano]."[20] Remarkably, the narrator distances himself from such an interpretation when he informs us: "I found out later they meant an old-fashioned globe of the world [*se refería* ... *a un baúl*; my emphasis], but at the time I thought they were referring to the world itself."[21] And yet, Daneri describes the aleph as "the only place on earth where all places are – seen from every angle, each standing clear, without any confusion or blending [el lugar donde están, sin confundirse, todos los lugares del

---

[18] On the intentionally paradoxical use of proper names in Borges, see Balderston (1993). The word Daneri contains reminiscences of both Pablo Neruda and Rubén Darío. On intertextual reference on the level of the signifier in Borges, see Núñez-Faraco (1997).
[19] Borges (1971), p. 10.
[20] Ibid.
[21] Ibid.

orbe, vistos desde todos los ángulos]."[22] If this were the case, the aleph would not just be *a* world, but *the* world seen from all angles. Let us call "metaphysical" any interpretation of the short story according to which (a) it presents the reader with the task of imagining an aleph and (b) the reader can carry out this task in a quite coherent way.

The first problem with the metaphysical interpretation is that the proper name "the aleph" is introduced in a fiction.[23] This means that we need an account of the reference (if any) of fictional terms. A straightforward difference between "Carlos Daneri" and "Graham Priest" is that my use of "Graham Priest" is tied to my causal interaction with Graham Priest, whereas my use of the term "Carlos Daneri" cannot be thus grounded in non-fictional reality because, *ex hypothesi*, Daneri never made an appearance in Buenos Aires (or elsewhere on our planet). To be sure, FOS expresses this by saying that Daneri does not exist (on our planet), which does not mean that he does not exist elsewhere (such as in Borges' "The Aleph").[24] In contrast to Priest, Daneri has the properties relevant to being someone who lives in a city called "Buenos Aires" only in virtue of exercises of the imagination relative to which readers of the short story are entitled to complete the otherwise incomplete fictional object they are initially presented with by the text. What the text of the short story leaves open has to be completed by exercises of the imagination. Non-fictional reality, by contrast, is also complete in those regards left open by the fictional text, such that Priest's location, say, is not imagination-dependent in any way like that of Daneri. For instance, where Daneri is exactly located between the lines, as it were – i.e., where the text contains no report – is largely up to us, as much as the size of his shoes. The text alone does not settle these issues, and there is no place in non-fictional reality where we might simply look to find the answer to those questions.

A crucial difference between Daneri and Priest is that Daneri can have different mutually exclusive properties depending on how various readers imagine him (short vs. tall, say) whereas Priest has the properties he has as a concrete object regardless of how anyone

---

[22] Ibid., pp. 10f.
[23] Apart from "The Aleph's" explicit reference to Cantorian transfinite set theory, there might be a further intertextual link to Vaihinger's "Alpha body" [Körper Alpha]. Borges quotes Vaihinger elsewhere (in *Tlön, Uqbar, Orbis Tertius*). The "Körper Alpha" is a fictional object: "the immovable central point of absolute space" (Vaihinger (1925), p. 72). In line with my non-metaphysical reading of Borges, I interpret *Tlön, Uqbar, Orbis Tertius* as a fictionalized presentation (and rebuttal) of Vaihinger's "Metaphysik der Empfindungen." See Vaihinger (1922), p. 99.
[24] For a discussion of the notion of not being as being elsewhere, see Jocelyn Benoist on Gabriel in Benoist (2017) and my response in Gabriel (2020d), §3 as well as Gabriel (2018c).

imagines him. Even though actual human beings also have imagination- and concept-dependent properties, whether they are currently in London or in Sydney is not open to interpretation.

In this context, in a comprehensive account of the ontology of fictional objects, I have recently argued that there are two related objects associated with the word "Daneri." On the one hand, there is the inscription "D-a-n-e-r-i," which is part of the text of a short story. The inscription triggers exercises of the imagination in suitable readers competent to engage in mental story-telling based on texts. I call this kind of object *the metahermeneutic object*. On the other hand, there is the fictional object Daneri, which we are invited to imagine as we read the short story. This object's existence is essentially tied to interpretations, which complete the information provided by the text. My term for this second kind of object is *the hermeneutic object*: its existence is its being imagined to be a certain way.

Applying this distinction to the aleph, there is an inscription "a-l-e-p-h" and an accompanying invitation to engage in exercises of the imagination. While I roughly know how to imagine Daneri (as a human being living in Argentina, etc.), the aleph is much trickier, as there is no comparable object outside of the fiction such that the aleph is similar to it. If the arguments for the no-world-view are correct as they stand, we can even know that the aleph is impossible for us to imagine, as this leads to incoherent thought. So how would we manage to imagine it within the fiction?

Against this background, I stick to my guns and maintain that, even within the fos of "The Aleph," the aleph cannot be sufficiently characterized so as to make even an appearance within the fictional city called "Buenos Aires" embedded in the fos of the short story named "The Aleph." There is an aleph neither within "The Aleph" nor elsewhere.

The aleph is too nebulous to become an object of proper fictional reference that does more than attempt to engage in an exercise of the imagination triggered by a relevant textual inscription. Reading "The Aleph" does not catapult us to the God's-eye point of view of a total vision of all objects. The aleph's impossibility is not only a function of its having contradictory properties (unlike the infamous round square and its ilk), so it does not help the metaphysician's case that we could draw on a semantics of impossible worlds.[25] For "The Aleph" to contain an incoherent thought is not for it to be about strange events in an impossible world.

---

[25] Berto and Jago (2019). For discussion of realism about *impossibilia* in the context of ontological pluralism, see McDaniel (2017), pp. 69–71.

Arguably, Borges himself rejects the metaphysical interpretation according to which an exercise of our imagination triggered by his literary text lends support to the conceptual possibility of a total vision. In general, the research literature on Borges suggests that he was intentionally playing with various metaphysical notions of reference, truth, falsity, and reality in a specifically non-philosophical way.[26]

In sum, it is not evident that Borges' short story is "quite coherent," as Priest claims when formulating his first case against the no-world-view in favor of the object e. Rather, there are good reasons to prefer the poetological view according to which "The Aleph" is deliberately incoherent.

Regardless of the details of Borges scholarship, however, it is possible to construct a case against the no-world-view of the following form: if we can show that there are exercises of the imagination that permit us to think about an object – such as the aleph – that corresponds to object e such that e is essentially embedded in a fiction, FOS would be obliged to endorse the existence of the world after all. If we successfully specify any fictional fos – such as "The Aleph" – and introduce the world as a fictional object, we are apparently able to say what it is for the world to exist.

Countering this objection, I maintain that the case of "The Aleph" generalizes. Objects that essentially appear in a fiction depend for their completion on exercises of the imagination. There is no exercise of our imagination such that we literally achieve a total vision of absolutely everything so that no story-telling or poetical genius can produce a text which helps a reader to achieve a metaphysical insight. Thus, recourse to actual or possible short stories apparently dealing with metaphysical objects appearing within their fos turns out to be a red herring.

Thus, Priest has yet to provide an actual case for his overall claim that it is possible to substantiate his metaphysical model for FOS, according to which FOS is translatable into a slightly heterodox because non-well-founded mereology. Recourse to fiction alone does not do this job.

Now let us look at the formal part of his objection. Axioms of foundation in set theory and mereology alike prohibit the construction of loops: in set theory this means that there aren't any structures of the following form: $x_1 \in x_2 \in \ldots \in x_n \in x_1$. In particular, this rules out that a set is a member of itself. In standard mereology, antisymmetry serves the function of ruling out loops:

---

[26] See again Núñez-Faraco (1997).

- (Anti-symmetry) If x is a proper part of y, y is not a proper part of x.

This axiom covers many plausible cases of actual part–whole relationships. My hand is a proper part of my organism, but my organism is not a proper part of my hand; Helgoland is a proper part of Germany, but Germany is not a proper part of Helgoland; the word "Helgoland" is a proper part of this sentence, but this sentence is not a proper part of the word "Helgoland," etc. Yet, not assuming (anti-symmetry) has the potential advantage of making room for mereological loops such as the following: object a is a proper part of its fos and its fos is a proper part of a:

- ... < fos(a) < a < fos(a) < a ...

On this basis, Priest offers a simplified model of the mereological architecture he extracts from FOS. His crucial assumption is the notion that, in FOS, objects are proper parts of their respective fos such that fos are wholes composed of objects. The arrow in "$x \to y$" indicates that x is a proper part of y. Applied to object e, Priest's simplified tree looks like this:[27]

However, the mereological model of FOS has serious shortcomings.

Firstly, Priest's model is extensionalistic: it identifies fields of sense with wholes composed of parts without considering the intensionalistic idea that fields of sense are only wholes of parts if their unity can draw on a furnishing function in virtue of which the objects appear in that field of sense rather than in some other. A sense is a rule that governs the structure of objects in a given field. Senses are intensional objects: they are modes of presentation of objects. In the paradigmatic case of a thought directed at an object in a given field, the mode of presentation of the object is typically not on the level of the object.[28] In any event, senses are the paradigms of intensional objects. What there is essentially appears within the range of senses only some

---

[27] See ch. 1, p. 28.
[28] Gabriel (2015a), ch. 9, in particular, pp. 254–6. To be somewhat more precise: in some cases the mode of presentation (the sense) of an object appears alongside an object in the same field of sense, whereas in other cases modes of presentation of an object are such that they cannot appear alongside the same object.

of which are *de re* accessible to human thinkers.²⁹ Any mereological model of FOS based on extensionality misses this essential intensionalistic component of the proposal.

Another problem is that metaphysical mereology has some notorious weaknesses when it comes to the issue of change and identity over time. Mereological essentialism – i.e., the view that a given whole is necessarily composed of its proper parts – is, to say the least, counterintuitive.³⁰ Similarly, what about vague objects or objects on the quantum level of the universe that are not easily thought of in terms of neat extensional models that impose identity conditions for the reidentification of two epistemic episodes of the same whole?³¹ And if this were not enough evidence that metaphysical mereology at least does not obviously fit the bill of respecting its target system, reality, there is the fact that temporal reality as we know it is an open system: we do not even have compelling evidence that the physical universe is an atemporal block such that all physical entities can be regarded as stable parts of a single "frozen" whole.³²

More importantly, Priest ignores my explicit rejection of mereology as a metaphysical discipline. My objections (some of which Priest endorses) against metaphysical interpretations of set theory extend *mutatis mutandis* to metaphysical interpretations of mereology insofar as it is formally regimented in any of the recent standard ways. In chapter 4 of *Fields of Sense* I argued against Badiou's attempt to read the structure of reality (its ontology) off of set theory, noting that, "[i]n ontology, set theory does not speak for itself."³³

Set theory unaided by philosophical reflection does not prove anything of any importance for philosophical reflection. Set theory by itself is not a candidate for ontology, as it only contains information about the meaning of "existence" under some sort of interpretation of its results.³⁴

---

[29] Trivially, all senses are *de dicto* accessible, minimally in virtue of being accessed under the guise of senses that cannot be accessed *de re*. See the discussion of unknowable propositions in Gabriel (2020a).

[30] The locus classicus in recent metaphysics is Chisholm (1973) and Chisholm (1975).

[31] For the quantum case, see the discussion in Maudlin (1998). Thanks to Jan Voosholz for emphasizing the points now explicitly made in this paragraph.

[32] Last but not least, one could invoke the phenomenon of hermeneutic openness, which plays an important role within the ontology of fictional objects. Fictional objects are essentially interpretation-dependent. How we interpret – i.e., specify the open spots in a given score of an artwork such as to compensate for the fact that no fictional object resembling a non-fictional object is ever completely described by a text – varies from interpretation to interpretation and cannot be fixed once and for all. For such a strictly ontological reading of an important point in hermeneutics, see Gabriel (forthcoming c).

[33] Gabriel (2015a), p. 117.

[34] Gabriel (2015a), p. 120.

From this standpoint, the ontological situation vis-à-vis a plurality of axiom systems for mereology is the same: we need a reason for choosing among the available mereological systems in order to show that mereology has metaphysical or ontological import. Mereology by itself does not provide us with metaphysical insight. Independent of philosophical interpretation, its symbols do not have the kind of meaning required for metaphysical insight into the architecture of a reality that is at least in part independent of the models provided by mereological theory-construction.[35]

The more specific problem with mereology that I identified in earlier work is familiar from similar debates in the grounding literature in analytic metaphysics.[36] How can we justify the assumption that there is a univocal, overall part–whole relation if the part–whole relationships with which we are acquainted on a pre-ontological layer of our dealings with reality do not as such speak in favor of such a metaphysical treatment? In other words, the idea of a univocal part–whole relation that binds my cells together to form an organism in exactly the same way in which we ought to account for the unity of the proposition, say, cannot be justified by mere recourse to the fact that we can devise a host of formal systems for mereology that seem to suggest the feasibility of such an interpretation of both the theory-independent facts and the formal systems available.[37]

Thus, just as in the case of metaphysical interpretations of one's preferred choice of axiom system for set theory, it is not sufficient to point to a given mereological formal system in order to produce a metaphysic. For this reason, Priest needs to present an actual *case*, independent of an axiom system choice, that could motivate the FOS theorist to adapt that mereology and substantiate it with a metaphysical interpretation.

In this context, it is not sufficient to maintain that e itself, insofar as it appears in a slightly heterodox mereology, thereby exists (in my sense of existence). For, *ex hypothesi*, everything is a proper part of e, which means that all objects (including chairs, tables, numbers,

---

[35] Things might get trickier when looking at Husserl's mereology in the context of his *Logical Investigations*. It would take me too far afield here to show that Husserl's metalogical vocabulary brings him much closer to FOS than to contemporary formal regimentations of mereology. For Husserl tries to connect logical symbolization and meaning (*Sinn*) in a way potentially more suitable for making an intensionalistic case for the existence of the world than the one presented by Priest.

[36] See my explicit rejection of metaphysical mereology as a model for FOS in Gabriel (2016a), pp. 235–9, and Gabriel (2015c), pp. 57–72.

[37] Thanks to Joline Kretschmer, Laura Michler, and Jan Voosholz for pushing me to clarify this point.

Is There Such a Thing as Everything? 51

and objects we currently cannot conceptualize, etc.) appear within mereology. But how does this work? How do we map all objects onto mereology in that way? Given the dialectical position of the introduction of metaphysical, heterodox mereology in the context of a debate with the no-world-view, it would have to be shown first and foremost that e is conceivable in a manner demanding more than a stipulation or definition of an operation of mereological fusion of all objects into e.

In light of this, let me conclude this part of the discussion by highlighting that the Borges case rather speaks in favor of FOS. For, contrary to the metaphysical reading, there is evidence that Borges does not believe in the existence (or conceptual possibility) of e. Remarkably, Borges repeatedly characterized metaphysics as a "branch of fantastic literature."[38] In our specific case, the narrator explicitly describes the aleph which he sees in the basement in Buenos Aires as "a false Aleph [falso Aleph]."[39] The whole report is therefore "contaminated by literature, by fiction."[40]

There are many other passages in Borges where paradoxes of absolute totality play a role. For instance, in the very short piece "The Yellow Rose" we read about a revelation which occurred to Giambattista Marino, Homer, and Dante.

> Then the revelation occurred: Marino saw the rose as Adam might have seen it in Paradise, and he thought that the rose was to be found in its own eternity and not in his words; and that we may mention or allude to a thing, but not express it; and that the tall, proud volumes casting a golden shadow in a corner were not – as his vanity had dreamed – a mirror of the world, but rather one thing more added to the world.[41]

The world-whole is incomplete insofar as any mirror we use in order to represent it modifies it by adding something to its reality. The

---

[38] See Borges (1964), p. 10: "They [the metaphysicians on Tlön; MG] judge that metaphysics is a branch of fantastic literature." To be sure, the speaker of this utterance is not Borges but a fictional narrator.

[39] Borges (1971), p. 16. As Jon Thiem pithily puts it in Thiem (1988), p. 112: "Daneri trivializes the Aleph. He reduces it to the order of such modern inventions as the telephone, the moving picture, and the astronomical observatory.... Using the Aleph as a kind of panoptic videotape machine, he fails to view it as anything more than a total repository of real life images. He ignores its truly marvelous feature: the capacity to annihilate the limits of human spatial perception, to convey visually a transcendental order of space. Narrator and reader alike recognize that this Aleph, the Aleph that 'The Aleph' makes us see, is far more fascinating than Daneri's universal peephole."

[40] Borges (1971), p. 13.

[41] Borges (1970), p. 38. Both the aleph and the encyclopedia in "The Yellow Rose" are located in a corner (ángulo) of their respective site.

world, if it existed, would be (ever so slightly) modified through our grasp of it simply because our alleged grasp of the world adds something to it we have not yet represented.

Of course, the deep conceptual structure of the problem of how we can represent the world as a whole is not adequately analyzed in those literary terms, as the narrator of "The Aleph" indirectly concedes when he classifies Daneri's ideas as "foolish," "pompous," and "drawn out."[42]

In sum, I deem actual literary cases such as "The Aleph," to the extent to which they are of philosophical importance, to be further grist to my mill rather than evidence of the conceptual possibility of the world.[43] When dealing with the world, it is not sufficient to introduce it as an object which might be modeled in the terms of a heterodox, consistent metaphysical mereology. For the world cannot be grasped without taking our access conditions into account, precisely because the world is supposed to be absolutely everything and, thus, has to include our access to it.

In the case of the world, its ontology and its epistemology cannot diverge in the way in which they do for more mundane objects. We cannot isolate the thinker from the world in the way in which this makes sense in the paradigm case of objective thought directed at mind-independent objects. The epistemological and semantic problems associated with any attempt to get the world in view cannot be circumvented by way of the introduction of the term "the world" or with recourse to the unrestricted quantification over a domain of absolutely everything.

In this context, I would like to address a question to Priest: What exactly is the relationship between his earlier insight that no theory of totality can be closed and his more recent attempt to provide a metaphysic which has room for a totality object such as e? If any attempt at closure for a theory of absolute totality generates an element of transcendence – i.e., something that is excluded from the alleged absolute totality – as he argued drawing on a long history of arguments concerning the limits of thought, then how can the operation of a mereological fusion of all objects escape the fate of inclosure?[44]

---

[42] Borges (1971), p. 5: "So foolish did his ideas seem to me, so pompous and so drawn out his exposition, that I linked them at once to literature. . . ."

[43] See my analysis of a similar looping scenario in *Escape from the Planet of the Apes* (USA, director: Don Taylor) in Gabriel (2015c), pp. 76f.

[44] In other words, how does Priest's metaphysic presented in *One* circumvent the problems identified in Priest ([1995] 2002)? For an in-depth discussion of recourse to dialetheism as the most likely tool here, see Moss (2020). In particular, for a discussion of Hegelian dialetheism vs. the no-world-view, see pp. 286–306. Moss intends to show that the

To sum up my discussion of the "The Aleph" objection, fictional or mystical reports of the *multum in parvo* are not "quite coherent."⁴⁵ They are incoherent, because they do not manage to get anything into view. The aleph is thus a pseudo-object. Or, rather, like any other fictional object, the term used in a fictional text to motivate exercises of the imagination is not by itself in good enough semantic shape to refer to anything. As soon we imbue it with reference within the fos of our imagination, it turns out that we are not able to get absolutely everything in view, as would happen if we actually encountered an aleph (or any other fictional object allegedly representing the possibility of metaphysical cognition of the world as an object). The *prima facie* plausibility that we can introduce a fictional object that plays the role of the world (albeit restricted to a fictional scenario) cannot be cashed in because we lack a conception of the relevant world-object, which is the very point of the no-world-view.

To be sure, at this stage of the dialectic, Priest is free to respond with his alternative account of fictional objects so as to show that thought about fictional objects is not restricted by the ontological difference between the text and our imagination, between the metahermeneutic and the hermeneutic object. He could defend a kind of "blind fictional realism" about fictional objects, as I have labeled this elsewhere.⁴⁶ According to such a view, the following realist claim applies to fictional as much as to non-fictional objects: "Imagining new things about an object does not change the object in question."⁴⁷ While I take it that this is true about paradigmatically non-fictional objects such as the moon or bosons, I do not believe that it applies to fictional objects. I can change Faust, the fictional object, by imagining him to have almost any kind of hair-cut, say. Faust's properties left open by fictional texts can be filled in by the imagination in indefinitely many ways, which does not mean that the fictional object thereby becomes arbitrarily contradictory. For the different completions of the incomplete metahermeneutical object depend for their existence on the details of an imaginary fos. To be sure, I happily admit that fictional objects can be produced that inevitably invite contradictory imaginings. But this does not save the world, as Moss maintains as part of his attempt to move from my relative dialethe-

---

world (which he also calls "the absolute") "can only exist as a *true contradiction*" (p. 287).

⁴⁵ Zipfel (2001), pp. 109–112, rightly classifies "The Aleph" in terms of fantastic and not realistic narratives, which means that criteria of coherence are intentionally undermined by the set-up of the text itself.
⁴⁶ Gabriel (2020d), pp. 220–25.
⁴⁷ Priest (2016), p. 120.

ism, as he calls it, to an absolute dialetheism about the world. For we do not even succeed in imagining the world in such a way that we would be able to ascribe contradictory properties to it. I will return to this in the last section of my chapter.

2.1.2 Two Propositions

Priest's second objection draws on the mereology of two propositions, p and q, which have each other as proper parts:

$p := q$ or snow is white.
$q := p$ or grass is green.

If there is such a case, which we could call "mutual appearance" (in that q appears in p and p appears in q), we might find a way to let the world appear within itself at some point in a mereological loop.

Now, I accept that p is a proper part of q and q is a proper part of p. I see no reason to reject the idea that regions of logical space are populated by structures of the following non-well-founded sort:

- ... $< p < q < p < q <$ ...

The arguments in favor of the no-world-view take this into account. Priest explicitly draws on a passage from *Fields of Sense* but does not provide a full reconstruction of the argument presented in the pages he refers to.[48] What follows is an abridged version of the considerations of some relevant missing pieces from the context of the argument.

First of all, some fos appear in themselves. For instance, I can refer to this sentence within this sentence in various ways (such as by way of the description that it is the second sentence of the paragraph you are currently reading). In some sense, the sentence exists within itself. In general, FOS does not rule out cases of *self-containment*. The no-world-view does not reject self-containment in general but raises specific problems for the combination of absolute totality and self-containment. In this context, I distinguish two kinds of concepts of absolute totality: *additive* and *unified totality*. If the world were a merely additive totality, it would take the shape of a merely disjunctive heap of fos. In this case, it would be unclear in which way we

---

[48] Priest refers to Gabriel (2015a), pp. 188f., where I endorse the proposition "that some field can appear within itself." For a reconstruction of my argument which takes this into account, see Hill (2017). Hill establishes the right connection between Gabriel (2015a), p. 140, and the arguments presented at pp. 188f. For a defense of FOS against Hill's objections, see Gabriel (2020d), pp. 371–90. Moss has offered a succinct reconstruction of my argument based on the correct point "that Gabriel does not posit a universal rule precluding self-containment" (Moss (2020), p. 297 and pp. 294–301).

could think of this disjunctive architecture as a totality, because the concept of disjunctive co-existence of fos does not provide us with any instruction (with any sense) that justifies any contentful metaphysical claim about the world – unless the metaphysician contends herself with the view that the world is a merely disjunctive heap of ultimately disjoint fos.

Yet, for good reasons, metaphysicians are more ambitious in that they try to specify a world field such that the organization of all the fos that appear within it is intelligible in virtue of their appearance in the world. Let us call a given specification of a world-view *a metaphysic*. A metaphysic delivers a rulebook for the unification of absolute totality and thereby posits a unified totality.[49]

This puts the metaphysician at the crossroads of at least the following two options: assuming that the world exists, it either appears within itself or it appears in some other fos. As seen, in Priest's mereological transformation of FOS into a metaphysic, the world appears within itself. This architectural proposal leads to the following scenario. If all fos appear in the world, and if objects appear in their respective fos, the world can appear within itself only if it is either one of the fos or one of the objects in a given fos. Priest chooses the option that the world is an object in a given fos. But how ought we to specify the fos in which the world appears?

The metaphysician searching for an instantiation of the mereological looping structure in order to save the world from paradox has to find some way of specifying a rulebook for a world architecture that makes it intelligible to the theorist how absolutely everything "in the broadest possible sense of the term hang[s] together in the broadest possible sense of the term,"[50] to borrow Sellars's famous phrase. Insofar as Priest himself kindly declares "a great deal of sympathy"[51] for FOS, he ought to accept that e has to appear in some fos. In the context of his neo-Meinongian ontology, a possible option would be to think of it as an ontological commitment of Priestian neo-Meinongian object-theory. In that sense, the world would turn out to be a logical or semantic object.

As long as there is no actual case in favor of the existence of the world that goes beyond the formal framework of a non-well-founded mereology, what Priest's logical rejoinders show is, at most, that FOS does not provide any purely logical reasons against the existence of the world – which should not come as a surprise, as we are dealing with

---

[49] Cf. The concept of a rulebook in Gabriel (2020e).
[50] Sellars (1963), p. 1.
[51] See the concept of a context in Priest (2016), pp. 112f.

a factual issue of existence or non-existence that cannot be settled *a priori*. The no-world-view does not intend to demonstrate the logical impossibility of the existence of the world. The issue of the existence of the world is not *a priori*. The world is not a logically impossible object whose non-existence somehow flows from its concept.

Rather, the no-world-view is a corollary of a model of our pre-ontological experience. Respecting the phenomenological evidence is part of the theoretical virtues of FOS.[52] I regard it as a serious shortcoming of any first-order metaphysics that it needs to show that, despite appearances, reality is an all-encompassing, unified totality composed of surveyable parts subject to an intelligible set of principles or laws that structure the world field.

Neither empirical knowledge nor the concept of empirical knowledge-acquisition force us to accept a world field.[53] Our causally anchored modes of information-processing, without which we could not know anything about the observable universe, does not presuppose that the universe is either itself an absolute totality or part of a larger totality (comprising abstract – i.e., non-spatio-temporal – objects, say). On this level, physics and metaphysics are independent from each other.

Similarly, advanced purely theoretical research in the formal sciences tells us that we can do mathematics or theoretical computer science without assuming that there is a mathematical totality comprising all mathematical objects and structures. At the very least, we know from the various incompleteness and independence results in twentieth-century metamathematics that there is no complete formal system such that all mathematical propositions are axioms or theorems within it.[54] Mathematics has long learned to live without an absolute totality of its objects. Similarly, Priest has shown that there is a plurality of logical formal systems, including paraconsistent systems. This makes it hard to see how there could even be a totality of purely logical objects – i.e., objects in the domain under investigation by the logician. Yet, even if there were a totality of logical objects subject to some most encompassing laws of being true (be they consistent or paraconsistent), this would, of course, still not entail the existence of the world, because the world, if it exists, comprises many more types of objects than those recognizable by logical investigations.

---

[52] For a discussion of this methodological aspect of FOS, see Gaitsch et al. (2017).
[53] In Gabriel (2020a) I tried to show that the world field plays a constitutive role in acquiring the concept of knowledge-acquisition. Since then, I have come to believe that this is optional – i.e., that we can dispense with the notion of the world field on this meta-epistemological level as well.
[54] For a discussion of the halting problem in this context, see Gabriel (2020b), p. 140.

The no-world-view generalizes these insights beyond the frame of natural science and metamathematics by introducing a notion of relative existence – i.e., of appearance in a fos that differs from the notion that there is such a property of existence *tout court*. This results in the rejection of an all-encompassing fos. The world's non-existence is ontological, not logical. There cannot be a meaningful rulebook for our account of reality which contains all other rulebooks within itself. Knowledge of what there is is fragmented, which corresponds to the piecemeal structure of reality itself.[55]

2.1.3 FOS and (Neo-)Meinongian Object-Theory

In this section, I argue that Priest's (neo-)Meinongian object-theory needs to address the problem that it does not seem to offer an adequate account of intentionality that makes intelligible to finite, fallible thinkers how they could successfully think about the postulated totality of objects.

Meinong himself resorted to the strategy of postulating an idealized thinker, without providing an epistemological account of how we are able to grasp metaphysical thoughts about all objects. Taking a closer look at Priest's own framework, neo-Meinongianian object-theory, I now want to formulate a metaphysical problem of reference tied to the expression "object": How can we think of the world as an object if we admit that there is an indefinite number of objects that we can only name *de dicto*, without being in a position to characterize them sufficiently to think about them in an informed, *de re* manner? If the world is e, and if there are indefinitely many parts of e we cannot think about *de re* (for lack of concepts, contingent epistemic barriers, or simply due to spatial isolation), it is unclear which parts of our conceptual machinery are applicable to the world as a whole.

Meinong is acutely aware of this kind of problem, which he softens by making use of the traditional theological conception of a perfect, ideal thinker who grasps all objects *a priori*. He explicitly introduces his version of a theory of objects, his *Gegenstandstheorie*, as a "theory of objects of knowledge"[56] rather than of objects *tout court*. Responding to the question of how we can secure the epistemic

---

[55] Here, I will not go into the issue concerning the modal structure of the world's non-existence. I believe that it is necessary – i.e., that it is impossible that the world exists. However, the relevant modal vocabulary for this claim is provided from within FOS and, therefore, does not easily translate into contemporary standard ways of modeling this impossibility in terms of possible worlds, which should not come as a surprise. If the actual world cannot exist, then how should there be other possible ones? For my account of modality in FOS, see Gabriel (2015a), chs 10–11, and Gabriel and Krüger (2018).

[56] See Meinong (1960), §6, pp. 76–117.

accessibility to the totality of objects, he draws on what he calls an "instructive fiction":[57]

> Assuming an intelligence of unlimited capacities, there is nothing unknowable; and what is knowable, is. However, since the preferred usage is generally to apply "it is" (es gibt) to things which have being, and particularly to existing things, it would perhaps be clearer to say: All that is knowable is given – namely, given to cognition. To this extent, all objects are knowable. Given-ness as a most general property can be ascribed to Objects without exception, whether they are or are not.[58]

Meinong's concept of an object is tailored to idealized conditions of intelligibility unavailable to any actual human theorist. Remarkably, Meinong himself has to resort to his own brand of metaphysical fictionalism based on the notion of an idealized, fictional thinker to whom all objects are given. Yet, he owes us an answer to the question of whether the idealized thinker's epistemic position is intelligible to us.

The main strength of Meinongian object-theories is that they are promising candidates for delivering a convincing ontology of different kinds of objects (fictional, ideal, concrete, non-existing, incomplete, impossible, etc.). In light of this, I have characterized FOS as an instance of "formal Meinongianism" – i.e., as "the view that we cannot claim that something does not exist without thereby committing to its existence."[59] More specifically: "to claim that something does not exist is to claim that it exists in some field of sense other than the one originally under consideration,"[60] an amendment designed to accommodate the no-world-view.[61]

The trick of Meinongianism is to detach intentional reference from ontological commitment: to successfully think about something, to turn it into an intentional object, does not commit one to the existence of the object picked out by a suitably referential term. Meinongian thought promises to be about objects that do not exist

---

[57] Meinong (1960), p. 92.
[58] Ibid.
[59] Gabriel (2015a), p. 180.
[60] Ibid.
[61] In contrast to formal Meinongianism, substantial Meinongianism, which I attribute to Meinong, is "the view that we cannot claim that something does not exist without thereby committing to its subsistence, where this is a form of intentional inexistence, that is, a being in our realm of thoughts" (ibid.). I would now hasten to add that I should probably not have said "in our realm of thoughts" but, rather, "in the realm of thoughts," given that the relevant realm of thought is that inhabited by the idealized thinker.

without thereby performing the miracle of bringing them into existence.⁶² If successful, this strategy solves the Eleatic riddle of how to think about non-existing objects without thereby contradicting one's claim that they do not exist.

But what, if anything, is an object? What is the topic-neutral concept of an object such that all objects (regardless of their specific ontic status of appearing in their fos) at least share the feature of being objects? In this context, Priest offers a *flat formal ontology*, as I call it, according to which an object is

> the kind of thing that one can name, be the subject of predication, be quantified over, be the object of an intentional mental state. Thus, Australia is an object, since one can refer to it by the name "Australia." It is an object, since one can say "Australia has six states," so predicating "has six states" of it. It is an object, since one can quantify over *it*, as in saying that some continents (such as Australia) are entirely in the southern hemisphere. And Australia is an object, since one can think about it, wish one were *there*, and so on.⁶³

This informal elucidation of the concept of an object threatens to be circular because it defines objects as what can be "the object of an intentional mental state." Yet, this is probably not a serious problem, as the circularity can easily be avoided by defining an object as the kind of thing that can be the target of an intentional mental state. Anyhow, Priest's formal definition of an object is the following:

- $Gx := \mathfrak{S}y\; y = x$

As he tells us, "G" stands for "Gegenstand" – i.e., object – and $\mathfrak{S}$ is the particular quantifier "some", which he rightly distinguishes from the existence property and a properly existential quantifier.⁶⁴ In ordinary language, his definition of "object" then becomes: "To be an object is simply for there to be something which is identical to it or, more simply, to be something."⁶⁵

This widespread conception of an object is problematic, though. For one thing, it owes us an answer to the identity riddle: How can

---

⁶² Unfortunately, this raises a series of problems concerning the totality of objects. See Meinong (1960), pp. 83–4. Meinong wants to solve the looming paradoxes articulated by Russell's criticism by introducing the concept of a "pure objects" (ibid., p. 86), which is "by nature indifferent to being" (ibid.). He believes that this "finally eliminates the appearance of paradox" (ibid.). However, the "principle of the indifference of pure Objects to being" (ibid.) seems to be a case of *obscurum per obscurius*.
⁶³ See ch. 1, pp. 19f.
⁶⁴ See also, Priest (2014b).
⁶⁵ See ch. 1, p. 20.

identity statements, such as "$x = y$," be both informative and non-contradictory?[66] This is not harmless, because trivial self-identities such as "$a = a$" do not lend themselves to the application of any characterization principle that might help us to distinguish two senses under which we could think of the same object.[67] If there is an (alleged) object about which we are merely entitled to say that it is itself, how can we distinguish a from b so as to rule out that $a = b$? If the meaning of "a" cannot be stated with recourse to a characterization of a that goes beyond the claim of self-identity, a cannot count as an object we can meaningfully introduce into thought and discourse. Characterizing or proper properties (as I call them) distinguish an object in a given fos from other objects in the same fos. They serve a discriminatory function.[68] Proper properties differ from the properties an object has simply in virtue of being an object. There cannot be objects that do not have any proper properties, as these objects would be indistinguishable from other objects in their respective fos.

In this context, Priest rightly puts his finger on one of the major problems of any kind of Meinongianism. The eye of the conceptual storm is the following principle, which Priest calls the Characterization Principle (CP).

- (CP) An object has those properties that it is characterized as having.[69]

(CP) is quite attractive in the context of an account of non-existing objects, because it allows us to characterize a non-existent object in such a way that it turns into an intentional object without thereby having to exist. Notoriously, this highly welcome feature of Meinongian object-theories is not sufficiently generalizable. For one thing, it threatens to make it too easy to prove the existence of everything, insofar as we can *prima facie* characterize any object as existing. Secondly, and more importantly, an unrestricted (CP) can be used to prove absolutely everything. As Priest succinctly puts it:

> For let B be any sentence, and consider the condition $x = x \wedge B$. Let t be the object characterized by this condition. Then the CP gives us: $t =$

[66] For a discussion of the riddle and its ontological pedigree, see Gabriel (2014a).
[67] Priest (2016), p. 60, points out that identity is not existence-entailing: "It is clear, however, that some non-intentional predicates are not existence-entailing. Thus, logical predicates, such as identity, are not: even if a does not exist, it is still true that a is self-identical, $a = a$."
[68] Gabriel (2015a), pp. 43–71.
[69] See Priest (2016), pp. xviii–xix, and chapter 4, where Priest offers his own solution. Much discussed neo-Meinongian proposals include Routley (2018); Zalta (1983, 1988); Parsons (1980); Berto (2013).

$t \wedge B$, from which B follows. It would seem, then, that only a restricted class of contexts, $A(x)$, can be used in the CP. The problem is, which? This is the characterization problem.[70]

At this point, I surmise that Priestian neo-Meingonianism and FOS shake hands. For Priest resolves the characterization problem by taking recourse to an object-theoretical contextualism. He accepts the unrestricted validity of the principle while distributing objects over a plurality of worlds, a maneuver translatable into the strategy of spreading objects over a plurality of fos: "The CP *can* hold unrestrictedly, provided only that its instances may hold, not at this world, but at others."[71] What is an object in one world is not an object in another, and *vice versa*.[72] This is structurally similar to FOS's account of non-existence, according to which some things exist in some fos and do not exist in some other fos, such that existence is ontically relative to a fos. Nothing exists in all fos because there is no successful way of unifying all fos into a landscape suitable for assessments of possible worlds semantics.

At this stage, a decisive difference between neo-Meinongianism and FOS comes to the fore: Priest commits to there being "the set of *objects*."[73] Thus, there is an all-encompassing domain of being (the set of objects) which is identical across all worlds. But, again, what is it exactly to be a member of that set? Which predicate allows us to construct such a set? And what is the metaphysical relationship between the set of objects and the mereological fusion of objects? Does e make a double appearance after all, one in set theory and one in mereology?

One reason why I see a problem here is as follows: if an object is something we can think about, there are some objects we can think about *de re* (by characterizing an object in intelligible terms or actually perceiving it) while there are some other objects we can merely think about *de dicto* (which includes the objects *we* cannot think about except by thinking about them under that very guise). There are some objects such that all we can know about them is that they are beyond our ken, which includes objects that are contingently unknowable by us.[74] Thus, not all objects are objects insofar as there is a mode of presentation graspable by a finite human thinker endowed with a limited set of concepts.

---

[70] Priest (2016), p. viii.
[71] Ibid.
[72] Ibid., p. 13.
[73] Ibid.
[74] Gabriel (2020a), pp. 80f.

One way of putting this is that being and thought come apart – they are not identical – which is the principle of *ontological realism* in contradistinction to *absolute idealism*.[75] Absolute idealism ties the concept of an object to the concept of objective thought such that there cannot be any objects that are unthinkable by us.[76] I believe that Meinong himself was an absolute idealist in some sense, as he ties being to being thinkable.[77] He identifies the "objects in their totality" with the "totality of the objects of knowledge."[78] On this basis, he distinguishes between "metaphysics" as the theory of "the totality of what exist"[79] and his novel *Gegenstandstheorie*, which is famously not limited to the actually existing. He explicitly concludes that there cannot be an object

> which could not at least in possibility be an Object of cognition; at any rate, we may say this if we adopt the instructive fiction [!] that the capacity for knowledge is not impaired by limitations, such as stimulus thresholds and thresholds of discriminations, which are laid down by the constitution of the subject and are never entirely absent. Assuming an intelligence of unlimited capacities, there is nothing unknowable; and what is knowable, is. However, since the preferred usage is generally to apply "it is" (*es gibt*) to things which have being, and particularly to existing things, it would perhaps be clearer to say: all that is knowable is given – namely, given to cognition. To this extent, all objects are knowable. Given-ness as a most general property can be ascribed to Objects without exception, whether they are or are not.[80]

This passage ties the concept of an object to a fiction, the fiction that the totality of objects is given to an idealized thinker. This is either metaphysical fictionalism or absolute idealism, depending on how we conceive of the being of the idealized thinker and the associated most general ontological category of givenness (*Gegebenheit*).

There are some objects that are objects only in virtue of the fact that some thought is about them. Classical candidates for this category of being are mind-dependent objects such as pains, qualia, sense data, or even conscious mental states in general.[81] For the sake of argument, let us call objects whose being is their being thought about "ideal objects." They differ from real objects whose being is

---

[75] See Rödl (2018). On the concept of idealism at stake here, see Gabriel (2009), pp. 69–96.
[76] See Rödl (2018), pp. 55–8.
[77] Meinong (1960), p. 90.
[78] Ibid., p. 79.
[79] Ibid.
[80] Ibid., p. 92.
[81] See Koch (2016), pp. 69–87.

mind-independent.[82] Some real objects are embedded in evidence-transcendent facts, whereas some other objects are known to us.

This leads us to the question as to whether the object which is the fusion of all objects is an ideal or a real object. If it is neither ideal nor real, we need an account of its specific category of being. Simply put, is e mind-dependent or mind-independent? Clearly, e has to have both mind-dependent and mind-independent parts. But what about e itself? If it is mind-dependent, we wind up with the claim that the world-whole would not have been an object had no one ever thought about it, which is a form of ontological idealism.[83] If it is mind-independent, then how can it have parts that are mind-dependent?

FOS offers a way out of these metaphysical conundra by circumventing the construction of a fusion of all objects such that all objects are proper parts of it. But does this not commit me to the claim that there is nothing which is true of all objects, which seems to contradict the claim that all objects appear in a fos? And what about the claim that all fos are fos? Is this not a truth about all fos such that there has to be a way to think about the entire landscape of being after all?[84]

My answer to this worry is that the universal quantifiers sometimes used in the articulation of FOS are unsurprisingly restricted – i.e., bound by the domain of objects found within the fos of formal ontology. *Ex hypothesi*, the fos of formal ontology is itself one of indefinitely many fos without being all-encompassing (which follows from the no-world-view). The universal quantification in some of the formulations of FOS itself is thus meaningfully restricted to a domain of formal objects. In the fos of FOS there aren't any fos that aren't fos. Here, everything is a fos. Yet, there are fos in which there are only objects that aren't fos. For instance, set theory is such a fos. Insofar as the axiom of extensionality is accepted, the objects of set theory differ from fos. In some systems of set theory there aren't any fos, only objects (such as in those preferred by Badiou). The quantifiers used in the articulation of set theory are restricted to sets (and associated objects), those used in FOS to fos (and associated objects).

I regard it as a theoretical virtue of FOS that it repudiates the idea of a totality of objects and replaces it with an unsurveyable proliferation of fos. Notice that, according to this picture, the fact that there is no view from nowhere is not epistemic, but ontological: there just

---

[82] For some of my reasons for rejecting the mind-dependence–mind-independence distinction as ontologically relevant, see Gabriel (2015b). My use of a version of this distinction here is dialectical – i.e. designed to explore some of the consequences of ontologically committing to e in Priest's framework, as I understand it.
[83] Gabriel (forthcoming a).
[84] For more on this, see Gabriel (2014b).

is no maximal, God's-eye point of view, no ontologically independent judge, because the world (which would be its object) does not exist.

2.2 Metametaphysical Nihilism

FOS is an anti-metaphysical doctrine to the extent to which "metaphysics" is supposed to deal with the world as a unified and complete domain containing absolutely everything. There is no fos over which we could meaningfully quantify with a metaphysically unrestricted universal quantifier.

However, FOS is still a metaphysical doctrine in many other, less demanding senses of the term "metaphysics."[85] If by "metaphysics" we intend to pick out any doctrine committed to there being things which are neither material nor physical, FOS as depicted here is a metaphysical doctrine. Also, if "metaphysics" refers to a discipline attempting to characterize how things would have been had no one ever evolved to notice how things are, FOS is also a metaphysical doctrine. It is a point about existence itself which is reflected in the fact that pre-ontological experience reveals a reality to us which contains many different kinds of objects that are not *prima facie* reducible to a single layer of pure objects.

Metaphysics typically rests on ontological absolutism to the extent to which it draws on a combination of two directions of thought. The first direction of thought is an *aspiration to unrestricted objectivity*. Qua study of ultimate reality, the fundamental nature of reality, the basic furniture of reality or what have you, it aims at a world-view that is free from potentially distorting factors, free from mere appearances. The second direction of thought is an *aspiration to unrestricted unity and totality*, which I call the commitment to the unity of reality, or the existence of the world. These two directions are typically combined in such a way that they make it hard to see how we could avoid *heavyweight existential quantification* – that is, claims of the form that some *X* exists or does not exist full stop – where this contrasts with *lightweight existential quantification*, such as that there are indefinitely many unicorns in the world of the movie *The Last Unicorn* or that a virgin birth occurred exactly one time in the Bible.[86]

The task of listing all possible arguments for and against the existence of the world cannot be redeemed because we cannot even hope to achieve a complete overview of the actual arguments discussed over

---

[85] See Gabriel (2016b).
[86] Thomasson (2014).

thousands of years of the histories of metaphysics in the manifold traditions of what we call philosophy. As far as we can tell, humans on all continents have been puzzled by the issue of how things hang together "in the broadest possible sense."[87] The range of answers to the deep issue of how we, human thinkers, fit into the landscape of what there is cannot be exhausted by any feasible project.[88] This means that we cannot hope to decide the major metametaphysical issue of the very feasibility of metaphysics by way of judging the possibility or impossibility of metaphysics in terms of a complete account of our options. Metametaphysics shares the overall fate of philosophy and arguably of any large-scale epistemic project (such as physics) that it cannot culminate in a single overarching world-view. At the very least, the no-world-view then has the virtue of accounting for this constitutive incompleteness of metametaphysics without lapsing into metaphysical dogma.

According to metametaphysical nihilism, the "position" of nothingness is occupied by the world, as it were. Once we realize that it simply does not exist, we face nothingness. But *pace* Priest, what we thus face is not an object but, rather, the fact that there is nothing to be thought about when we try to make metaphysical sense of our oceanic feeling of belonging to a whole. Our oceanic feeling at most corresponds to our habitable position in our ecological niche.

Metaphysics is a kind of temptation grounded in a combination of the oceanic feeling and our human capacity to transcend any given conceptual horizon that seems binding to us from our parochial positions. But it always ends up running into specific difficulties characteristic of a metaphysic developed in a seriously systematic way. Contemporary metaphysicians typically avoid this form of incoherence by merely suggesting a metaphysic without delivering their system.

Nothingness is what you experience when you begin to realize that metaphysics is impossible due to the absence of its alleged object, the world as a whole. FOS offers us a way of accepting the non-existence of the world by letting go of the desire to see ourselves as part of an all-encompassing whole.

In this context, Priest (and, in his wake, Moss) challenge metametaphysical nihilism by arguing that I should have admitted that the noun phrase "the world" cannot be meaningless. For, if "the world" is meaningless, "Gabriel's own claim that the world does not exist [is] meaningless."[89]

---

[87] Sellars (1963), p. 1.
[88] On this see the discussion in Gabriel (2018a).
[89] See ch. 1, p. 29.

Before I explore the space of responses to this *expressibility objection*, let me briefly rehearse my official claim that sentences such as "the world is the world," "the world is not my left hand," and "the world does not exist" are "plain nonsense, like saying the following: 'XCEANNR$_{s12*}$' or the following: '.'."[90] The use of an apparently meaningful noun phrase "the world" in "the world is not my left hand" is purely dialectical – i.e., it takes place on a lower rung of the ladder, designed to lure in the metaphysician who believes herself to be in cognitive, epistemic, or, at least, semantic touch with the world as an object.

The expressibility "objection" in my view is not really an objection but a rehearsal of what happens on the last rung of the ladder to the first-order metaphysician who finally achieves an insight into the very meaninglessness of her earlier endeavors. The ontologist of fos takes herself to lead a life freed from metaphysics and is kind enough to offer a path of liberation to those still stuck in the world.

Thus, I do not regard the expressibility "objection" as a problem for FOS but, rather, as a problem for the first-order metaphysician who believes she has a spectacular object of remarkably pure inquiry in view. To be sure, Priest argues that his cognitive state when directing his thought at e (his version of the world-object) is well formed and meaningful. At this juncture, he points out that "the most plausible suggestion here is that I am thinking, not about the object, but about a representation of the object, such as a word, picture, or concept."[91] To me that seems indeed to be the case. For Priest claims to "know full well that the world is the mereological sum of everything; it is not a representation."[92] Above, I have argued that mereology, after all, is a discipline which provides models for how to think about reality. It would be surprising to me (and to everyone who has not heard the view before) that the world is the mereological sum of everything. That view, if anything, is the result of philosophical theorizing about the purview of the formal discipline of mereology regimented in light of a slightly heterodox formal system which allows Priest to fix a meaning for "the world" such that he can claim to know full well what he is thinking about.

Yet, above I argued that even this much is an illusion. Remember: How is it possible to draw all objects that exist outside of mereology as a target system of its models into mereology? How do they make their entry into the discipline? How do we secure reference

---

[90] Gabriel (2015a), p. 200.
[91] See ch. 1, p. 29.
[92] Ibid., p. 29.

for the term "the world" in such an extraordinary context? And how could we "know full well" that the world "is not a representation"? After all, a view of the form that the world as a whole is a representation whereas more specific objects, such as my left hand, are not is not *a priori* outrageous.[93] For one thing, Kant and many philosophers before and after him actually thought that the world was a representation without thereby thinking that everything in it was a representation. In a word, Priest has not demonstrated how he is actually thinking about a well-delineated object that really is the mereological fusion of all objects. He owes us a realist demonstration that e is more than a representation.

To be sure, there are many complications here, some of which I have explicitly addressed in the critique of the foundations of first-order metaphysics in the first three chapters of *Fields of Sense* and elsewhere. More specifically, in this chapter I have argued that the first-order metaphysician owes us an account of how he gets the world as a whole in view. I regard this as a perfectly legitimate request in light of the fact that it takes quite some training for human thinkers to wrap their head around the notion that there might be an object such that all other objects are proper parts of it (not to mention the additional twist brought to this form of inquiry by the demands of a non-well-founded mereology).

At this point, Moss offers a reconciliation by suggesting that the *pars destruens* of FOS (which I call "negative ontology") might "further function as the groundwork of meaningful claims in positive ontology that are true."[94] This would indeed place me "very close to the mystical traditions."[95] As Moss rightly maintains, the mystics believe in something like the existence of the object of their insight, which would distinguish my view from theirs. Yet, the situation is actually much more complicated. For those of the apophatic tradition – in particular, Plotinus and his fellow Neo-Platonists – precisely do not believe that the object of their ultimate insight is the world as a whole. On the contrary, the One is both not identical to the world-whole and explicitly does not exist. It is strictly speaking beyond the world-whole and, therefore, beyond being (ἐπέκεινα τῆς οὐσίας).[96] The

---

[93] For more on such a view, see Gabriel (forthcoming a).
[94] Moss (2020), p. 295.
[95] Ibid. For my take on the mystical traditions, in particular, Plotinus, see Gabriel (2009).
[96] Plato (1997), 509b9-10. On this, see the *opus magnum* Halfwassen (2005). Jens Halfwassen, my teacher in metaphysics, passed away prematurely in February 2020. For some recent reflections on the relationship between his Neo-Platonism and FOS, see Gabriel (forthcoming b). For a logically sophisticated appropriation of these themes in the opposite direction, see Priest (2014b) and (2018a).

Neo-Platonic One is neither an object nor does it exist. Interestingly, Plotinus himself arguably holds the view that the world as a whole exists only in thought (νοῦς) and that thought finds itself in the One, which transcends its capacity for reference, as the One is not an object. In that sense, my view is actually somewhat closer to the apophatic tradition than Moss surmises. At the same time, I have avoided presenting FOS in light of a discussion of the limits of thought, because I believe that the apophatic tradition kicks in much too late. Rather than transcending first-order metaphysics for good, the apophatic tradition in the so-called West clings to the hopeless task of turning the absolute into an object at almost any cost.

It would take me too far afield to spell out my view about the Buddhist and Advaita traditions in India as well as the Chinese Daoist tradition of apophatic thought, which I see as attempts to block the desire for metaphysics.[97] This would require a different kind of engagement with Priest's way of seeing Buddhism as metaphysics.

Let me conclude by saying that I regard the ontological pluralism of FOS as an important step towards overcoming the desire to turn everything into an object. Overcoming the world, if anything, has always been part of the salvation offered by religious thinkers of both West and East. However, FOS's metametaphysical nihilism promises to deliver a novel way forward in the perennial attempt to let go of the idea that absolutely everything can, in principle, become the object of human thought and language. Where we were expecting the world, we found nothing.

---

[97] I owe the idea of seeing central parts of so-called Asian philosophies as anti-metaphysics to the Heidelberg seminars on Nagarjuna and on Wang Bi's influential reading of the Dao de jing co-taught with Lothar Ledderose and Rudolf Wagner during the first funding phase of the research cluster "Asia and Europe in a Global Context." Unfortunately, Rudolf Wagner also passed away in 2019. For a sophisticated reading of the Dao de jing's philosophy of language, see Wagner (2003).

3

Some Thoughts on Everything

Graham Priest

3.1 Introduction

Gabriel and I agree on a number of things. We also disagree on a number of things. Some of those disagreements are, I think, merely terminological; some are certainly not. It would take several books to explore all these matters. And there is only one of this book. So in this chapter I will focus on what I take to be our central (non-terminological) disagreement: whether the world is an object – or, to put it in Gabriel's terms, whether it exists in a field of sense (fos).

Gabriel claims, centrally, that it does not – indeed, that the thought that it does so is deeply metaphysically incoherent in some sense. In §1.3 I objected to his arguments that this is so. I noted that in standard mereology there is an object which is the mereological fusion of all objects, **everything**, and averred that we may take this to be the world. In §1.4 I argued that Gabriel himself appears to be committed to the existence of the world in his practice of writing and thinking. In chapter 2, Gabriel objects to my arguments. In this chapter I take up his objections.

Here, and in what follows, I boldface the word "everything" when I am using it as a noun phrase. Without the bolding it is the quantifier. The same goes for "**nothing**." In fact, to keep matters visually simple, in what follows I will often abbreviate **everything** to **e**. It should be noted that whether **e** is an object and whether one can quantify over everything are quite distinct issues which are not to be conflated.[1]

---

[1] For what it is worth, I note also that **e** is not the same as being. The first is a totality of a certain kind. The second is a property of the things in that totality. This is quite different. In the same way, the totality of red things is not the same as the property redness.

3.2 Borges' Aleph

Let us start with the discussion in §1.3. We will come to §1.4 in due course.

Gabriel's first objection to what I say (in §2.1.1) concerns an object, the aleph, which occurs in Borges' short story of the same name. Gabriel takes me to be advocating some variant of an objection proffered by Mehlich and Koch, to the effect that the world occurs in the field of sense provided by the story, and so is an object (exists in that field of sense). He takes me to hold that the aleph is the world, and so is an object.

Now, this is not my objection. The aleph is not the world. It is, as Borges puts it, "a point in space that contains all other points" – and so, presumably, their contents. This is not the world, since there are many things that it does not contain: abstract objects, such as numbers, non-existent objects, such as Sherlock Holmes, and so on. So it is not true in the story that the aleph is the world. In fact, it is not even true *simpliciter* that the aleph contains all physical objects – that is, that all physical objects are part of it. *The Aleph* is a work of fiction. The statement about the aleph is true in the story. That does not make it true. You may tell a story in which Graham Priest is a woman. That does not make it the case that I am a woman.[2]

So what is the point of the aleph example? Let us agree that to be an object is to occur in a field of sense. I am, in fact, perfectly happy with this claim. If e is an object, then it occurs in a field of sense. And one field of sense in which it occurs is, then, itself. This shows that the *proper part* relation of the mereology, $<$, is non-well-founded. That possibility is accommodated in standard mereology. More radically, it shows that $<$ is not anti-symmetric. That is, that $x < y \rightarrow \neg y < x$ fails. Since anti-symmetry is an axiom of standard mereology, this is a different matter. However, it is not one that is a problem, *per se*. There are, as I point out in §1.3, well-known mereological theories in which anti-symmetry fails.[3]

---

[2] Even if it is true that to exist is to be an object that occurs in a fos, there is an important difference between a fictional and a non-fictional fos, however one might think best to cash out this distinction. For example, it is true in *The Hound of the Baskervilles* that the hound exists on Dartmoor. It is not true *simpliciter*. Someone who refused to take their holidays on Dartmoor because they feared the hound would be sadly misguided.

[3] On p. 42 Gabriel notes that fos's are not extensional, in the sense that having the same parts does not make them the same. Extensionality fails in non-well-founded mereologies. See Cotnoir and Varzi (2021), 3.2. He also says that the *occurs in* relation is not transitive. But neither does the parthood relation of mereology have to be so. We will come back to this briefly in due course.

Of course, that there are perfectly consistent mereological theories where the parthood relation is not anti-symmetric does not show that parthood really is not anti-symmetric. It might be held that such theories are incoherent in some way other than inconsistency.

Now, the point of the *Aleph* story (at last) is that the story told in *The Aleph* is a perfectly coherent story. Of course, it is only a story. It does not show that things actually are like that. But there is nothing impossible (logically, physically, etc.) about the situation it describes. Hence it shows that the situation described in the story is coherent.

Gabriel suggests (p. 28) that the story itself is incoherent. Obviously, the fact that the aleph is a fictional object does not make it so, or all fictions would be incoherent. Neither would the fact that the aleph is an impossible object – if indeed it were – make it so. We can tell perfectly intelligible stories about impossible objects.[4] Given that these matters are irrelevant, Gabriel's argument for this view would seem to come down to this:

1 The notion of the aleph and the notion of the world are the same.
2 The notion of the world is metaphysically incoherent.
3 So the story of the aleph is incoherent.

Whether a story about an object whose notion is incoherent is, *ipso facto*, incoherent is somewhat moot. However, the first premise of the argument is false, as I have noted. And the second premise is question-begging. It is exactly the major claim that Gabriel is advancing and that I am disputing.

3.3 *Propositions*

§1.3 uses another example to make the point that a mereology where anti-symmetry fails is quite coherent: two propositions which refer to each other and so (at least on a very common understanding of the nature of propositions and their parts) are part of each other. Clearly, matters of fiction are irrelevant to this. In response to this example, Gabriel agrees in §2.1.2 that it is perfectly acceptable for the relation here to be anti-symmetric ("some fos appear in themselves," p. 54). He thus agrees with the point I am making!

The issue, then, is not about whether anti-symmetry is coherent but about whether the special case that $e < e$ is coherent. As Gabriel says (p. 54): "The no-world-view does not reject self-containment in

---

[4] See Priest (1997).

general but raises special problems for the combination of absolute totality and self-containment." But what? In the rest of §2.1.2 he addresses the matter.

First, Gabriel says that, for there to be a field of sense, one must be able to characterize it in some way, and he asks how to characterize the world. I don't actually see why a field of sense needs a characterization. (That seems a rather odd thing for a self-confessed realist to say.) But, in any case, e is easily characterized: it is the fusion of all objects. And, indeed, all things hang together in "the broadest possible sense of the term" (p. 55): they share the most fundamental property of being an object.

A second argument is to the effect that we have no legitimate ground to believe in the existence of e anyway: "neither empirical knowledge nor the concept of empirical knowledge-acquisition force us to accept a world field" (p. 56). Perhaps; but lots of our knowledge goes beyond this, for example in mathematics. It is true that, in the orthodox set theory of our day, there is no totality of all sets – though it is mathematically problematic just because of this.[5] But much of what we reasonably believe goes beyond both the empirical and the mathematical. In particular, there are philosophical discussions that make it reasonable to believe that things are thus and so, and it is just such a discussion that Gabriel and I are engaged in here. Indeed, I find his claim that the existence of the world "cannot be settled *a priori*" (p. 56) particularly surprising. That seems to be exactly what Gabriel is trying to do. He is, after all, writing from the philosopher's armchair.

To bolster his argument about mathematics, Gabriel refers to incompleteness results such as Gödel's theorem. This strikes me as somewhat irrelevant. The theorem has nothing to do with totality at all. It shows that any axiomatic (that is, recursively enumerable) theory of arithmetic is either inconsistent or incomplete. In particular, there is a totality of all the statements which are true (in the standard model); but it is just not recursively enumerable. He also suggests that the fact that there is a plurality of pure logics problematizes the thought that there could even be a totality of purely logical objects investigated by logicians (let alone something much more generous). That doesn't seem to follow. The objects of pure logics investigated by logicians are just a certain kind of pure mathematical object, and so part of that totality. (Even orthodox set theory takes there to be a totality of all mathematical objects; it is just a proper class, not a set.)

---

[5] See Priest (2006a), ch. 2.

Note, finally, however, that none of these considerations addresses the matter of the specialness of e with respect to self-parthood. They therefore seem to be beside the point at this stage in the discussion – namely, the regress argument of §1.3.

3.4 Mereology as Such

In the second half of §2.1.1 Gabriel turns to a number of objections to the argument of §1.3, concerning the use of mereology itself. Let us take these one by one.

First, Gabriel says that mereology ignores the intensional aspects of fields of sense. Now, I don't think that this is true. In standard mereology, *any* bunch of things (as long as it is not empty) has a mereological fusion. However, this need not be the case; there are plenty who hold that, for a bunch of objects to have a fusion, they must fall under a concept which, as one might say, ties them together.[6] Thus, the three objects Markus Gabriel, Saturn, and the number π have no fusion. They are just too disparate. For myself, I am inclined to accept this view.

How to cash out the notion of being tied together is a somewhat disputed matter. However, whatever it is, there is no reason why the sort of intensional relations that Gabriel requires of the objects in a field of sense should not satisfy this notion.

But suppose that mereology does ignore intensionality, as Gabriel says. The theory of mereology ignores several things: it contains no modal or tense operators, numerical language, and so on. It is none the worse for that. For the claim that something is ignored to be of relevance, it has to be shown how, exactly, this omission is relevant to present matters, viz. whether my objections to Gabriel's regress argument that there is no world fails. In other words, the point has to be brought to bear on the specific issues at hand – which Gabriel does not appear to do. And, in the last instance, that $x < y$ is interpreted as "x is a (proper) part of y" is beside the point. It could be interpreted, equally, as "x is in the field of sense y." As far as I can see, the arguments concerning regress deployed (on each side of the issue) are exactly as good or as bad when transposed to this new key.

The arguments in the next paragraph are several. First, there is an objection to mereological essentialism: the view that an object necessarily has exactly the parts that it does have – that is: $(x < y \to \Box x < y) \land (\neg x < y \to \Box \neg x < y)$. Mereological essentialism is a somewhat

---

[6] For a discussion of matters, see Cotnoir and Varzi (2021), 5.2.

implausible view. (There would seem to be perfectly possible worlds in which I was born missing a finger.) But, in any case, mereology is not committed to it. As observed, the usual language of mereology has no modal operators and so cannot even express it. Such operators can certainly be added to the language, but how they interact with the mereological machinery can be adjusted to taste. For the same reason, specific theses about time are irrelevant.[7]

The next objection is to the effect that one cannot read off substantial philosophical theses from formal systems ("we need a reason for choosing among the available mereological systems in order to show that mereology has metaphysical or ontological import" (p. 50)). I agree entirely. There are many formal systems. Indeed, there are many formal systems of mereology which differ with respect to the properties they attribute to the parthood relation, fusions, etc. If we wish to use a system of mereology to tell us something, we have to get the system right.[8] Indeed, the dispute that Gabriel and I are having now is naturally seen as part of such a debate: Does the correct system have a top element? So I do not ignore this issue at all.

Nor, as Gabriel suggests, is mereology committed to the claim that there is a unique part–whole relation. The mereological relation between my appendix and me might well be thought to be different from the relation between me and New York. If so, one could, of course, have a different mereology for each notion of parthood. Alternatively, one can simply form the union, $\cup$, of all these different relations – that is, $x \cup y$ iff for some (parthood relation) R, xRy – and take this to be the parthood relation of an overall mereology. If one does this, the relation will not be transitive, of course; but one can have a perfectly fine mereological theory (with a top element) without transitivity.[9]

Let me end this section by replying to Gabriel's explicit question (p. 52) of whether my own "earlier insight that no theory of totality can be closed" itself provides an argument against e. The reference is to what I say in *Beyond the Limits of Thought*. There is no page reference, and I am not exactly sure what Gabriel is referring to. It is true that I say that certain structures instantiate the Inclosure Scheme, and for such totalities there is an operator, δ, which, when applied to a totality of objects of kind K, generates a new object of

---

[7] For a discussion of modal and temporal essentialism, see Cotnoir and Varzi (2021), 6.2. The matter of vagueness that Gabriel raises is also irrelevant. There is nothing in mereology which requires the objects with which it deals to be precise – whatever, indeed, that might mean. (For a discussion, see Cotnoir and Varzi (2021), 6.3.)

[8] Thus, much of the discussion in Cotnoir and Varzi (2021) comprises such a discussion.

[9] For a discussion of the whole matter, see Cotnoir and Varzi (2021), 3.3.

kind K. But that a structure instantiates the Inclosure Scheme *presupposes* the existence of a totality of all objects of kind K. And if e is the totality of an inclosure, all this shows is that e is an inconsistent object.

3.5 *Noneism*

Next: I hold that some things do not exist – Sherlock Holmes, Vulcan (the planet postulated before the General Theory of Relativity to explain the rotation of the perihelion of Mercury), God (any one you like). The view is defended at length in *Towards Non-Being* (hereafter, *TNB*).[10] It is often called *Meinongianism*. I prefer the term "noneism." A version of the view was indeed held by Meinong. But it was widely held before him. Indeed, it is the most standard view before the twentieth century. It was held, for example, by all the great medieval logicians.[11]

Now, mereology is standardly formulated with the assumption that all objects exist; however, my formulation presupposes noneism. In §2.1.3 Gabriel raises a number of issues specifically concerning this. In this section, let us walk through these.[12]

First, for x to be an object, Gx, is for it to be something. That is, we may take for Gx, $\mathfrak{S}y\ x = y$ (where $\mathfrak{S}$ is the particular quantifier, read as "for some"). It is not difficult to see that Gx is logically equivalent to $x = x$. Identity is a binary relation which everything bears to itself and nothing else. Hence, whatever x is, $x = x$ is a logical truth.[13] Gabriel worries about the old chestnut as to how, if that is the case, identity statements such as "Hesperus = Phosphorus" can have informative content. My answer is the one that most contemporary logicians, following Frege, would give. "Hesperus" and "Phosphorus" have different senses but the same referent – however one chooses to cash out the notion of sense. In this way, the statement in question is different from "Hesperus = Hesperus."

---

[10] Priest (2016).
[11] *TNB*, 18.2; Priest (2020).
[12] I shall not discuss the views of the historical Meinong, though Gabriel does so. I note only the claim (fn. 61) that, according to Meinong, things that don't exist subsist (*bestehen*). This is a common misapprehension. That was the view of the early Russell, not Meinong. Meinong held that some things have *Nichtsein*: they neither exist nor subsist. See *TNB*, ch. 5.
[13] To say that something is an object is also equivalent to saying that it can be the object of an intensional state. Any circularity here is harmless, since, as Gabriel notes, this use of "object" can simply be replaced by "target."

According to me, e is the mereological fusion of all objects. Gabriel worries about how one can think of such an object if there are parts of it that can be referred to only *de dicto*. The answer is that I can think of it simply by using the name "e," in the same way that I can think of Markus Gabriel by using the name "Markus Gabriel." Perhaps one might then worry about how I can refer to e *de re* if there are parts of it which can be referred to only *de dicto*. This is a non-issue. I can refer to the apple in front of me *de re*. The apple is the fusion of all its molecules. I have no way of referring to some of these (actually, any of these) *de re*. Indeed, I have no way of referring to most of these at all.

The next point concerns the properties of objects which may not exist. If one characterizes an object, g, by the condition $A(x)$ one cannot conclude that $A(g)$. That way lies triviality. According to me, $A(g)$ does hold – but not necessarily at the actual world; only at those worlds (possible or impossible) where something does satisfy the condition $A(x)$. Note: this notion of world has nothing to do with Gabriel's notion.

Indeed, Gabriel is correct that there is an alignment between this theory and his theory of fields of sense. There is a certain analogy between something having its properties in a field of sense and its having them at a world. However, Gabriel holds that, outwith an object's fos, in which it has its properties, it does not exist. According to my account, a characterized object can be an object at a world in which it does not have its characterizing properties (and whether or not the object is an existent object there is another matter entirely).

The next worry concerns the set of all objects. Gabriel says that I take there to be a set of all objects. He refers to p. 13 of *TNB*, but no such claim is made there. What is done there is to use noneism to rebut an argument to the effect that worlds must have different domains of quantification. There is then a legitimate question as to whether they do so. My preferred view is indeed that they do, though one could certainly go the other way on the point. I will return to this matter in due course. But, whatever the outcome of this, one may take the domain of the actual world to be the set of all objects. It is this fact which allows me to say, for example, that all objects are self-identical – and mean it.

Gabriel asks whether the set of all objects is the same at e. It is not. As I note in §1.3, being part of a mereological fusion is not the same as being a member of a set. The mereological fusion of all objects is not even a set. So, if there are problems with the set of all objects, this does not, in itself, raise problems for e.

However, if there is a set of all objects, it is certainly an object, and so a member of itself. How to handle this matter raises issues in the philosophy of set theory. In the standard set theory of our day, Zermelo–Frankel set theory, such an assumption leads to contradiction. As I note in §1.3, however, there are perfectly consistent set theories where there is a universal set, the set of all things, which is a member of itself. There are even paraconsistent set theories in which there is a universal set which is a member of itself; in these, contradictions arise, but they do so in a perfectly controlled way. I will not go into matters here, since these are not the problems that worry Gabriel. He asks, instead, what predicate is used to "construct" the set. Answer: the predicate *x is an object* – if you like, $x = x$. He asks what it is to be a member of that set. Answer: to satisfy that predicate – i.e., to be an object.

Finally, since sets and mereological fusions are quite different kinds of things, unless a very tight connection is built between fusions and sets (which I have never seen attempted), remarks about sets bear no relevance to the present matter.

Returning to e itself, Gabriel asks whether it is an ideal object or a real object – where ideal objects are ones "whose being is their being thought about" (p. 62) – since it has both real and ideal parts. This is an interesting question, though its sense is not entirely clear. The best I can make of it is this: Would e still have been an object if no one had ever thought about it?[14] That is, assuming a standard analysis of counterfactuals: in those (possible) worlds where no one thinks about e, is it an object? That is, would it be the case that "$e = e$" is true in such worlds?[15]

This takes us back to the question of whether all worlds have the same domain. If the domain of quantification is indeed the set of all objects, the answer is: yes, it is still an object – that is, "$e = e$" is true at such a world – though, if one is not a mereological essentialist, e may not have the same parts at those worlds as it does at the actual world. There is another possibility, however. A natural thought is that certain things are in the domain of quantification of a world only because of acts of cognitive agents at the world. Since such acts may vary from world to world, so can the domain of quantification. Thus, Sherlock Holmes is an object only because of the cognitive activity of Arthur Conan Doyle. Had he never written the stories, Holmes

---

[14] I think this is better than: Would e still have existed if no one had ever thought about it? – since it is not at all clear that it is an existent object at all.

[15] Where "e," here, is to be understood as a rigid designator, not a definite description, whose denotation may change from world to world. We want to be sure that we are talking about the same thing at each world.

would not be in the domain of the actual world. If e is like that, then, in a world where no one ever thinks of e, it is not in the domain of quantification; so it is not true that e = e.[16] Both constant-domain and variable-domain versions of noneism are technically viable; so, in a sense, one may go either way on the matter, depending on one's philosophical proclivities – though my own preference, as I have already said, is to take the domain to be constant.[17]

Gabriel goes on to explain that, according to him, there is no totality of all objects and worries that this commits him to a fos containing all objects. His solution is that you cannot quantify over everything. That is a problem, since he would appear to do so himself. To give but two examples, he says (p. 40, my emphasis) that we may think of metaphysics "as the discipline studying the architecture of *absolutely everything*," and (p. 41, my emphasis) there is no object "whose architecture or structure could be investigated by the methods (if any) of metaphysics *qua* theory of *absolutely everything*."[18]

Perhaps a better way to go is to endorse the view that quantifying over a bunch of objects does not commit you to there being a totality of them. A number of people, for example, hold the view that one can quantify over all sets without there being a set of all sets.[19] That view is not entirely without problems either,[20] but it poses a special problem for Gabriel. According to him, a literary work provides a field of sense in which the objects it countenances exist. So if he does, indeed, quantify over all objects, his own work provides a field of sense for all objects. There is, then, a world.

So Gabriel's view seems to run into a wall whichever way he goes.

3.6 "The World Does Not Exist"

So far I have been discussing the issues of §1.3 and Gabriel's response to them. In that section, I argued against the adequacy of Gabriel's arguments that there is no world. So far, I have been arguing that his replies do not succeed. Let us now move on to the issues of §1.4. There, I argue that Gabriel cannot himself maintain that there is no

---

[16] Whether the statement is false or neither true nor false is an issue we do not need to settle here.
[17] The issue is discussed in *TNB*, ch. 14.
[18] On the difficulties of someone who does not believe in universal quantification to express their own view, see Priest (2007).
[19] See a number of essays in Rayo and Uzquiano (2006).
[20] See Priest (2007).

world – or at least that he cannot do so consistently.[21] (Indeed, this matter has already surfaced at the end of the last section.) In his discussion of metaphysical nihilism in §2.2, he replies, in effect, to these arguments. In this section I will consider his response.

The problem here is that we – Gabriel included – say and think things which presuppose that the world is an object. Indeed, the claim which is at the centerpiece of Gabriel's philosophy, "the world does not exist," is just such a claim. In fact, at one point he even says that his view is an instance of one according to which "we cannot claim that something does not exist without thereby committing to its existence" (p. 58). Realizing that this is incompatible with the no-world-view, he rephrases this as: "to claim that something does not exist is to claim that it exists in some field of sense other than the one originally under consideration." However, even this rephrasing implies that the denial of the existence of the world implies that it does, after all, exist in a field of sense.

However, setting this matter aside, how can one accommodate the fact that claims are made which presuppose that the world is an object? In §1.4 I offered Gabriel a way to do this. "e" has no referent, and atomic sentences (that is, sentences without connectives or quantifiers) with non-referential terms are false. In particular, then, "the world does not exist" is true. The main problem with this strategy is that there seem to be atomic sentences about e that are true, notably those deploying intentional relations. The problem is a quite general one for those who hold, as might seem to be the case, that there are true statements of the form "I believe/fear/worship a," where "a" does not refer.

One possible solution to the problem is to take the target of such intensional states to be, not the object itself, but a representation of some kind; but I point out there that, generally speaking, an object and a representation of that object are not the same thing. A picture of the Brandenburg Gate is not the Brandenburg Gate; and I can think of the one without thinking of the other. What holds for the Brandenburg Gate holds equally for the world. Gabriel asks for an argument that the world is not a representation (p. 67). In fact, I give

---

[21] I think that there is a great deal to be said for the thought that the world is indeed a contradictory object – and none the worse for that! But I will not go into the matter here, since it appears to have no appeal to Gabriel. He says (p. 53, his emphasis), "I happily admit that fictional objects can be produced that inevitably invite contradictory imaginings." But this does not save the world, as Moss maintains as part of his attempt to move my relative dialetheism ... to an absolute dialetheism about the world." In fact, holding it to be true in a story that there are contradictory objects is not dialetheism, since it does not follow that it is true *simpliciter* that there are contradictory objects.

one: representations may well be mereological fusions (they usually are), but they are not the mereological fusion of *everything*. If you don't like that argument, that is, in fact, irrelevant. The Brandenburg Gate would work just as well as a counterexample to the view that I was suggesting. And if you don't like that view at all, that's fine by me. I was offering it as the most promising way out of the problem that faces Gabriel. Rejecting it is all grist to my mill.

In fact, Gabriel's preferred solution is quite different. It is to reject all discourse about the world – his included – as literally meaningless, "plain nonsense" like "XCEANNR$_{s12*}$" as he puts it (p. 66). But how can one, with a straight face, write books the central claim of which one takes to be pure nonsense? In reply, Gabriel appeals to a metaphor: his statements are rungs of a ladder that one must ascend, and from the top of which one can see the statements to be nonsense.

The move is, of course, a very familiar one: it is the turn that Wittgenstein makes at the end of the *Tractatus*. And Gabriel's application of it is no more successful than Wittgenstein's.[22] Patently, "the world does not exist" is not plain nonsense, like "XCEANNR$_{s12*}$." We understand it, discuss it, disagree about it. Clearly, it is meaningful. The claim that e does [not] exist, in particular – whether it is true or false – has a perfectly good meaning as spelled out by the appropriate mereology. It can be defined in terms of parthood, and parthood is a perfectly meaningful notion. If I say that a part fell off my bike as I cycled home, only a sadly benighted person would say that that claim is meaningless.

Moreover, the claim that statements about the world are meaningless is self-undercutting. If the claims are meaningless, they can establish nothing. In particular, they cannot establish that there is a problem if they are meaningful. The very case for Gabriel's view about the meaninglessness of such claims therefore collapses. To use his metaphor: we cannot ascend the ladder, because the first rung breaks when you put any weight on it.

I think that, far better than taking his own words to be meaningless, Gabriel would be better off taking a dialetheic position to the effect that the world (like **nothing**) both is and is not an object.[23] However, as I noted, he is not inclined to go dialetheic.

---

[22] On Wittgenstein, see Priest (1995), ch. 12.
[23] How so is explained for the case of the *Tractatus* in Priest (2019).

3.7 *Nothing and Emptiness*

Let me end with a couple of comments on other matters on which Gabriel touches in §2.2. Much of chapter 1 is about nothing. Gabriel says little about this topic. What he does say is summarized in the following quotation (p. 65):

> According to [my view], the "position" of nothingness is occupied by the world, as it were. Once we realize that it simply does not exist, we face nothingness. But *pace* Priest, what we thus face is not an object but, rather, the fact that there is nothing to be thought about when we try to make metaphysical sense of our oceanic feeling of belonging to a whole.

The thought here is that the world is nothing, no thing. That is, of course, Gabriel's view. But it does not follow from this that **nothing** is no thing as well. One cannot infer that the object **nothing** is no thing from the fact that **everything** is no thing. The fact that a mereology has no top element does not imply that it has no bottom element. Whether or not there is a fusion of no objects is a question independent of whether there is a fusion of all objects. Gabriel certainly thinks there is no such object: "I maintain that there is ... no such thing as nothing or nothingness" (p. 40, fn 7), but he provides no reason for this in the chapter.

Indeed, Gabriel does not maintain his view about **nothing** consistently. He says two paragraphs later (p. 65):

> *Nothingness* is what you experience when you begin to realize that metaphysics is impossible due to the absence of its alleged object, the world as a whole. FOS offers us a way of accepting the non-existence of the world by letting go of the desire to see ourselves as part of an all-encompassing whole.

In the first sentence, "nothingness" cannot be a quantifier. You experience nothing (no thing) when you are unconscious (or dead). That is not what happens in the moment of *satori* Gabriel is talking about. In such a moment, you experience **nothing**, so you experience something (some thing).

Speaking of *satori*, Gabriel indicates at the end of his essay that there are certain interesting connections between his view and views in some traditions of Asian philosophy. Indeed there are. I will not go into the matter here; but let me just say that it is perhaps at this point that our views are closest to convergence.

I endorse the Madhyamaka view that all objects are empty (*śūnya*). That is, they are what they are only in virtue of relations that they bear to other things.[24] Given some object, x, this will be a part of the totality, $f(x)$, containing x, all the objects it relates to, all the objects they relate to, and so on (plus the relation-instances of all the relations in question – yes, these are objects too). One may naturally think of this as the field of sense of x. Everything, then, is indeed in a field of sense.

In Indian Madhyamaka thought there is no suggestion that, given an object, x, the relations in question spread everywhere. That is, that $f(x)$ will include all objects. Thus, *Madam Butterfly* and Puccini may be co-related in this way. But *Madam Butterfly* and Sherlock Holmes are not. Different objects may well, then, be in different fields of sense. So far, Gabriel and I concur.

However, in Chinese Huayan philosophy, those relations are held to spread everywhere. Every object is in a *single* vast network of relations. This is illustrated in the beautiful metaphor of the Net of Indra. Objects are like jewels spread through space. Every jewel reflects every other jewel (reflecting every other jewel, reflecting every other jewel, etc.). This is also a view which I endorse.[25] And, if this is right, there *is* a global field of sense.

We are not yet at the thought that this field of sense is a member of itself – that is, that the whole network is also a node in the network. At least some important Huayan thinkers held this view, however. In one of his discussions, Fazang (643–712), the third patriarch of the school and arguably the most important Huayan philosopher, says the following.[26] (Note that, in this quotation, the planks, tiles, etc., are metaphors for the parts and the building is a metaphor for the whole. Identity, here, does not mean numerical identity. It refers to the relationships of interdependence in the net of relations.)

> *Question*: since the building is identical with the rafter, then the remaining planks, tiles, and so on, must be identical with the rafter, aren't they? *Answer*: generally speaking, they are all identical with the rafter.

And this seems right on my account as well. The whole (the network) is indeed an object, so it is one of the objects in the network of objects. In this case, then, the global field of sense is an object in the global field of sense. Moreover, using non-well-founded set theory, one can show that such is mathematically quite coherent.[27]

So Gabriel's view and mine converge only to diverge again.

---

[24] See Priest (2014b), 11.5.
[25] See Priest (2014b), 11.9.
[26] Cook (1977), p. 82.
[27] See Priest (2014b), 12.8.

4
Some Thoughts on "Some Thoughts on Everything" (Which Are Not about Everything)
Markus Gabriel

Priest maintains that our central philosophical disagreement boils down to the question of whether the world is an object. He interprets FOS in such a way that existence according to FOS is the same as being an object in Priest's neo-Meinongian theory of objects. However, this does not seem quite right to me. For, like Priest, I endorse a version of noneism, according to which some objects exist (relative to a fos = fos_j) and some do not (relative to fos_i). On this level, there might seem to be the option of arguing that the world is a non-existing object. To be sure, I do not hold the view that Priest recommends to me. I only mention it here because it shows that being an object and existing are identical neither in FOS nor in Priest's overall theory of objects. In many contexts, the difference between being an object and existing plays no important role. Yet, as we shall see in due course, because it takes more to exist, in my ontology, than to be an object in Priest's sense, there are additional considerations in the discussion of the world's existence or non-existence that Priest should not ignore in his interesting attempt to marry FOS with a form of metaphysics – i.e., a metaphysical interpretation of non-well-founded mereology.

In this chapter, I will stick mostly to the philosophical material adduced in Priest's reply to my chapter 2. In so doing, I will follow the order of his considerations.

4.1 Borges' Aleph

Priest replies that his objection differs from the Mehlich–Koch objection. He does not believe that the existence of the world in fictional fos would be sufficient to establish that the world exists after all. He draws a distinction between truth *simpliciter* and being true in the story. According to him, statements about the aleph in the story are not true. I disagree in that I reject the true-in-the-story vs. true *simpliciter* dichotomy. Yet, this does not mean that I believe that we can turn Graham Priest into a woman by telling a story about him in which he is a woman. My account of the existence of fictional objects has it that fictional objects exist in fos that are isolated from us in such a way that objects that appear in fictional fos differ from objects that do not appear in fictional fos. According to my preferred view of fictional objects, therefore, we cannot tell a story about Graham Priest in which things are true about Priest that are not actually true. Stories about Graham Priest are not about our Graham Priest but about some other object which might seem to be quite similar to Priest (depending on the details of the story).

At this point of the dialectic, this has no important consequences for Priest's way of specifying the impact of his point on FOS, but it has consequences for the relationship between the Mehlich–Koch objection and Priest's objection. For, if the aleph were an object which exists in the fos of *The Aleph*, then the world would exist.

Another minor disagreement has to be flagged: I believe that Borges thought of the aleph as the world and not just as a physical object which contains all physical objects. According to my interpretation of the short story, it shows that the world's existence cannot be coherently formulated – which is not a metaphysical or metametaphysical view defended by Borges, the Argentinian author, because it is part of a short story presented by a narrator (who happens to be called Borges too). Here, Borges the narrator is not identical to Borges the author, and this in turn is important for my non-metaphysical reading of the short story, which I have laid out in some detail in my *Fiktionen*.

Arguably, the short story is not only incoherent if we already accept FOS together with its no-world-view. Rather, it is arguably incoherent by its own account, which is why the aleph which the narrator finds in the basement is precisely a merely "false Aleph."[1]

Thus, I disagree with Priest that the story is coherent. It is not. And this is not irrelevant, because the story is supposed to provide an example of a situation (a possible world, if you like) that could be modelled in terms of a non-well-founded mereology, where the parthood relation is not anti-symmetric.

Given my independent reasons for thinking of fictional fos as meontologically isolated (isolated from us by the non-existence of their objects as judged by our non-fictional lights), Priest could not resort to the maneuver of writing a metaphysical short story

---

[1] Gabriel Ch. 2, p. 51.

according to which the world exists, unless he provides independent reasons for thinking that the story is coherent on the very level of its attempted reference to such a strange object.

My objection to Priest's objection, therefore, does not come down to the two-premise, one-conclusion argument Priest ascribes to me. For I do not accept premise 1, albeit for reasons that differ from Priest's. Also, the second premise of the argument he ascribes to me is not question-begging. It is simply the conclusion of the arguments for the no-world-view. There is nothing question-begging if one uses a premise to establish a conclusion that differs from the premise.

4.2 Propositions

It is correct that I do not object to the possibility of crafting a mereology without anti-symmetry. It is also correct that there has to be something special about e, such that the case where e would be a proper part of itself should be ruled out. Actually, I provide a whole battery of reasons for the view that e raises special concerns. Priest considers only a subset of those reasons. I will not repeat myself here, only reply to the parts of my argument that Priest explicitly discusses.

First, he wonders why fos need a characterization. My reply to this is simple: senses are characterizations. For there to be a fos, there has to be a sense (or a bunch of senses) that constitute the fos. This is what it is for fos to be intensional objects. Nothing odd here for a realist who is a self-confessed realist about senses![2]

To be sure, Priest believes it is possible to characterize e: "it is the fusion of all objects" (Priest, p. 26). I disagree with Priest that all objects "share the most fundamental property of being an object" (p. 72). My reasons for rejecting views of the form that existence (or being an object, for that matter) is a first-level or even a fundamental property of objects are laid out in my *Fields of Sense*.[3] My arguments that establish those reasons evidently hang together with the no-world-view, but they do not presuppose it.

Among other things, I still disagree with Priest's notion of an object in at least the following sense. Identity conditions for an object are field-relative in such a way that there can be no God's-eye view of all the fields. Even if they co-existed in a single, unified field and there were a God somehow surveying this totality, we would not thereby be in a position to occupy this epistemic position. Epistemological

[2] Gabriel (2015a), ch. 12.
[3] See ibid., ch. 2.

and semantic considerations pertaining to our knowledge-acquisition and contentful contact with objects must, therefore, not be ignored. We cannot abstract away from them in an account of objects as such. Thus, I deny that the operation of fusing all objects into a super-object e has enough grip on the realm of objects to actually perform the operation. The performance of the operation for the kinds of thinkers that engage in the activity of philosophizing has to be taken into account in a context where one attempts to talk about absolutely everything (which includes the finite position of the thinker as one of the objects in the envisaged panorama). Priest does not tell us how we achieve his overview of all objects so that he can guarantee that they fuse into e. On this level, it is certainly not sufficient to point out that we can stipulate an operation that would do the trick for a thinker who is capable of solving these problems.

Priest struggles to find an argument in the section he discusses. That is surprising. There are many arguments in the section, which I will not repeat here (see pp. 48ff). The reader can judge if those Priest is not willing to consider are convincing or not.

One of my arguments indeed hinges on a worry about identity.

Priest rightly assuages this worry by maintaining that the identity of a whole that has itself as a proper part just is a case of identity in non-well-founded mereology. Yet, in my view, he still owes me a case in favor of believing that reality corresponds to non-well-founded mereology – i.e., that reality is such that there actually is exactly one largest whole such that the largest whole counts everything (including itself = e) among its proper parts. I will get back to this point when I discuss mereology as such. There is no appeal to Ockham's razor at any point. I ask only for some kind of evidence that the world field actually exists. For this, it is not sufficient to point out that it might exist, namely in a scenario in which there actually is an object e which can be modelled in terms of non-well-founded mereology. Neither the Borges case nor the case of the propositions provides me with any reasons in favor of such a metaphysics.

I am not engaged in the activity of settling the existence of the world *a priori*. My argument is not that there is no formal system that describes a possible scenario where something exists that resembles the world. There are formal systems (such as orthodox set theory as well as the standard apparatuses used by practicing mathematicians, computer scientists, and physicists) according to which there is no e and there are formal systems (including the one sketched by Priest with recourse to Cotnoir and Bacon)[4] that beg to differ. As I see

---

[4] See Cotnoir and Bacon (2012).

the dialectics, Priest needs to demonstrate that things are such that orthodox set theory, say, is metaphysically less adequate than non-well-founded mereology because it excludes the world field.

It would lead too far afield to discuss the question as to how to interpret the scope of Gödel's theorem, which some (including Gödel himself and Roger Penrose, to name but two prominent examples) have interpreted as establishing more than the "official" point about the axiomatic theory of arithmetic.[5] But that is indeed largely irrelevant for our discussion here.

Not so the issue of logical pluralism. Priest famously discusses this in *Doubt Truth to be a Liar*.[6] In this context, Priest's rejection of logical pluralism in one sense comes with an explicit acceptance of the sense of "logical pluralism" I was drawing on. Priest writes:

> Given a fixed application to some domain, there may be many different applied logics which constitute theories about the behaviour of that domain – and correspondingly, disputes about which theory is right. I will call this, for want of a better term, *theoretical pluralism*.[7]

The question, then, is which applied logic (dialetheism, quantum logics, classical logics, or what have you) describes the behavior of the world field. But that means that the logical systems themselves, which exist in the plural (with or without a stronger form of validity pluralism in the background, which Priest and I both happen to reject), will not settle the issue of the existence of the world. In that sense (the one I was drawing on), the world's existence cannot be settled *a priori*.

Priest ends his discussion by claiming that I have been begging the question in my discussion of his objections. That is obviously false, because I have been arguing against some of the assumptions that I take to be operative in his explicit objections and in the theoretical background they draw on. His claim that my replies invoke the no-world-view ad hoc is utterly unfounded and thus dialectically unjustified.

---

[5] Gödel himself sometimes presents his theorem as evidence against Hilbertian formalism as a philosophical doctrine. For him, then, the implications of the theorem go beyond the narrow scope of the proof and motivate his sympathy for Husserlian phenomenology, in particular. See, for instance, his reflections in Gödel (1995). See also the much discussed use of an interpretation of the theorem in Penrose (1989).

[6] Priest (2006b), ch. 12.

[7] Priest (2006b), p. 196.

4.3 Mereology as Such

Priest argues that it is not necessarily true that mereology ignores the intensional aspects of fos. Let's see. It would not, as Priest rightly points out, if it contained a structure that allows us to think of wholes as bound together by falling under a concept. Given the bundle theory of objects that I offer as an account of objects that works well within FOS, senses play the relevant role. Thus, if non-well-founded mereology were the metaphysics for FOS, it would have to include this notion of the function of a sense. Priest is wrong when he maintains that I have not adduced reasons that show that this is relevant for our discussion. Among other things, this is important and explicit in my discussion of the distinction between an *additive* and a *unified totality*, as well as in the context of the need to characterize the world field (pp. 54f.). Hence, it is also false that the arguments on either side "are exactly as good or as bad when transposed to this new key" (p. 73).

Concerning modal operators and issues about time and identity, it seems odd to deny that they would play a crucial role in any detailed assessment of the prospects for a metaphysical interpretation of non-well-founded mereology. A metaphysic without modality and time is wildly inadequate. Hence, these issues are certainly not irrelevant. The same applies to vagueness.

Priest agrees with me that "[t]here are many formal systems of mereology which differ with respect to the properties they attribute to the parthood relation, fusions, etc." (p. 74). That makes him a (mereo)logical pluralist in the sense I was drawing on. I agree with him that our dispute turns on whether the correct system has a top element. However, I read this dispute as also being about the question of whether it makes sense to search for a correct system. I think there are many equally correct systems of mereology, where this just means that there are many such systems that work in a particular case. If "being correct" amounts to more (say, correspondence with metaphysical reality), Priest owes me reasons to believe in the existence of e that go beyond the claim that e's existence is logically possible according to one of many formal systems.

Next, the topic of mereological pluralism in the sense of the view that there are many part–whole relations: I am happy with the idea that there is a plurality of different part–whole relations. I explicitly reject transitivity for specific cases. I do not accept the possibility of forming a union of all part–whole relations. *Mutatis mutandis*, my arguments for the rejection will repeat some patterns of my arguments for the no-world-view. In particular, we would have to discuss in more detail how the union operation is supposed to work, which is not clear from Priest's short presentation of the view. Among other things, he does not offer reasons to believe that we can form the union of all actually existing part–whole relations. This repeats the epistemic problem of coming to know **e**: for us to form the union U of *all* different mereological relations, we have to be able to think of *all* of them. But how do we manage to establish the relevant connection between the supposedly existing different mereological relations and the formal apparatus, such that we know that the apparatus is the correct theory for such a domain? The answer to this question cannot be given from within a given formal apparatus – at least not without further ado – i.e., by adducing metaphysical, interpretative reasoning.

Priest's reply to my question concerning the Inclosure Scheme is interesting in that he both accepts that there is an issue (if we take **nothing** into account) and that there is no issue (if we do not take it into account). After rereading *Beyond the Limits of Thought* (which includes a discussion of expressibility objections against Grim's incompleteness universe,[8] which to some extent resembles a no-world-view), it seems to me that our disagreement concerning **e** depends, among other things, on whether it is true "that totalization is conceptually unavoidable."[9] It should not come as a surprise that I disagree. Spelling out the potential for (dis)agreement concerning the issue of the domain principle (as one way of motivating closure) significantly goes beyond the argumentative stage-setting of the conversation at hand. However, let it be noted in passing that my remarks about vagueness and temporality on p. 49f. are relevant for this topic, because the world field cannot be thought of (if it can be thought of at all, which is, of course, part of our disagreement) without providing an account of the unfolding of the temporal parts of reality as well as the vague parts of it. Given that **e** is not a purely mathematical object, it is not sufficient to retreat to Cantorian territory, which deals only with mathematical quantities of a particular form.

4.4 Noneism

Priest and I are both noneists, though very different ones. Potential disagreement concerning non-existence (which is not nothingness) are consequences of the relativity discussion I offered in my earlier

---

[8] Grim (1991).
[9] Priest (1995), p. 124. For a discussion of my no-world-view in the context of a slightly different reconstruction of the dialectics between Kant, Cantor, and Hegel, see Kreis (2015) and my replies in Gabriel (2016a), §6, which differ slightly from earlier remarks in the English edition, which I wrote before Kreis's Bonn Habilitation thesis was published.

chapter. Priest does not take up the issue, so I will not repeat myself (see pp. 61f.). Suffice it to say that I can say everything the noneist wants to say with some additional conceptual resources from FOS. We also agree that we need a notion of Fregean senses for our account of the old chestnut concerning informative and non-contradictory identity statements. That is reason enough to suppose that Priest also needs a notion of a sense such that a sense-less mereology would be wildly inadequate for the tasks at hand.[10]

Now, if "e" is sense-less, it cannot be identical to itself. The main issue concerning *de re* and *de dicto* reference arises from this. There is a categorial difference between an apple and the world. I have reasons to believe that there is an apple in front of me that allow me to refer to it without thereby being in a position to refer to all of its parts in the same way. These reasons are grounded in my perceptual relation to the apple. However, I do not stand in a perceptual relation to the world (for one thing, it does not contain only the kinds of objects that can be the object of perceptual states). What is more, I do not stand in any other unproblematic or obvious epistemic relation to the world. While the apple is an object in the world (one of its parts), the world is not in that sense an object in the world. If it is a proper part of itself (as non-well-founded mereology would have it), it is not thereby a perceptual object (unless one is committed to some form of mysticism, which is precisely one of the topics in Borges that he discusses in relation to world, as I point out on p. 53). There is more I have said about the problem of the thinkability of the world field (pp. 62f.) which Priest does not take up in his reply. Again, I will not repeat myself here. There is also the further claim that Priest believes to be able to think of e by just using the name "e," which to me seems question-begging (to say the least). In any event, defending this would require a lengthy defence of a semantic internalism and a demonstration that no relevant contribution by semantic externalism is to be expected in the case of the meaning of "e," which would be very surprising given that all the cases that motivate externalist accounts are supposed to be proper parts of e. Hence, I cannot believe that Priest is capable of thinking of e by using its name in the way in which he thinks of me by using my name, unless he has had a special mystical encounter with e.

Priest and I disagree about the proposition that "a characterized object can be an object at a world in which it does not have its characterizing properties." He accepts it and I reject it. We have reasons

---

[10] For a discussion of the issue of whether $x(x=x)$ is a metaphysical thesis, see Gabriel (2020d), pp. 371–82.

Some Thoughts on "Some Thoughts on Everything"   91

for our choice which have not been made sufficiently explicit in this book. Thereon hangs a tale.

Here is what Priest says in *TNB*, p. 13: "If one is a noneist, there would seem to be no reason why the domain of each world should not be exactly the same, namely the set of all objects – whatever an object's existential status at that world." In his reply he clarifies the position of this conditional in the argument he unfolds. The result is the same, as he maintains that, "whatever the outcome of this, one may take the domain of the actual world to be the set of all objects. It is this fact which allows me to say, for example, that all objects are self-identical – and mean it" (p. 76).

Priest adds that this set of all objects (which according to me does not exist, but this is indeed a different matter) differs from e, because e is a mereological fusion and not a set. Alright. Given that he agrees with me that we cannot read our metaphysics off from set theory (p. 26), I will leave it at that.

Footnote 15 might be read as evidence that the issue of the meaning of "existence" is not purely terminological. For Priest there seems to accept that the following propositions might be true (because it is not entirely clear if it is not):

- (No-e-view) e does not exist.

If e = the world, at last, then, Priest accepts that the world does not exist. Or, rather, he has not entirely made up his mind in that regard. Now, he will, of course, reply that he reserves a special meaning for "existence" which differs from "appearance in a fos," which he takes to be tantamount to being an object. But I do not. Hence, there is much more potential for agreement and disagreement here, because Priest comes at least as close to accepting that e does not exist as I come to accepting that it does.

His discussion of the identity conditions of e on p. 75f are sufficient counterevidence against his earlier claim that the issue of mereological essentialism is irrelevant. His brief response to my question concerning whether e is an ideal or a real object to my mind reveal why it is not sufficient to insist that non-well-founded mereology does the job of putting pressure on my view that e does not exist. The issues lie elsewhere, as Priest's own considerations demonstrate. Next, Priest claims that, despite myself, I clearly quantify over everything. However, he misrepresents what I explicitly say in my chapter. Here is the relevant statement: "There is no fos over which we could meaningfully quantify with a metaphysically unrestricted universal quantifier" (p. 64). My points about universal quantification in that chapter all deal with the issue of unrestricted universal quantification, not with universal quantification as a grammatical or logical form *per se*. Therefore, if universal quantification is restricted in the way in which I introduce its use in the chapter and elsewhere, it is false that I am damned if I quantify over all objects and damned if I don't.

4.5 Intentionality

It is false that I have claimed that the no-world-view is an instance of formal Meinongianism (which I accept). The move is not *ad hoc*; it does not stand alone but is supported by the no-world-view which dialectically precedes my account of non-existence.

Priest raises specific objections along the lines of expressibility worries concerning the no-world-view and its slogan "that the world does not exist." He offers me a way to express the slogan as a meaningful proposition – that is, to assert that "e" has no referent, so that the atomic sentence "the world exists" comes out false and "the world does not exist" turns out to be true. He provides me with good reasons (known from the Wittgenstein on nonsense literature on which I do indeed draw) for preferring this to my solution (more about this in a second).

Whether I can accept his offer again depends on the issue of whether e is an object. If it is not an object (which I am inclined to accept), it might indeed be more attractive to think of "the world" in "the world does not exist" as non-referential. But this raises expressibility problems by itself. For are we not indeed talking about something when we say of the world that it does not exist?

If the world is an object, it certainly must not be a representation (the world is neither will nor representation, if you allow me the pun). But now we are back at the issue of a theory of objects and our relations to them. In order to achieve more clarity on the issue of whether the world is an object (and thereby to get a better grip on what I would deem an attractive theoretical move), I would require more details about Priest's referential position vis-à-vis the world which brings us back to the topic of how exactly he refers to the world in such a way that his reference is more than the occurrence of a word in a grammatical position where reference is to be expected, which is one of the worries I raise in my chapter.

To be sure, I have room for forms of cognitive illusion when we deal with (apparent) objects such as e where Priest thinks that he knows that he has managed to refer to e in virtue of his impression that he is thinking about it. We might have a coherent notion of object and a coherent notion of totality or fusion, but this does not mean that we are necessarily targeting an object when we think (or try to think) of a fusion of all the objects. And if there are reasons to think that the coherent notion of an object precludes there being something like a totality of objects – which is a large part of what is at issue here – then when we think we are thinking of e we have an illusion of understanding only.[11]

I admit that our discussion contains many meaningful details, but I disagree that we disagree about the truth of the proposition "that the world exists." My central claim is not metaphysical; it is not the claim that, surprisingly, the world does not exist. My central claim is meta-metaphysical: it is the claim that we get mired in plain nonsense when we assume that the world exists. We cannot successfully construct a contentful theory of absolutely everything. We cannot even achieve a theory of everything in the universe. Incompleteness is our epistemic fate. I take this to be a consequence of the non-existence of the world, which does not mean that we are looking for a specific object (the world) which we simply did not find (as a result of empirical shortcomings or a knock-down formal argument). The slogan "the world does not exist" is dialectical by its very nature.

What I have argued in my chapter and in this second set of replies to Priest's replies (whether successfully or not) is precisely that parthood is a perfectly meaningful notion, but none that helps us to construct a metaphysical theory. For that, we need the kind of substance which no formal system can deliver. Thus, we need more epistemic and semantic resources. And the grammatical stability of the phrase "the world does not exist" does not provide them.

Notice that the slogan "the world does not exist" is not at all the first rung of the ladder, which marks one of many significant differences between FOS and Tractarian ontology. Not all ladders are the same.

The lower rungs are stable pieces of ontological theorizing (the ontology of fields of sense) which provides accounts of existence, knowledge, modality, the irreducible existence of the mind, the mode of existence of fictional objects, and so forth. It's just that the ontology does not have a top element. When we try to ascend to such a high level, the last rung breaks down and we are back in the midst of an intrinsically pluralistic reality.

However, intellectual honesty requires that I look much deeper into the issue of sense and nonsense and its relationship to an account of subjectivity – i.e., the position from which we theorize about reality

---

[11] I owe the thought expressed in this paragraph as well as some of its sentences to written comments by Alex Englander.

(as one of its thinking denizens, not as proper parts of an already established maximal whole), and this is my next project. I hereby promise to spell out the alternative route Priest offers me in order to see what suits the dialectics of worldly thought better: an account of nonsense or one of sense.[12] In sum, the plain nonsense interpretation of "the world does not exist" might not be my last word on the issue (mostly thanks to Priest's and Moss's interventions concerning that part of FOS).

4.6 Nothing and Emptiness

At the end of his chapter, Priest is right when he concludes that, on this important issue on the lower level of reality, our views first converge (in India, as it were) only to diverge again (in China). This geographical reminder, of course, does not settle anything but opens up possibilities for further discussion.

Though I have serious interests in classical (and contemporary) Indian and Chinese traditions of philosophy, I am far from being an expert, which is why I am careful concerning more detailed pronouncements about emptiness and nothingness. I thank Priest for drawing my attention to the Chinese Huayan philosophy. I am familiar with Madhyamaka thought (which is part of the motivation of my view which, biographically speaking, though, is more influenced by early encounters with Hinduism and Advaita philosophy). Indeed, Priest and I agree entirely with the idea that relations might not spread everywhere (which is another way of stating what is central to my view without the slogan stating the no-world-view as a singular negative existential). Arguably, many classical Indian systems stick to the view that the network of entities consists of partly disjoint structures that cannot hang together in an all-encompassing network. Priest moves north, as it were, and sides with an interesting Chinese intellectual development. So far, I am happy to stay in the South – i.e., with Advaita: there is no such thing as the one; at most there is a non-duality at the heart of subjectivity, which is not evidence of the presence of a special object (the One).[13]

I disagree with Priest's claim that in the moment of *satori* you experience an object, namely nothing. Hence, my distinction between

---

[12] This will be an essential part of my book project *Being Wrong: Sense, Nonsense, and Subjectivity*, under contract with Harvard University Press.

[13] I have discussed this in detail with respect to Plotinus and his development of the relevant themes from the Platonic Parmenides in Gabriel (2009).

nothing (which is Priest's name for an object that exists in his preferred mereology) and nothingness. Śūnyatā comes closer to what I point to in the passage Priest quotes. It is an experience and not an object of an experience. Hence, in my view there is no such object as **nothing**. And, even if there were, it would be irrelevant to the discussion of nothingness, which precisely does not assume that there is anything left when we eliminate the furniture of reality (the substances), namely nothing. Exercises such as the act of abstracting from objects by showing that substances are empty, and so forth, are stepping stones towards a different kind of insight, one that overcomes the temptation to turn everything (including **everything**) into an object.[14]

The experience is one of being part of a flux of realities that have no overall focus: the phenomena are grounded neither in an all-encompassing whole nor in a self that unifies them into a whole (and would therefore have to unify the whole of the phenomena and its unification into a further whole). The phenomena just are what they seem to be: intrinsically manifold, sometimes disjoint, sometimes overlapping. They come in the shapes they assume and are not embedded in an overall frame from which we could derive overall patterns. These statements are all part of what I call positive ontology, which is the *pars construens* of FOS. They do not form a world-view. There is no object they have in view whose architecture could be articulated by any specific discipline (be it mereology, physics, metaphysics or any other kind of theory). The reason for this is not that the world is too huge, as it were, to be comprehended by us, finite creatures, but – let my mantra be repeated – that it does not even exist.

---

[14] It would lead too far away from the details of our agreements and disagreements to show in detail why Heidegger and many thinkers from ancient Indian traditions would classify any kind of metaphysical object theory as the paradigm target of the charge of the forgetfulness of being. Given that I reject that charge for FOS, Priest and I both might have to clarify our (very different) takes on what is going on in Heidegger and Hegel, which would be a topic for too many unwritten books to be fully discussed here. Suffice it to mention the elephant in the room: I do not think that Hegel and Heidegger were dialetheists.

Part II
Bonn Discussions

5

Discussion about Existence

August 16, 2021

Gabriel: Which topic should we start with?
Priest: Maybe it would be a good idea to start with existence, because I suspect our differences here are merely terminological. If that's so, we can clear the matter up and set it aside.
Gabriel: Then let's start with existence, at least insofar as you think it's a terminological issue. You use "existence" such that it means: being a member of the causal order, a view nowadays known as Alexander's dictum. That's still your take on existence, is it not?
Priest: Yes, I'm happy with that.
Gabriel: And you translate what I call existence into being an object. And then you read fields of sense ontology as a certain take on what it is to be an object. Correct?
Priest: That's right. I think that what you call existence is what I call being an object. We have a disagreement about many things, such as whether you can quantify over all objects, whether there is an object *everything*, and so on. Those differences are real enough. But, just as a matter of terminology, I'm happy to say that what you mean by existence is what I mean by being an object.
Gabriel: How important then is existence in your sense, for your view? A lot will depend, of course, on what role existence in your sense plays in setting up your ontology.
Priest: Sure. So, to begin with: why is it important for me? Let me give you one major reason. I used to be a Christian when I was a kid. Now I'm an atheist. What did I change my mind about? Well, I decided that God does not exist, and that was a major difference. So, the change there from existence to non-existence was a significant one for me – and for most people. Now that particular sense of existence, I think, is best cashed out in terms of being able to have a causal role in the universe. I think God is a perfectly good object. I can think about God, quantify over God, and so on. But God is like Sherlock Holmes, just a non-existent object. I guess

you think that God exists in a Christian field of sense or an Islamic field?

Gabriel: Yes, I do. God exists in those fields, at the very least. But I happen to think that theology, at least philosophical theology, has never believed that God exists in your sense. I think very few people held that view. Maybe some authors of the Bible did. Anyway, it is not constitutive of what it means for God to exist according to monotheists.

Priest: Well, I don't know. Christians think that God intervenes in human affairs from time to time, such as by being incarnated. That's the kind of cause I mean. I don't mean simply scientific causation. I mean actually doing things which have an effect in the physical world. Since we are on this topic, let me ask you about something else. You think that God exists in the Christian field of sense?

Gabriel: No doubt.

Priest: But I presume that you'd call yourself an atheist.

Gabriel: Well, I really haven't made up my mind. For instance, in your sense of atheism, I'm very clearly an atheist. I do not believe that anything that is causal in any relevant physical sense, say, is such that God is a cause for it. God leaves no immediate causal traces in the universe. Physics doesn't need a God parameter. He is nowhere to be found in the equations or the measurements.

Priest: Sometimes people ask me the following question: you think that God is an object which exists in some possible or impossible world. Since you think that, why don't you worship God? My reply is that to exist in a world other than the actual world is not actually to exist. Just as I am a woman at some possible worlds, but I'm not actually a woman. Now, let me ask you the same question. You think that God exists in some field of sense. So why don't you worship God?

Gabriel: As a response, I would start with the problem that there are too many gods, too many conflicting commitments. Interestingly, I hold the same view as my six-year-old daughter. She thinks that, for every God who is represented in a museum, there is a God in something like my sense of existence. Therefore, she tells her religion teachers in her school – religion is a mandatory subject in not-so-secular Germany – that there are obviously many gods. If they say there's just one God, she tells them: "You're wrong. There are many, I've seen them in the museum." So, that would make her a polytheist. Ontological joking aside, there are clearly many Gods, but they cannot be found here, as it were.

Priest: Here?

Gabriel: Yes.

Priest: Where are you pointing?

Gabriel: I am pointing to the fields of sense we occupy, so as to draw a distinction between us and what happens with fictional objects. I call this part of my view about fictional objects *me-ontological isolationism* (me-ontology being the theory of nothing, of non-existence). I think that fictional objects are isolated from us in an important sense.

Priest: So, this use of the word "here," being isolated from us, is interesting, because what you're gesturing at is a really important distinction. I would draw it in terms of the difference between the actual world and other worlds. I know you don't accept that framework exactly. But you're suggesting, I take it, that there is a difference in some sense between our reality and fictional reality.

Gabriel: Definitely. I want to be able to express, in the jargon that I'm using, everything that you want to express at this point with world-talk. Possible-worlds talk gives us ways of saying the following: in the actual world there is no Sherlock Holmes; he's not here. I would just say he is not "in our fields of sense." He is in another field of sense, but is thereby isolated from us. Now one might ask "What's our field of sense?" Fair enough. And then if I wanted to, I could say all the indexical things that people have said about the actual world, if I were inclined to use possible-worlds talk.

Priest: OK. I have heard Greg Moss say that you are a dialetheist, and that surprised me. I've read you saying that of course there can be contradictions in a fictional field of sense, but that doesn't imply there are contradictions *here*, as it were. But dialetheism is the view that there are contradictions *here*, however you cash out that idea. So, have I got your view wrong?

Gabriel: No, you've got that absolutely right. That's why I avoid contradictions when I say sometimes – using my sense of existence – something like Sherlock Holmes exists and doesn't exist. I think there's a parameter to be made explicit in the following way: Sherlock Holmes doesn't exist *here* and Sherlock Holmes exists *there*, and that's not a contradiction.

Priest: OK, good. Then I hadn't misunderstood you.

Gabriel: As to whether there are true contradictions *here*, I don't know. But there are some contradictions in fictional fields of sense.

Priest: Interestingly, you used the word *true* then. And I take it that you mean true *simpliciter*. But somewhere in one of your pieces you said you don't buy the distinction between truth *simpliciter* and truth relative to a field of sense. It sounds to me as though you are now buying that distinction, in effect.

Gabriel: Well, I don't know if my theory of truth is sufficiently developed yet. I tend to think that truth has to be truth everywhere. I'm very monadic about truth. When I say something like "true in a field of sense," I want to locate the parameter in existence, not in truth. That's certainly a tendency I have on this issue, and once again me-ontological isolation can be helpful in avoiding unnecessary contradictions. For there is a worry which David Chalmers once put to me in this way: there are unicorns in *The Last Unicorn*. That's fine. What about *The Last Unicorn II*? In *The Last Unicorn II*, the last unicorn reads Gabriel's *Why the World Does Not Exist* and decides to disturb the conversation with Chalmers. But it's not here, so we can't claim that something is true or exists just because it is presented in fiction. In response to this, my idea is to say that it's still true that the unicorn does these things. When I say something like "It's true in *The Last Unicorn II* that the unicorn travels to New York and so forth and crosses boundaries between fields of sense," then this does happen, but it still does not happen here. It's true, we might say, about a certain field of sense. If I say "true in," then this sounds like a form of relativism about the truth predicate. But if I said "true about," then I can have my cake and eat it. In general, my inclination is towards minimalism in the theory of truth.

Priest: OK, I wouldn't express it exactly the same way, but I think we're on the same page here. Instead of fields of sense, I talk about worlds. And I'd say truth is relative to a world – such as truth in the world of Sherlock Holmes's fiction, truth in the story.

Gabriel: Exactly.

Priest: Truth in the actual world is truth *here* as you put it. I'm happy to identify that with truth *simpliciter*.

Gabriel: Yes, that's fine. Well, the point might not be entirely terminological, because there are associated ontological issues. But I'm certainly inclined to accept the way you've just put things.

Priest: OK. So, this is a useful discussion, because I think it clears up lots of what are really non-issues, but simply differences of terminology.

Gabriel: Just one question about existence at this point, though: Do you think that it's relevant for existence to be in the causal order *here*? Because Sherlock Holmes is also, of course, a causal agent elsewhere. Hence, what distinguishes the actual world from Sherlock Holmes's world is not existence in your sense, but something else.

Priest: Right, but Sherlock Holmes is in the causal order of the worlds that realize the Holmes stories. In *this* world, Holmes doesn't causally affect anything. In the same sense that it's not true *simpliciter* to state that Holmes exists, it's not true that Holmes is in the causal order. But, if you go to a different world, the fictional worlds, then Holmes exists, Holmes is in the causal order. So, again, this is parameterization between worlds.

Gabriel: Yes, exactly. I parameterize in terms of fields of sense. This is why, on this level, I think we can probably perform similar maneuvers out of similar motivations.

Priest: I agree with this. Maybe there's not much more to be said about existence, but let's come back to that. Last night I was rereading some of your work. I was actually looking for a definition of "field of sense," and I couldn't find one. Maybe I missed it. I wanted to ask you about your understanding of the notion of a field of sense; not just examples, but a sort of a characterization.

Gabriel: Well, in *Why the World Does Not Exist* I draw a distinction between domains of objects, sets, and fields of sense.

Priest: Right, you certainly draw a distinction between fields of sense and sets.

Gabriel: And domains. So, I would like to define fields of sense in the following way: a field of sense is an arrangement of objects under a description, such as the arrangement of this white cup of coffee on the table in front of me right now.

Priest: Does this include relations between them?

Gabriel: Yes. And I think that the field of sense contains the qualities of the object, the whiteness of this cup, my perspective on it, and so forth. Fields cover full reality, and they come with a sense as the arrangement of their objects. Senses are modes of presentations. Given that this does not require someone to whom they are presented, I sometimes also speak of arrangements, which includes qualities.

Priest: OK. So, am I right in thinking a field of sense is a bunch of objects, plus the relations between them, plus characterizations of these things?

Gabriel: Yes, absolutely. I think the relations have to be characterized. Not within all fields of sense, though: there are some fields of sense which are constituted precisely by an abstraction from their sense – for instance, sets. Generally, mathematical abstraction might have this shape. There are certain elements from the characterization of a given object that I'm allowed to abstract from in order to look at relations that obtain elsewhere. For instance, I do not think that these objects here on the table in front of us exist in the quantum universe. This has certain consequences for our account of the relationship between macroscopic objects and quantum events. In this context, I do not believe that it makes sense to wonder in which way this bottle is constituted by its elementary particles, because it isn't. I think that elementary particles are an abstraction function on this bottle.

Priest: OK.

Gabriel: I then need some philosophy of physics for this; thereon hangs a tale.

Priest: But a field of sense is an aggregate of objects plus the relations between them, plus some characterizations?

Gabriel: Yes.

Priest: All right. So, one thing I wondered about in our discussions back and forth about *everything* (the object) was whether mereology is just the wrong bit of apparatus to capture what you mean by a field of sense, and I persuaded myself that it was OK. Because, with a mereological whole, you have a bunch of objects; that can include the relationship between these, and that's OK. And then, each object, each mereological sum can have a description, which collects together its parts, so to speak. Thus, there is an intensional element there given by this characterization. I'm sure we have disagreements about what the appropriate mereological structure might be. I think that's probably our big difference. But I don't think that I'm doing your view a great deal of violence by thinking of it in mereological terms.

Gabriel: Well, at this level, my initial worry was a version of my worry about set theory. Where we entirely agree, I think, is that there are different set theories, and so you need an interpretation of set theory in order to obtain metaphysical results (if any). Similarly, my tendency is to think that, *mutatis mutandis*, mereology fares no better.

Priest: Look, I think we agree here, first, that, whatever it is, be it a field of sense or a world, it is not a set. We're not living in a set. So set theory here is irrelevant, but I think that mereology is not irrelevant. I'm happy to interpret your view about fields of sense as a mereological one. Of course, there are different mereologies – different formal theories – and we may well disagree about what the appropriate mereology is. So, we need more than just a piece of formal apparatus. And I'm sure we'll discuss that later this week. But, at the moment, we're just getting the ground rules straight. So that's all good. Let's return to the matter of existence. And now I really do think that this is by and large a terminological issue; namely that what you mean by existence in a field of sense is what I mean by an object.

Gabriel: Is the following necessary for objects to exist in your sense?

As you know, I take the etymology of "existence," which is not just Indo-European, very seriously. It means "to stand out." Plato coined the term by using the Greek verb *exhistasthai*. It then enters Latin (*existere*) via various translations and other languages. Literally, to exist means to stand out. Now someone might say, "Oh, this is just an Indo-European concept with an Indo-European intellectual background," and so forth. But to make a trivial observation: you find the idea in contemporary Chinese, for example, as *cúnzài*, which means "to be contained in," and the Chinese characters express precisely that as well. And there are further examples. So, the idea is widespread. It's not, as it were, linguistically parochial. Now the question is something like: Do objects need a background for them to stand out from or to be contained in? Visual objects do; you look around, and there's always a background for them. I take this as my basis, as it were. And I think that's what we experience in perception. That's why, as you know, sense for me is both Husserlian noema and Fregean mathematical architecture. I think that the sense in sense modality and the sense in Fregean sense are the same concept. Senses on this level of analysis are directions in which we can identify objects (which is well preserved in the Roman languages, where "sense," "sentido," "senso," and so forth still mean direction). There has been a big debate in Husserl and Frege studies as well as a back and forth between the two about these issues. I think it can easily be resolved by just thinking of *sense* as having the same sense in both the perceptual and the logico-semantic cases. Frege did not entertain the thought that Fregean thoughts are operative in perception. I think that they are, and Husserl thought that. If you go for full-blooded Fregeanism, you wind up with a weird philosophy of mathematics, but that's a debate between the two of them as I understand it. In any case, I think of sense as covering both. So, I generalize on the case of perception, where you need a background, a context for objects. Does this line of thought play a role for you? Can there be an object for you without a context?

Priest: No. I mean, in the first chapter of this book, I said that to be an object is to stand out against the background of nothingness. So, I'm quite happy with this idea. And, no, of course that's not existence as I use the term.

Gabriel: But that's existence as I use it.

Priest: Right. Etymological considerations are interesting. But then they're nuanced. As I understand it, the Greeks, for example, have only one way of expressing existence and truth, and that is the verb *to be*. And I think the verb *to be* is actually ambiguous – this is a lesson that Greeks learned the hard way – for example, between predication and existence proper.

Gabriel: Yes, this is a famous line of thinking about the multiple meanings of the Greek *einai*.

Priest: So, etymology is interesting, but in the end, we're doing philosophy in the language that we speak now, and words are words. You can mean anything you damn well like by them. The important thing is to be clear how you use them, so that you don't just argue at cross purposes. And, I think it's just silly to say you *must* mean *this* by a word.

Gabriel: Indeed. But if you think that it's necessary for something's being an object that it stands out against a background, then that's the notion of existence that I'm working with. There we entirely agree. And then I would just think that, you know, intension enters the picture with the standing out – what I call appearing. Hence my ontological formula is: to exist is to appear in a field of sense. I take this to be the core concept of existence, and I analyze it into different components where the word "appearing" plays the intensionality role. It's also designed to draw phenomenologists into my game.

Priest: All right; then that all sounds good. So, let's take it, until it appears otherwise, that what I mean by "is an object" is what you mean by "exists in a field of sense."

Gabriel: I think, after all, that this is correct.

Priest: And, in fact, I'm even quite happy with the thought that something is an object only with respect to a field of sense. Indeed, for me, that's almost trivial just because it's an object in e, everything. So, if it's an object, it's an object in that field. Maybe in others as well. But, again, I don't think that's a difference very relevant to whether or not e is an object.

Gabriel: Indeed.

Priest: At any rate, I'm happy with the thought that things are objects with respect to a field of sense.

Gabriel: And I think you're also happy that your object e (everything) clearly has parts which are wholes. And the parts which are wholes can then be fields of sense as well. Right? That's no problem for you.

Priest: Absolutely. Incidentally, when one discusses these things, it's very easy to slide from the noun phrase "everything" to the quantifier "everything." The same goes for "nothing." And I think this can cause all kinds of confusion. What I suggest for our discussions is that, when we're referring to e, the guy that I like and you don't like, we stick to using "e," and we use "everything" for the quantifier.

Gabriel: On board. And clearly you want to say that e is a field of sense – maybe the field of all fields of sense?

Priest: You can look at it that way. It certainly includes everything. So, it includes all fields of sense and itself. We'll come back to that.

Gabriel: That is to be expected.

Priest: Let me ask you one more question about fields of sense: What are the identity criteria for fields of sense? I know roughly what sort of thing fields are. How do I know when two fields of sense are the same or different?

Gabriel: Well, I think that it depends on the field. For some fields the identity conditions will be *a priori*, by definition. In mathematics, identity criteria are established by way of definitions. And then, of course, the question is always going to be: What does this mean? We can have an additional philosophy of mathematics discussion about this, but this is of course what the mathematician will do in order to enter their fields: they use definitions and then begin the work of analyses, proofs, and so forth. Once you then have a system of equations, you generate new objects or find them, depending on how you think about what you are doing in mathematics. For other fields of sense, identity criteria are going to be empirical. Someone will think "There's impressionist painting," and now we have a field of sense of impressionist painting. Then one can ask: How did you know? How did you coin the term? Why do you think that these paintings belong together? As a consequence, there will be a discussion about genre, and the art historians will disagree and argue about it. So, the issue in that case will be empirical in a fairly straightforward sense. I don't think that there's an overall answer to the question of how we individuate fields. Some senses are like *this* and other senses are like *that*.

Priest: It must be more complicated than that because, I presume, you think that a mathematical field of sense and an artistic field of sense are different.

Gabriel: Clearly.

Priest: So, then you've got to have criteria of identity and difference which explains why those are different.

Gabriel: Well, here, I could just draw upon an *a priori* versus empirical distinction. The identity criteria for mathematical objects are *a priori* and the identity criteria for artistic objects are empirical.

Priest: OK. But what's the identity criterion that tells you that, say, category theory and romantic art are different fields of sense? There's got be something that separates those two.

Gabriel: Well, I think it's going to be their respective senses. I can tell you in particular cases what it is. For instance, there are colors in

— you know, I will only come up with examples, right? — I would say something like: there are colors and paintings. There's a certain surface structure to the colors. You need biochemistry in order to analyze this and to authenticate paintings, and so forth. And none of this applies to category theory. Instead, here is what we do in category theory, stuff with functors, and so forth, and then I give you an introduction to category theory — in just the way that I could give someone an introduction to the history of art.

Priest: OK. So, it sounds as though at least this is a sufficient condition for difference: namely, that the fields deploy different concepts or a different family of concepts.

Gabriel: I go piecemeal from field of sense to field of sense, so to speak, which to my mind is a consequence of the no-world view. At least, you can think of it as a consequence. Of course, I cannot have an overall account of fields of sense which is both *a priori* and synthetic.

Priest: Agreed. I don't think so. But, in any case, this is a view independent of whether there is an e. Just because, even in mereology, if you haven't got anti-symmetry, the identity of two objects in the mereology isn't determined by their having the same parts. You've got to say something else. I don't know if there's a standard answer in this case, but certainly there's an issue here about when two mereological totalities are the same or different, and the answer is not going to be an extensional one in terms of having the same parts.

Gabriel: What's your take on what differentiates one world in your sense from another? I assume that the worlds will be parts of e, right?

Priest: Yes. That's a fair question. I think that worlds are mereological wholes. I'm even happy with the thought that two worlds can contain the same objects. What differentiates the two worlds is that the objects will have different properties. Therefore, the worlds themselves, those mereological wholes, would have different properties because their parts do so. The identity criterion that I would give for these things is then a very standard one — but a rather boring one. Namely it's the Leibniz criterion that two things are the same just if they have the same properties. That's a rather boring criterion, but I don't know how to say anything more informative.

Gabriel: Nor do I. I just think that senses are properties, as I say in the last chapter of *Fields of Sense*. Senses are ways for things to be. Hence, senses are, as it were, categorial properties. They are what join objects in one field of sense and distinguish them from others.

So, in this respect, I'm a Leibnizian about matters of identity as well.

Priest: Look, I don't know how big a difference this is between us, but certainly some properties – or concepts; we needn't draw a distinction here – distinguish things from other things. So, being a work of art distinguishes the *Mona Lisa* from Donald Trump. I'm happy with that. But I don't think all concepts do that, because I think some concepts just apply to everything across the board.

Gabriel: What do you have in mind?

Priest: Self-identity, for example. This doesn't distinguish one kind of object from another, just because all objects have it. So, it may well be that what you call a property I might call a distinguishing property.

Gabriel: I call them *proper properties*. In my books, I distinguish between proper properties and other kinds of properties, such as logical properties (self-identity is one of these), ontological properties, which include existence and things that hang together with it, and contrast these with proper properties.

Priest: So we might take these to be what Kant means by determining properties "*bestimmendes Prädikat.*"

Gabriel: And you think that being an object is a property, right? You think it is, but it's not a distinguishing property?

Priest: You can put it that way.

Gabriel: And I think that existence is both an ontological property and a distinguishing property: it distinguishes one field of sense from another. I do not think that there's an overall concept of existence, which is non-discriminatory, as I call it. And I think you will argue in the mereological context, for example, that there are good reasons for me not to hold this view and just to adopt an overarching concept of existence, such that all these other forms of existence stand in some relation to it, maybe by being part of e.

Priest: Yes, pretty much, given that, when you talk of existence, I talk of being an object. But there is a disagreement in this area – namely, whether one can quantify over everything, every object. We'll discuss this later.

Gabriel: Good. I think existence is quite clear now.

Priest: I think the discussion today has been very useful, because it's allowed us to clarify a number of concepts and put aside some differences that are merely terminological. So, when we get to the things we do disagree about, we won't be talking at cross purposes.

Gabriel: Absolutely.

6

Discussion about Intentionality
August 17, 2021

Priest: I think the meeting yesterday was very good. We cleared a lot of ground and made sure that we're not disagreeing about things purely for terminological reasons. And this morning we have decided to talk about intentionality. I know that you think there are important issues here, and I think you should explain those.

Gabriel: The first issue, as I see it, is that there are different kinds of intentionality depending on various epistemic notions. For starters, let me draw the following very simple distinction: I can think about some objects, or my thought can be directed at an object, knowing certain things about some of its properties. For instance, I know that Angela Merkel is the chancellor of the Federal Republic of Germany, and I can thereby think of Angela Merkel by description. I actually think of Angela Merkel in a way that differs from my thought when it's directed at all the objects I do not know anything about, apart from the fact that they are objects in India. So, I think there's a difference here: while in both cases my intentionality is established via knowledge by description, I am in contact with Angela Merkel in ways that essentially differ from my knowledge by description that there are some objects in India about which I do not know more than that. And then there are more differences: the objects I don't know anything about at all, say, or the objects – maybe this is a fourth category – that are unknowable in principle, whatever those are. Philosophers have thought that there are many of those, such as the infinite, the One, God, etc. And then there's the fifth category: objects that, perhaps contingently, transcend our ability to know anything about them in particular, such as events beyond the event horizon as physicists understand it. This is not a complete list. This is a way of beginning to draw distinctions between different kinds of intentionality. Now, this plays a role in our discussion, I think, to the extent to which I might now ask what kind of intentionality is in play when we discuss our relationship to e. There are additional problems with our intentionality when it comes to e, given that the intentional state directed at e is part of e. This might complicate matters. If e exists (if it is an object), our thought directed at it has to be part of it. And it had better be tied to some rather demanding epistemic notion (such as philosophical knowledge) or other, because I assume that you are not just guessing that it is an object. But, before we get to that – which, I think, is a special topic connected to whether e exists, and so forth – I just want to have set out these distinctions which I think can be drawn with regard to intentionality. That's my starting point.

Priest: Yes, I don't think I'd put it exactly the same way, but I do recognize the distinctions you're drawing. I take the thinking relation to be univocal, but I can think of something in different ways. For example, I can think of it *de re*, under no particular description. I can think of that (*pointing to a chair*). But usually, when I think of something, I do think of it under some characterization or other. I can think of the German chancellor *de dicto*. Then I'm thinking of Angela Merkel under that description. As such, I may or may not know various things about her. If I think of Angela Merkel under the description "chancellor of Germany," then I presumably know that she's the chancellor of Germany. And I may know of other things about her; some things I may know very little about, and some things may be beyond my abilities to know anything. So, I recognize the various distinctions you're drawing. But, for me, that *a* thinks of *b* always means the same thing – though, when *a* thinks of *b*, this may be so for different kinds of reasons, with different kinds of epistemic consequences.

Gabriel: The question then is going to be how exactly we think of the relationship between philosophical concepts such as intentionality, knowledge, being, existence, identity, difference, and so forth – what it is for them to be univocal or to have a determinate meaning on a certain general level, and then be differentiated into different kinds? I assume that this is what you have in mind when you say "univocal" and then construct your theory of thought or thinking as univocal. I think that this plays a huge role in *Beyond the Limits of Thought* and in your past work. So, one way of thinking of what you've said is something like the following: there's a concept *thought* or *thinking about* – which is perhaps the paradigm of intentionality. It's clearly an intentional concept. And then there are these various kinds, which just fall under this concept, right?

Priest: You could put it that way. In terms of univocity, what I meant was that there is a single semantics at issue here. Namely, intentionality is parsed semantically as a relationship between a subject and an object. But that's only part of the story, because there are ways in which different things might follow from your thinking in a certain way. Hence, I think we agree here. We may have to come back and revisit this issue, but I suspect that we're enough on the same page that we can go ahead and come back if necessary.

Gabriel: Yes, we can. The question, then, is really going to be what kind of role intentionality plays or does not play in our philosophical activity when we are trying to direct, or are directing, our thought at surprising objects. What I mean by surprising objects are objects like e, identity, and intentionality itself. They're not surprising by your conception of an object. But, outside the philosophical debate we currently find ourselves in, people might be surprised to hear that there are objects like e, identity, intentionality, and so forth, though it just follows smoothly – at least for most of those objects – from your understanding of being an object and my concept of appearing in a field of sense. It also makes me very open-minded concerning the concept of an object. But I do hold that intentionality is not univocal, or, rather, that there are different kinds of intentionality, which cannot be brought under a single concept by just thinking about objects regardless of their respective fields of sense.

Priest: Well, one can certainly think of objects of different kinds – I mean, e, if it's anything, is a simple object – a saturated object, in Frege's terms. Whereas identity, if it's anything, is a binary relation. And, of course, you can think of relations and you can think of simple objects. These can both be the target of an intentional state of mind. But there *are* some surprising things about intentionality. And the most obvious thing, I think, for philosophers, is that we seem to be able to think of things that don't exist, in the traditional analytic sense, such as Sherlock Holmes, and so on. One might well think that there are problems with apparently true claims about the fact that one can think of e or Sherlock Holmes or possibly other things. I'm happy to discuss and explore these issues.

Gabriel: Are you worried about the following problematic, which I've spelled out in a paper about the famous master/servant chapter in the *Phenomenology*: namely, that, if we think of intentionality paradigmatically as a subject–object relation of aboutness, or whatever, then we must provide an account of how we can direct intentionality at itself.

Priest: Give me an example.

Gabriel: Well, I can think about myself thinking about Angela Merkel. Now, the target of my thought is a thought whose target is another object, and any level of nesting is in principle possible, right?

Priest: Yes, that's right.

Gabriel: But then some people worry that a paradox is looming here. If you think of this in terms of consciousness and self-consciousness, certain identity problems might seem to arise. And we are in a territory here that may, to some extent, be analogous to what we will discuss concerning e: we seem to be dealing with strange loops, as Douglas Hofstadter has famously called them. Someone might wonder – I don't – what happens if I move from consciousness to self-consciousness; and, in these debates, I assume that what people mean by consciousness is what we mean by intentionality.

Priest: It may be broader, but certainly it is one species of consciousness. But look, you're right. People do worry about this. How can something be the same thing, *qua* subject of thought and *qua* object of thought? I think Sartre thinks this is a problem. Certainly, I suspect Nishida sometimes thinks so too. Personally, I've never found a problem with this. I've spent so much of my life worrying about self-reference. There are many kinds of self-reference, and some of them lead to paradox, some of them don't. I don't think that me thinking about myself leads to paradox at all. Although, maybe if you tell a more complicated story, it can. After all, we're in the same vicinity as the liar paradox: someone who thinks "what I'm thinking is false."

Gabriel: And what about the following? I call this the paradox of self-consciousness. It's not really a paradox, though; I shouldn't have called it a paradox. I can just call it a problem of self-consciousness. Let's introduce another notion in order to be clearer: my overall mental state. If I'm in some overall mental state, I can begin to direct my attention to it, right?

Priest: It's very big!

Gabriel: Yes, it's a big mental state. I can nevertheless say things about it: I feel a certain way, I have a certain taste in my mouth, I'm awake, etc. I can write a long list about my overall mental state right now. That just means that part of my mental state now is directed at my overall mental state. So, whatever my overall mental state might have been before I directed my thought at it, I just changed my overall mental state in virtue of directing my attention to it. Therefore, I'm not capable of grasping my overall mental state without changing it.

Priest: OK, good. I think that's what worries people like Sartre. I don't find that argument persuasive, for the following reason. It makes perfectly good sense to me to say something like "I'm thinking this very thought." So, the content of the thought can be the thought enunciated by that sentence, as a form of self-reference. Now, is the fact that you're thinking the thought you mentioned a guarantee that you're changing your mental state? Well, it could be. Suppose you get up in the morning and have breakfast and suddenly think that, then clearly your mental state has changed; but once the state has occurred to you, you can carry on thinking and no further change happens. So, I don't see that thinking this kind of self-referential thought necessarily requires a change of state.

Gabriel: Yes, exactly. Clearly there are cases where this is not so, but the question is if those are cases where I direct my thought at my overall mental state.

Priest: Well, if your overall mental state contains that thought, then you don't change anything – if you're thinking that thought in the same way. If I write on a page: "All the sentences on this page are true," and one of the sentences on the page is "All the sentences on the page are true," I haven't changed the contents of the page. It just happens to be a sentence that falls under the description.

Gabriel: That will be the form of the solution. I think this clears up a lot of territory. But here's an issue about the notion of an object that you are using: I sometimes, in *Fields of Sense* and elsewhere, speak of the formal theory of objects, according to which an object is whatever can be the target of a truth-apt thought. That's one way in which I have put it in previous contexts. And this is where intentionality enters the picture. Then, I might already have created a basis which makes the commitment to e very hard to escape. For now it at least looks like I have a domain in front of my thought, which consists of all the objects. And sometimes I call a sense a furnishing function. Chalmers uses this notion in a different sense, having to do with possible worlds. But let a furnishing function just be the idea that we locate something in a field of sense. The objects in the field of sense have something in common; namely, that they're in that field of sense. And so, something maps those objects onto the field. And that's what I just call a sense. Now, the question is: Does being an object have a sense such that it necessarily generates the corresponding field, or is being an object too thin to come with a sense?

Priest: Right. This is good. I think there may be something here which does separate our thinking. Being an object is a property. How wide its domain is is something we probably disagree about. Let's leave it at that for the moment: being an object is a property. And *being an object* is a sense of that property. It has a clear sense, and so collects together all the things that fall under the property as specified by that sense.

Gabriel: There is something about this on which it would be good to hear your opinion. I have been thinking about whether the following is a problem for the view that to be is to be the value of a bound variable. If I say "There exists an x such that $x = y$," then, of course, x and y have to exist in order for them to be identical, right? So, if I clarify the notion of existence via identity or self-identity, I already assume things about existence. Hence, I don't really clarify the notion of existence. All I'm saying is that something exists. Thus, this formula is not a clarification of existence at all.

Priest: Well, I reject the Quinean thought that to exist is to be the value of a bound variable, so I would put your point in terms of being an object. But, that aside, there is an issue here. I certainly do think that you can define what it is to be an object as *to be something*. One of the ways to cash that out deploys the identity predicate $x = y$. Now, if it's true that $x = y$ – or even if it's false that $x = y$ – then x and y are objects. That is, the variables "x" and "y" pick out objects from whatever totality you're quantifying over. So, certainly in some sense, the definition of objecthood presupposes identity, which presupposes a notion of objecthood. I think you're dead right about that. But, as I think we agree, analysis has to come to an end somewhere; and there are lots of our fundamental concepts for which it's impossible to give some kind of non-circular characterization. A prime example is the notion of a set. You can say a set is a collection, or a group, or a bunch, or whatever. But, technical differences aside, these all come to the much the same thing. Similarly, the notions of falsity and negation are very intimately connected. You can define each only using the other. And I suspect that objecthood and identity are much the same. I think that's a place where analysis hits rock bottom, as it were.

Gabriel: At some point there's rock bottom. We all know this basically *a priori*, and it would be very surprising if philosophical analysis were infinitary.

Priest: Well, it's impossible, as Aristotle pointed out.

Gabriel: We agree that it would very surprising if someone came up with an infinitist view of philosophical justification.

Priest: Indeed. And, again, I don't think this is something that separates us. For you, to be an object is to appear in a field of sense. And, to explain the notion of a field of sense, you have to talk about objects. So that's going to lead to the same kind of issue.

Gabriel: Of course, at some point, but it matters where the point is. My rock bottom right now is the notion of sense, given the role it plays in my analysis of existence, or of being an object for that matter. I provide terminology – appearing, sense, field, etc. – and this is roughly where I stop. I can say more about appearing. There are things I can say about the elements of the analysis or definition, if you like, of existence – let's call it the definition of existence. But then, I'm currently really wondering about what a sense is. Again, we can clarify this by saying it's a description, it's a guise, a mode of presentation, an object's being thus and so. We have various kinds of formulae, and then we can, of course, connect the notion of a property, say, with a notion of a description. I would do that. But what's the relationship for you between properties and senses or descriptions. Do you think they are the same?

Priest: OK, so let's take those three things: properties, senses, and descriptions. A property is something that you attribute to an object, so it can be described by things like "x is red," "x is an object," "x is in Berlin." A description: well, you can describe properties, but more normally you describe objects. "The chancellor of Germany" is a noun phrase. It's not a predicative phrase. And, as you know, following Frege – and I think he got this right – when we speak of objects or properties (that is, concepts) our language has both a sense (*Sinn*) and a reference (*Bedeutung*). Frege's notion of sense is a bit unclear. But the way it's usually explained is that the sense is the way that the *Bedeutung* is grasped by a speaker. A pretty standard way would be to do this with a certain description. I guess I'm happy with that.

Gabriel: Yes, so am I, apart from the additional assumption I call realism about sense, according to which there would have been senses had there been no speakers. The good old idea of a mode of presentation is one I can easily wrap my head around. Now, I have one more question on this because I'm currently writing a chapter on sense for a new book: I want to think of senses as ways things are. So, if we put it by saying that a way for a thinker to think about an object or a property is a sense, then it's tempting to say that reality would be senseless had there been no thinkers, right? That looks very plausible, but Frege cannot be saying this. He believes that $7 + 5 = 12$ regardless of the presence of thinkers. Thinkers and speakers are not involved. As a mathematician, Frege thereby wanted to divorce sense from actual thinkers, let alone speech acts. And I'm inclined to think that this has to be correct. I would find it very strange if reality were senseless without thinkers. Does this strike you as a topic? I'm a realist about sense. Thinkers are not that important for the realm of sense; thinkers are just more senses: they bring more senses, complicated senses, to the realm of sense, but the realm of sense extends far beyond the presence of thinkers.

Priest: That's an interesting subject. So, take the name "Angela Merkel." The sense of this might be a description, "the chancellor of Germany." That description is itself an object. Can there be objects which would be objects even if there were no thinkers? We discussed this briefly in our written chapters. This depends on whether you're a realist about objects – in particular, non-existent objects – or a kind of conceptualist, shall we say. I change my mind on that sometimes, but generally speaking I'm inclined to think that all the objects are there, as it were, and would have been there even had no one actually existed to talk about them – because they could have done so had they existed. So, I guess I'm a realist about these things, in just the way you've described.

Gabriel: I think this is an important analogy between our views. There might be a reason why we incline in that direction. I don't know if there's a knockdown argument. I just think that it's very implausible to think the counterfactual thought that the objects wouldn't have been the way we find them to be had we not found them this way. There is something very odd about this thought. I can't find any way of making this thought more precise, though many have tried.

Priest: The main argument for some kind of conceptualism here comes from fiction. It's a very natural thought that Sherlock Holmes would not have been an object if Doyle had not – in some sense – created Holmes. That's a very natural thought. I think in the end that it's wrong, though. But of course, a case needs to be made for that.

Gabriel: I used to think that there are two kinds of senses or two kinds of objects. The ones that we, as it were, find and the ones that we produce in virtue of relating to them in a certain way, which would have opened a space for the view that Doyle creates Sherlock Holmes or that social facts are somehow socially constructed in that sense – i.e., where a bunch of people relate to a certain object in a certain way and thereby bring about the object as such. But then I became convinced that I ought to be what Davidson, for very different reasons, called "a realist in all departments" and reject the idea that sense is ever constructed or produced in a special ontological way. And now I tend to think that senses, and thereby objects, are indeed such that the realm of senses, the realm of objects, is laid out. That's something we also briefly discussed earlier, at least during our last meeting in Bonn a couple of years ago: about whether temporal relations can just be built into the realm of senses. So, the fact that I have thought about Angela Merkel is itself – i.e., that thought itself – in the realm of senses and objects. It's not that there is a flat realm of objects and then there are outbursts of thought.

Priest: It's clear that you can build time into senses. I mean, just consider the description: the first person I will think about when I wake up tomorrow morning. Tense is built into that. But it specifies a perfectly good object. It probably won't be Sherlock Holmes, but it might be well after this discussion!

Gabriel: OK, good.

Priest: I do think there is a difference in our perspectives, however. I have a very flat ontology – as you put it. The world comprises objects. They may be of different kinds and fit together in various ways. But they are all just objects.

Gabriel: This is tricky. What I call the bundle theory of objects in *Fields of Sense* is perhaps relevant here. This might get somewhat complicated, but let's see if we can get a clear-cut separation of issues here. I tend to think of objects – and sometimes I have thought that your gluon theory is in the same vicinity as the following line of thought – as bundles of senses. The natural Fregean picture is that there is the object, and now, as it were, the senses surround it like literal visual perspectives, right? There's the volcano. And then we can walk around the volcano, and every literal perspective on the volcano corresponds to a Fregean sense. And similarly for numbers: $3 + 1$ is one way of thinking about 4 and so is $2 + 2$, but then there just is the number 4 and its two guises. It makes its appearance in two ways on both sides of the equation. That's a very natural way to think. But, of course, the number 4 itself has a sense. So, I can also just write "$3 + 1 = 4$" or "the volcano is the volcano." The idea that there's a senseless object, that the *Bedeutung* is senseless and surrounded, as it were, by a corona of senses, cannot, I think, be correct. There's no rock bottom of reference where no sense plays a role, which is why I think of the sense/reference distinction as a functional distinction and not as a metaphysical one, meaning it's not a distinction that characterizes reality. Now the next idea is this: What if an object just is all of its senses? Then the object can be represented as a list of senses. Say, the number 4 is a list of all the equations, including equations where the number 4 itself makes an appearance. That's what I call the bundle theory of objects. And then what holds the bundle together? I think that's your gluon. What holds all of this together is just the fact that this is how they are, that this is how stuff is assembled. So, the table, the object table, in my picture is identical to everything that is true about it. It stands here, it has a white surface, and so forth. And if I were able to write down a list of all the true propositions where the object makes its appearance in the logical object slot, then this is what the object is. That's what I call the bundle theory. I hope this is sufficiently clear. I think that you hold a bundle theory.

Priest: No, I don't think I do. In general, I don't care for reductionist accounts – say, this object is the bundle of its properties or tropes or whatever. I think it's a perfectly bona fide object as it is. For me there are objects. If they have parts, there must be something which holds the parts together. That's a gluon. But gluons, objects, properties, senses, functions, these are all objects in some sense. And, of course, there are important connections between them, and those connections can be interesting because of things like the Bradley regress. But, in the last analysis, the pieces fit together – to use a Wittgensteinean metaphor, like links in the chain. So, we come back to this kind of flatness. Perhaps there is more to be said about these issues, and we can come back to them if necessary. But I think we have done sufficient by way of background clarification, and it is time to turn to issues where we clearly do disagree. Let's turn to these tomorrow.

Gabriel: I agree.

7

Discussion about Non-Wellfoundedness

August 17, 2021

Priest: What we've discussed so far are mainly clarificatory issues, I think. Now that we've got those sorted to some extent, let's turn to the main thing that we disagree about. I think this brings other things in its wake, but I take it to be the focal point of our disagreement. And that's about whether e is an object, or whether that statement even makes sense. We should get to the issue of meaningfulness or sense in due course; first, though, let's talk about whether or not e is an object, setting aside the meaningfulness of this discourse for the moment. So let me start by laying out the dialectics of the matter so far, at least as I see it. In the first chapter of this book, I claimed that one can think of e, the mereological sum of all objects, as the world in your sense. I didn't give an argument that e exists. I took it over from standard mereology. Whether that's a reasonable assumption or not is something we can come back to if you want. What I did do was reply to some of your arguments that there's no such thing. Given your assumptions, for e to be an object, it would have to be in a field of sense. But that field of sense has to be a part of e, by definition. Thus, the appropriate mereology is going to reject anti-symmetry. That is, you can have chains going all the way down, which repeat themselves. And then I said: that's fine; there's no particular reason why a good mereology should be committed to anti-symmetry. I then gave a few arguments as to why that's the case. Some of these arguments you've queried: the aleph argument, for example. But, in the end, I don't think that's an important issue just because you agreed that, in general, there's no reason why the mereology for a field of sense has to be well founded in this sense.
Gabriel: Yes.
Priest: So, the crucial question is why e, specifically, cannot be part of itself. I haven't yet seen an argument for this that I find persuasive.
Gabriel: My first question is: Are we in e? If you think of this visu-

ally, then e itself is smaller than itself, as it were, in virtue of being contained in it. And that can't be the case, of course.

Priest: Smaller? No, it's the same. It has exactly the same parts. It's exactly the same object, has the same definition. There's no difference in size, whatever that means. And notice that that consideration would apply to any field of sense that contained itself. There has to be something special about e, so we're not there yet.

Gabriel: Yes, that's right. I have to find some considerations that apply specifically to e.

Priest: Agreed.

Gabriel: In *Why the World Does Not Exist* and *Fields of Sense* I claimed that there are different kinds of part–whole relationships. So, as we know, Helgoland is a German island that stands in a part–whole relation to Germany, which differs very much from the part–whole relation in which my finger stands to my hand or the word "word" to the sentence I'm uttering. If reality, that is the scenario that we're in, were such that we're in e, I need reasons for thinking that this overall part–whole relationship is governed by anti-symmetry or, say, any kind of mereological axiom system. But here you might just say: look, if fields of sense are wholes, then we can get the field of sense of all fields of sense without any problems. I think this is your take on this. Is that correct?

Priest: Yes. And I agree that there may be several different part–whole relations here – though I take it that one can always consider the union of these. But we do not need to consider this matter here. The question concerns the parthood relation that e bears to itself – that is, the one in which e is to be taken as a part of itself. And you don't need to show that that relation is an anti-symmetric relation, just that e cannot be part of itself in that sense. So, what we are still looking for is an argument that e is special.

Gabriel: On this issue, my argument draws on the idea that e cannot appear alongside other fields of sense. If it is all-encompassing, it cannot be one of the several fields. Otherwise, these fields would be both in e and not in e. Yet, at this point you will rightly point out that this begs the question against non-wellfoundedness, which precisely allows us to identify e as a fos within which all other fields (and itself) appear and e, insofar as it appears within itself. You want to say that they are exactly the same e, one the container, the other contained, yet identical.

Priest: Yes. Consider the following diagram. The arrows indicate the parthood relation in questions. e is a part of itself; but there can be fields of sense, e_1, e_2, ..., which are also parts of e. Without anti-symmetry, matters are quite consistent. e_1, for example, is simply part of e, and so is represented as such, wherever "e" occurs in the diagram.

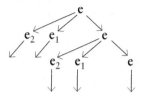

Gabriel: I doubt that this makes sense for the following reason, among others: in order to clarify some issues, in *Sinn und Existenz*, the German version of *Fields of Sense*, there is a twelve-step argument, which collects some of the main tenets of the ontology of fields of sense into an argument against world-views. A premise of that argument which is important for the matter at hand is the following (my own self-translation from the German): "If the world exists, there's a field of sense in which the world appears. Therefore, there would have to be a description under which everything that there is, including the world, falls – because senses are descriptions." And then what I reject is the claim that there is such a description. There is no sense attached to the picture of non-well-founded mereology as being the form of reality. The mereological picture is formally stable; we agree on that. But the question is about what the sense of the world field might be. What's the sense in which e exists? There would have to be a furnishing function, which maps e_1, e_2, and e to e itself. If one asks what that function is for artworks, I can say it's such and such, being an object which is essentially subject to interpretation, say, or whatever the right theory of the art field dictates. For physical objects, there is being measurable by instruments, plus mathematical apparatus. For the political field, it is being subject to constitutional procedures, or whatever. And what would be the sense of the world field? I think your answer would be that the sense just is the ontology of fields of sense. This is its own sense. Let's call this "this easy answer." Is that how you would reply?

Priest: Maybe. There are a few moving pieces before we get to that, however. First of all, note that we have now changed the subject. We were discussing your argument to the effect that there can be no e because of the ordering properties involved, and my reply to that. Now we have moved to a different argument against e, namely that it has no sense. In reply, I would say that it has a perfectly good sense, namely, that given by its definition as the mereological sum of all objects. You may well challenge the legitimacy of that characterization. I suspect you would, but that's the move that I'd make in the first instance. You characterize it by that description, which gives its sense. And that sense also tells you what the furnishing function is, in your terms. Because e is the fusion of all objects, the furnishing function maps each object into this fusion – that is, e.

Gabriel: Yes. That's what I mean by the easy answer. The easy answer is that mereology bursts with characterizations, as it were. Mereology itself gives you the characterization.

Priest: Well, the mereological definition gives you the sense. However, one might note here a possible objection from within the realm of mereology itself, before we even get to the fos considerations you mentioned. One might argue that the fusion does not exist.

Gabriel: And I take that issue not to be a minor problem, but evidence of the fact that metaphysical mereology is lacking in sense.

Priest: I wouldn't put it that way, exactly. The sense is fine. The thought is that it has no referent. In chapter 1, I characterize a fusion in terms of some condition, $A(x)$. But, as I point out there, there is a standard debate concerning when such a characterization delivers a referent. (Or at least, if one is a noneist, a referent which actually satisfies the characterization.) Some people, like David Lewis, thought that any condition will characterize a fusion. I am rather dubious about that. Some people hold that no characterization characterizes a fusion, because there aren't any. Peter Unger comes close to this view; and it is essentially the view of the Abhidharma Buddhist tradition. I think the truth lies somewhere in between. Some characterizations, such as "x is a physical member of Graham Priest" and "x is a movement of Beethoven's 9th Symphony," pick out a bunch of objects which have a fusion: me (or at least my body) and the symphony itself. The parts, in those cases, have a certain integrity. Contrasted with this are bunches of things with no such integrity. Thus, the condition "x is the Eiffel Tower or x is the number 3 or x is the property of being just" delivers a completely gerrymandered bunch of things. I think we are very close here to a distinction you draw in *Fields of Sense* between an additive and a unified totality.

Gabriel: Yes. That's right. A unified totality is one whose parts hang together. An additive totality is simply a bunch of unrelated objects.

Priest: Good. However one describes the distinction, it's not at all obvious how to cash out what, exactly, it is to have this kind of integrity.

Gabriel: No, it's not obvious. What I do in this part of *Fields of Sense* is indeed to say that a reality that lacks integrity is at least unattractive for the metaphysician. Typically, people who think that e exists, or that there is a discipline dealing with absolutely everything, do not think along those lines. That's at least part of the sociology of the discipline.

Priest: Yes, that's probably true.

Gabriel: As Aristotle put it: reality is not a bad tragedy. A bad tragedy would be one in which the parts don't hang together. You see Oedipus and then Donald Trump, and the one has a burger and the other one walks through the forest.

Priest: Yes, that's not very attractive!

Gabriel: This would be sad enough. Therefore, if e makes sense, it will be a unified totality, and it will come with a sense.

Priest: Yes, and I think that the condition I used to characterize the parts of e – the property of being an object, of being something – provides exactly what is required. The things that satisfy it are not a gerrymandered totality. The condition cuts reality at a joint, as one might say, the joint being perhaps the most fundamental joint of all: that between everything and nothing – though I suspect that you will disagree with this.

Gabriel: At the very least – which is why I raised the intentionality question. It is why the whole issue of intentionality or of the epistemology of the position enters the picture. Indeed, that is what I'm puzzled about.

Priest: I'm not seeing the connection with intentionality yet. What do you have in mind?

Gabriel: I think that our mental states, when they're directed at gerrymandered wholes, are defective in a way in which mental states that are directed at nice, good wholes are not. That's why, in a science class, you would have to leave the room if you pick out, say, only a bunch of things specified by some cobbled-together condition, as opposed to the sophisticated numerical conditions in algebraic geometry for which Peter Scholze in Bonn recently won a Fields medal. Peter Scholze gets the Fields medal, but, if I enter the room and I discover mathematical patterns of a gerrymandered kind, I don't even get a degree. I don't think they're making a mereological mistake in science and mathematics departments, and so I think that someone whose mental states were constantly directed at gerrymandered wholes – say a schizophrenic – would have a defective intentionality.

Priest: It's certainly true that it's hard to say what's gerrymandered and what's not, because some characterizations which appear gerrymandered may turn out as science develops to be actually a natural kind of some sense.

Gabriel: But the question then arises of how we can know independently of these considerations – considerations which give us something which is clearly formally stated – that this is instantiated. That's what I mean by the question "Can we base metaphysics on mereology?" This is a version of the *sense argument against the world*. So, imagine there's e. Perhaps there's no formal or *a priori* objection that ultimately rules out the logical possibility of e. Now, what would it be for us to know that this is the scenario that we are actually in? The issue of gerrymandering, and so forth, the content side of mereology, so to speak, needs to be addressed, and I don't see how we can fix this. I see this as a job for the metaphysician rather than for me.

Priest: Well, it's certainly a job. But it may not be a job for the empirical scientist. It may be a job for someone who wants to talk about being *qua* being or whether there is such thing as being *qua* being. Call that metaphysics if you want. However, it is often the case that general philosophical considerations determine some sort of philosophical natural kinds, so to speak.

Gabriel: Yes. They sometimes do. I wouldn't deny that. I would not want to get rid of philosophy as such. It's not an anti-philosophical stance that I'm advocating. That's the last straw I would pick before giving up.

Priest: Well, if you do, we're both out of our job!

Gabriel: Exactly ... we want philosophy and not full-blown Pyrrhonian skepticism.

Priest: Agreed. And it seems to me that being an object picks out such a philosophical "natural kind." The condition is clearly not gerrymandered.

Gabriel: But can we actually carry out the formal operation of fusing all objects?

Priest: We don't have to carry out anything, because, as we agreed in the last session, there's a realism about this.

Gabriel: In his account of our exchange, Greg Moss draws a distinction between a logical possibility and an ontological possibility. Maybe this is where it comes into play. One might say: yes, e is logically possible. Gabriel's arguments have not demonstrated the logical impossibility of e. Because, in that corner of logical space, it is perfectly possible; in other corners, it isn't, since, if you stick to wellfoundedness, you won't get e. Now, what reason do I have to make a choice between the two? My arguments establish only that, in one region of logical space, a theory can be formulated according to which e is possible. In some other region, if you don't have resources like non-wellfoundedness, you won't get to see this.

Priest: Yes, Greg does draw this distinction in some places, but I've never been sure exactly how to understand it.

Gabriel: This is how I read it.

Priest: Well, obviously there are lots of different theories of mereology. In some of them there's a top element and in some there is not; in some there's a bottom element, in some of them there's not; in some the parthood relation is well founded, and in some it's not; etc. All these are possible mathematical structures. But that doesn't tell you which one provides the correct picture of reality, as it were. One could say: Look, there are lots of pure geometries, Euclidean or whatever, and as pure mathematical structures they are all equally good. We have to look elsewhere to find out which is the geometry of the space/time of our own cosmos. That would be analogous. Now, with the geometric analogy, it's clear where you look: you'd look for an experiment. Question: where do you look in the case of the correct mereology? That's not so clear.

Gabriel: Indeed, I really wouldn't know where to look.

Priest: Well, I would look to concepts which "cut nature at the metaphysical joints," like being an object. Still, this at least puts our debate into a certain clear perspective. If one looks at things in mereological terms, you hold that the correct mereology has no top guy. And I hold that it does have a top guy – and, by the way, a bottom guy as well. In some sense, therefore, the correct methodology for choice between these is what we are discussing at the moment.

Gabriel: Yes. The question is going to be how we decide. What reason do we have to prefer one over another? I have officially preferred a "no top guy" mereology (if any). This has driven my thinking. If you ask me for a reason for this choice, then I would say that I cannot imagine the position taken from the God's-eye point of view or from cosmic exile, as people used to say in the good old Harvard days from Quine to Putnam. I cannot imagine such a position. This is maybe just part of an epistemological consideration.

Priest: Well, I don't think my view is a "God's-eye" view. I'm just talking about reality, using the linguistic resources at my disposal. I would have thought that you are doing the same. Actually, if you put matters in this way, I think it takes you into seriously troubled waters. In an obvious sense, what you're doing in *Fields of Sense is* presenting a God's-eye view. You are telling us how things in general are – even if you say that these things are such as to have no top element.

Gabriel: And I mean it.

Priest: OK. So, in some sense you are talking about the totality of objects ... Actually, we are in the vicinity of another important matter here. In your discussions, you *appear* to be quantifying over all objects. I think you would deny that you are. Maybe appearances here are deceptive. We should talk about that at our next meeting.

Gabriel: We will talk about exactly that. But my immediate response to this is: well, everything is an object in the domain of objects. But there are the things that aren't objects. And now that sounds paradoxical. So, this might get me into dialetheia land. But there's the idea that, in addition to the objects we have in view, there is, as it were, the dark matter of ontology, which we don't have in view, and we can't calculate its relationship to the matter we have in view.

Priest: Well, let's explore this next time!

8

Discussion about Everything, Nonsense, and Wittgenstein

August 18, 2021

Priest: I think the next topic on our list is really two topics: talking about everything – and that's "everything" the quantifier – and talking about e, or, in your phrasing, the world. Those are distinct questions although they are connected.

Gabriel: It would be a good idea maybe to hear how you think they might come apart. I have admitted that I'm willing to say that there are non-determining properties within a range of the quantifier, which is as big as it gets. At the same time I also think that there should be some limitations. I always think of this in analogy to the good old case: there's no beer in the fridge vs. there's no beer whatsoever. I think my quantifiers have the form of "there is no beer – i.e., no beer in the fridge."

Priest: Sure. In natural languages, quantifiers are almost always bounded by context, like that provided by objects in the fridge.

Gabriel: Exactly.

Priest: But there are, at least *prima facie*, times where the quantifiers are completely unbounded. So, for example, suppose I say, "after you die, you will experience nothing." In that context, "nothing" is a quantifier: there is no x such that you will experience x. And that really is an unbounded quantifier, because it's not that you'll experience nothing in the fridge or nothing in Bonn; it really means *nothing whatsoever*. So, at least *prima facie*, in a natural language you can have totally unbounded quantifiers. In that sense, you could quantify over everything.

Gabriel: So it seems.

Priest: OK. So, let's talk about whether or not you *can* quantify over everything. I think you can; I don't have a problem with this, and it seems natural to suppose that you wouldn't either, since you seem to do it yourself. For example, in your chapter 2, on page 40, you say that we can think of metaphysics "as the discipline studying the architecture of absolutely everything." Now, absent some fast footwork, that's an absolutely universal quantifier. And then there is another example, on page 41, where you say that there is no object "whose architecture or structure could be investigated by the methods (if any) of metaphysics *qua* theory of absolutely everything." Again, this is a universal quantifier with the broadest sense. Hence, I assumed that you would say that you can quantify over everything – particularly so, because people who claim you can't quantify everything seem to refute themselves in the very process. That's a really big problem for people who think you can't quantify over everything – namely, they can't express their own view. I'd assumed you didn't want to have to deal with that particular problem.

Gabriel: Yes, I'm not rejecting the content that the opponent is committing to. The opponents say: "absolutely everything is such and so." That's the metaphysician talking. She talks, and she thinks she has the universal quantifier and that she can do more with it somehow. Now this is what I'm denying. But, if I'm denying this, then the worry, which I would accept, is that I'm not specifying the relevant content.

Priest: Exactly.

Gabriel: Let the metaphysician be the person who, in addition to whatever she believes about semantics, logics, grammar, and so forth, also believes that there's e. Now we can also have the philosopher or the linguist or whoever, who is quite content with unbounded universal quantification. That person, by my own terminology, is not the metaphysician. So, this is a commitment that I might want to reconsider, and yet I tend to think that it's a short path from quantifying over absolutely everything to committing to e.

Priest: Oh, I think there is a very short path. We should come to that.

Gabriel: In order to block it, though, I'm inclined to try everything in my power not to commit to universal quantification in the first place. This is where I stand.

Priest: I understand that. At the very least, I think then you'd need to be more careful about how you phrase yourself. You need to express your own view without using a quantifier that appears to be absolutely unbounded. But can you do that? After all, you make claims such as that to exist is to appear in a field of sense.

Gabriel: Yes.

Priest: Now, even though there's no explicit quantifier there, you seem to intend a completely unbounded universal quantifier, since this is a claim about what it is for *anything* to exist.

Gabriel: I would reject that, because I think that, while there is a non-determining concept and therefore non-determining properties – so

I have no trouble with denying this relationship between property and predicates or concept and property – I do not think that that these two, determining and non-determining properties, are therefore on the same level. So, when I talk about an object, an actual object or a possible object for that matter, I'm moving from this top level downwards, but not in such a way that I'm going from a universal concept to one of the instances.

Priest: It's not that that I'm worrying about. The worry is about making universal claims about objects.

Gabriel: I do not think of the view that I'm propounding as making a claim about all objects, because the claim is that that cannot be done! Now, the question is whether this raises expressibility issues.

Priest: Well, let's look at one of these sentences more carefully.

Gabriel: That is exactly what we ought to do.

Priest: Take: "To exist is to appear in a field of sense." Now, what that appears to mean is: "For all x, x exists if x appears in a field of sense." And that is a quite general universal quantifier.

Gabriel: My immediate response would be that it's bounded by the things that exist. When I talk about the things that exist, I'm ruling out the things which don't.

Priest: But you think that everything exists in a field of sense.

Gabriel: Not the things that don't! But now the question is how the following two things hang together: the relativity about non-existence and existence. The picture is: if I say "a exists," then of course this formula tells me "in some field of sense, let's say, here"; but when I say it doesn't exist, then I'm saying, "it's not here." Let that be an absence. So, Angela Merkel exists *here*. But, in the Sherlock Holmes stories, she's not *there*. Hence, Angela Merkel exists and doesn't exist. Now, the next thing that I am committed to is that everything exists and doesn't exist in different fields. In field of sense ontology, this is tantamount to saying there aren't any necessarily existing entities.

Priest: I don't really see how that addresses the issue, but, in any case, it raises the same problem again. You say that all things exist in some fields of sense and not in others. Again, you're talking about all things, and now you cannot be talking about just some things, because you say they all exist in some field of sense. So, it looks as though you're quantifying over all of the objects there are in any field of sense.

Gabriel: Well, here, with this phrase "to exist is to appear in a field of sense," I'm saying that this particular instance of the universal quantifier is bound by the rule that you can replace an x only with an existing a, b, c, etc. I would think of this as restricting the domain of quantification. So, if someone now comes up with a non-existent thing, I would say that you can't do that. That would be the analogy with being in the fridge. Now the question is about the bigger claim – namely, that everything exists and doesn't exist.

Priest: You speak of "thing" here. But that is just another way of saying *object*. And, since we are talking about *any* thing, we have the same problem. Let's leave this one aside for a moment and come back to the statement of your view: for all x, x exists if x appears in a field of sense. That is, to make it absolutely clear, for all x, if x appears in a field of sense, x exists. What does this quantifier range over?

Gabriel: Of course, it ranges over things, say. But things do not exhaust what there is; there is also nothing, as you would agree, and this brings us back to a version of the difference between existence and non-existence.

Priest: OK. We can come back to the matter of whether nothing is an object in due course. Let us stay with the matter of what this word "thing" means. I take it to mean much the same as "object." You seem to be drawing a distinction between the two notions, and I wonder what that distinction is.

Gabriel: In my terminology, when I use the word "object," we enter different territory. I do draw a thing/object distinction. Sometimes the thing/object distinction is something like: "thing" is a large grammatical structure, so that we can say something like "all things." When we begin to say "things," we say this with the lowest possible voice. And when I say "object," specifically in the context of my theorizing, I mean something that we can be wrong about. I call this the epistemic concept of being an object.

Priest: We agreed that what it means to be an object is, for you, to exist in a field of sense. This might problematize that. But let's set that aside for now, as it would take us off track, since the problems now seem to appear with universal quantifiers ranging over things. Whether you use the word "object" or not, you're still quantifying. I mean – I presume you think that everything is a thing.

Gabriel: Yes, everything is a thing, except for nothing.

Priest: Then you're quantifying over everything.

Gabriel: Yes, I am quantifying over everything, but the quantifier is restricted, it rules out nothing.

Priest: Well, I thought *you* thought there was no such thing as nothing! But, in any case, the whole point of distinguishing between objects and things was to be able to talk about things that are not objects. But now we have to talk about things that are not things. So, the problem has reappeared in this new terminology.

Gabriel: Well, let's be more careful here. Let's look at this phrase: for all x, x exists (in one field of sense) and doesn't exist (in another). What can replace the variable? I would say that everything that gives me a field of sense can replace this variable. Now, what do we do with replacements of the variables that create nonsense? I think there are some of those, so I think there's a contrast class. The question is whether there's an unbounded quantifier somewhere in what I'm doing, right? If there is, I think it would be a quantifier with no contrast class, like "everything." In that case, there's no contrast class

Priest: Well, the question is: Is that quantifier quantifying over the things in just one field of sense or over things in every field of sense? And it certainly appears that you are quantifying over the things in any field of sense – that is, all objects.

Gabriel: The quantification is over the objects in all fields of sense in which the object can be considered to make an appearance. When I say there aren't any tables in quantum theory, what I'm saying is that the sense of the quantum field just excludes the availability of tables. If my mind were really just the mind of a quantum theorist, such that I couldn't even see reality, being a sensorially blind being capable of calculating everything in quantum theory, then there's nothing you can do to tell me that there are tables.

Priest: I'm not sure if that helps either. The claim you made a few moments ago was something like this: "when I say 'for all x,' I can replace the variable with the name of any object for which it makes sense to do so, given the field of sense." So, you seem to be saying of all things that some of them are of this kind, and some are not. So, the wide-scoped universal quantifier has reappeared. Hence, it seems to be that, to say whatever you want to, you need to quantify over absolutely everything. I understand that you don't think so, but I think we should now leave it to anyone who hears this discussion to make up their own mind on the matter. Let's turn to the other issue we mentioned: the connection between universal quantification and e. There is an issue for you here, and it's a matter of self-reference.

Gabriel: Agreed.

Priest: The fact that you quantify over a totality does not *ipso facto* commit you to the existence of that totality. There are lots of sensitive issues here, but just, for example, think about Zermelo–Fraenkel set theory. This quantifies over all sets, but notoriously there's no set of all sets. So, there's at least a distinction to be drawn here. Let's agree, at least for the sake of argument, that the mere fact that, if you do quantify over everything, this does not *ipso facto* commit you to the existence of e. But in your case there seems to be a special problem, which is this: consider your own texts. Now I've always assumed – and you can tell me if this assumption is wrong – that, if you've got a text, it constitutes a field of sense. And the things in that field of sense are the things which are mentioned or quantifiable over in that field of sense.

Gabriel: Yes.

Priest: So, if you, yourself, in your texts are quantifying over everything, as we've been discussing, then it would seem to follow that there is a field of sense of everything because your own text provides this. That's a problem for you.

Gabriel: Yes, unless I can perform a similar maneuver that has the structure of Zermelo–Fraenkel set theory, but for fields of sense. In fact, I think of myself as doing that. This is part of the explanation of why, when faced with a choice between different mereologies, I went for anti-symmetry because I had not considered non-wellfounded mereology. You pointed out this blind spot. Hence, I made a blind choice. But it's interesting that the choice was guided by some consideration, of course, which was, *mutatis mutandis*, inspired by maneuvers in set theory. This was clearly part of the genealogy of the view.

Priest: All right. There is a problem about how Zermelo–Fraenkel set theory can get away with this, because it means Zermelo–Fraenkel set theory has no semantics. Set theorists tend to ignore this, but an analogous problem *is* there in set theory. But let's stick to your case. There are only three premises, and the three of them land you in the conclusion you don't want. The first is that any text provides a field of sense. The second is that the field of sense contains everything that is mentioned or quantified over in that field of sense. And the third is that, in your texts, you quantify over all things. The third is what we've just been discussing. I'd always assumed that you held the first two, but, if you endorse all three, you've got e. Therefore, one of those has got to go.

Gabriel: Well, I think my preferred option would be to give up the third.

Priest: OK. That takes us back to the problems we've just been discussing. Here's a move you could have made in that context, though you didn't: you think that talk of e is meaningless – though you yourself talk of it. You could also say that absolutely universal quantification is also meaningless, though you yourself do it. That puts us squarely in *Tractatus*-land. Though since we are going to end up there anyway, you might go there a bit earlier and declare that part of your discourse meaningless as well.

Gabriel: Yes. I have sympathies for that. Generally, in terms of the overall dialectical situation, I want to be as close to the metaphysician as possible, to someone who believes in both quantifiers of the widest possible scope and e. And I want to stop committing to the metaphysician's world-view shortly before she jumps into e.

Priest: The thing is that you might find that you don't have to jump, but you're pushed by your own words. In the *Tractatus*, Wittgenstein ends by declaring most of his book meaningless. He rather likes this; there's a mystical side to Wittgenstein in the *Tractatus*; you can see him sort of grinning with pleasure when he gets to the end. But most people who read it have not had the same reaction. There are very obvious problems. The first is that, *prima facie* at least, we do understand very well what's going on in the *Tractatus*. It's not meaningless. Or, at least, if it's nonsense, it's very well-hidden nonsense. And the same, I think, must be true for you. At one point you analogize talking of the world with a nonsense string, XCEANNR $_{s12*}$. I don't think that's a good analogy, because what you say is not an obvious nonsense string. *Prima facie*, it has a sense, whereas the nonsense string doesn't even have that. So, what you need is some account of things that are nonsense but *prima facie* sensible. There's work that needs to be done.

Gabriel: OK, so here's one difference. As you have pointed out in several of your published takes on the Tractarian strategy, it's unclear whether the whole building breaks down; it's unclear to what extent it's even a ladder. You think you're on the first rung and then it might turn out you're not even climbing. My picture, by contrast, is one where you're really climbing. And when you try to use the upper rung, you find there just isn't one. You're climbing, climbing, and then there's just nothing. This is on the level of a metaphor, of course, but it makes a significant difference. Thus, claims like "to exist is to be in a field of sense" or "all things exist and don't exist" – none of these break down until the last act. Whereas I read Wittgenstein as basically saying that everything breaks down. But then there are contradictions, it's unstable, and no one has solved those worries.

Priest: Okay. Let's try to think through this thing non-metaphorically. I mean, the ladder is a metaphor, and it's a nice metaphor, but what it means is something like this: that when you read the *Tractatus*, you have this illusion of understanding but, once you get to the end of the *Tractatus*, you realize that it was an illusion. And that's the bottom line of the *Tractatus*. I think that's a cleaner way of putting the point which avoids metaphors. Now, there's a problem with that line, which I think is a problem that you might face as well, which is this: Why does one claim that certain things are meaningless? Because it follows from certain things in the *Tractatus*. This move of Wittgenstein is not capricious. In some sense his very theory appears to force him into this situation: according to his own theory, his own words are meaningless. Now, meaningless claims can't establish anything. So, what we see is that the move has undercut the ground for making this claim that there are meaningless claims. The English have this expression – there is probably something similar in German – "sawing off the branch on which you're sitting."

Gabriel: We have the same expression in German.

Priest: That's essentially what Wittgenstein is doing, and I worry that you face the same problem, that you're undercutting your own ground by making this move.

Gabriel: I don't see this. I think that all the claims are fine as I climb up, as it were, as I approach the metaphysical field, the world. I'm approaching the world topic and, as I'm approaching, everything is stable enough. I'm saying what a field of sense is, why reality is disorderly, what an object is, what facts are, and so forth. I do all this theorizing, and, with respect to my theorizing, I don't take this Tractarian self-undercutting attitude at all. I'm just constructing a theory of fields of sense in the usual way; and, at some point, someone might ask about the field of all fields, and I have to point out that that's meaningless.

Priest: OK. But the question is how to understand your own theorizing. For the theorizing doesn't just tell you that talk of the world is meaningless, but much of your own theoretical machinery.

Gabriel: There's a little more architecture to my work. I don't want to be a complicated writer, but there is a reason why *Fields of Sense* has two parts. I start with destructive propositions there, and then I end Part I with negative ontology, and then we get positive ontology.

Priest: OK. I just looked at the index, and you make references to the world in both parts. So neither part is innocent.

Gabriel: That's correct. The book as it stands is not kosher; it still addresses the metaphysical desire, as though it were largely intact. I should either rewrite some parts of it in order to really separate the positive from the negative ontology much more strictly than I've done in the book. I shouldn't be so accommodating to what I call the metaphysician in Part II.

Priest: Well, I'd like to see how that trick could be turned, especially if one is to avoid absolutely universal quantification as well.

Gabriel: Presently, one might think of the book as being written as a dialogue with my reader. There's a dialectic going on in the ancient sense: I'm engaging with my opponent, I'm talking to someone. Sometimes I think of this – as did Wittgenstein – in analogy to psychoanalysis or more mundane psychotherapy: someone is coming to see me with a metaphysical problem.

Priest: That makes it sound less like the Wittgenstein of the *Tractatus* than the Wittgenstein of the *Investigations*, who says he wants to cure us of philosophy. He does say almost exactly that it's a therapeutic book. Once you get what his point is, then you stop worrying about philosophical problems. I don't think you want to go that far.

Gabriel: No. I want to say that, once you get what the point is, you are doing philosophy. There's nothing Carnapian or whatever. There is no suggestion that we replace philosophy or give it up.

Priest: Well, I'm glad to hear that! – though I felt that your book was giving me problems rather than taking them away!

Gabriel: Well, here's a problem you might have: Do you think that e (in your sense) exists (in your sense)?

Priest: That's an interesting question. In my terminology, e is an object. Maybe it's a contradictory object. That's not something I've argued for in our discussion; but I think there are good arguments for this once nothing, n, comes on the scene, and I'm happy to go there. If it turns out that the world is this paradoxical thing, that wouldn't surprise me, just because these big totalities are often paradoxical things. But setting that issue aside, is it an existent object?

Gabriel: Yes. Is it part of the causal order?

Priest: I don't know whether I have a stable view on that – though I don't think that the answer (whatever it is) is going to affect anything that we disagree about.

Gabriel: It's just that if you say "e does not exist," that doesn't mean what "the world does not exist" means in my terms, but you certainly might wind up defending the view (in your language) that e does not exist.

Priest: Agreed: it could happen. However, the general situation concerning your question is as follows: suppose you've got a mereological whole, and suppose some of its parts exist (in my sense) and some don't . . .

Gabriel: That will be the case with e.

Priest: Yes. Does the whole exist or not? I was teaching in Turin before the pandemic, and a student came up with the following argument for the existence of e, which I rather like. (I'm embarrassed to say that I can't now remember who it was.) Let us suppose that, when people wrote the constitution of Athens, they believed in Atlantis, and so they defined Athens or Greece, the Greek territory, as the various bits, including Atlantis. Some bits obviously exist. Atlantis, it turns out, does not. So, it turns out that Greece itself has both existent and non-existent parts. What should one say about Greece itself? It seems very natural to say that Greece exists even though some bits of it don't. If the argument is good, it shows that something that is composed of existent and non-existent parts can well exist. I think I'd be happy with that conclusion. After all, if you have causal contact with something, you never have causal contact with the whole thing. I have causal contact with this teacup, but obviously there's lots of it I don't have any contact with – the bits inside the china, for example. If one takes this point, then e exists.

Gabriel: What about the following: imagine some version of dualism is correct, and I'm a sum or a whole with existent and non-existent parts. My mind does not exist; it's not in the causal order, says dualist epiphenomenalism, which is still a serious option, right? Now I see the soccer player kick a ball: then I would say that his body scored the goal, but he didn't. That might not be a problem. We could say that this is similar to the Greece case: the whole does not exist, but a part does.

Priest: That would be analogous in a way.

Gabriel: Where we say the whole does not exist, though.

Priest: Perhaps. I'm not sure.

Gabriel: I think both examples are plausible.

Priest: Well, I think I prefer the conclusion suggested by the Greece example. But if some objects composed of existent and non-existent parts exist and some don't, I don't find that a problem. I don't see why there has to be a uniform answer on the matter.

Gabriel: Also, I assume both possibilities are at least *prima facie* compatible with non-wellfounded mereology. Any problems would, then, lie elsewhere.

Priest: Yes, it seems so.

Gabriel: Perhaps this is a good place to stop for today. We have spoken a lot about everything, **e**. We haven't yet discussed nothing, **n**. Let's do that in the next discussion.

Priest: Yes, let's move to **n**.

9

Discussion about Nothingness
August 20, 2021

Gabriel: My suggestion for today is that you introduce the topic of **n**, because **n** is perhaps even more heterodox in your way of thinking about these issues than **e**.

Priest: I think that that's true, at least from the perspective of standard mereology: **e** is a regular guy and **n** isn't. So let me introduce the issue. According to the definition that I give in chapter 1, **n** is the fusion of the things in the empty set, the fusion of no things, if you like. That goes against standard mereology, because the standard assumption is that, if things have a fusion, there must be some of them; you can't put together no things. I find that view groundless. Now, you can actually have a fairly regular mereology with the bottom guy, with the fusion of no things, and it's perfectly consistent. Then, assuming that every bunch of things has a fusion, you just get a Boolean algebra, and so a perfectly consistent structure. The way I do it, if you throw the bottom guy into the ordering, it isn't a consistent structure because **n** turns out itself to be an inconsistent object. So, you don't have to do it that way; you can preserve consistency if you want. But I rather like doing it in such a way that **n** turns out to be a contradictory object, precisely because there's an intuitive paradox about nothingness. It's something; after all, we can think about it. To put it in your terms, I guess it's an object in a certain field of sense, namely my text. But, by definition, it's the absence of everything. It's what you get when all objects have been removed, so to speak. Hence, it's not an object. It's therefore a paradoxical object; it wears its paradoxicality on its face, as it were. And this paradox exactly follows from the definition I gave. This is a virtue of the account in terms of traditional philosophy of science: the account "saves the phenomena." It explains why we have this paradox. That's why I think it's good to have **n** in the mereology, and the explanatory work that this does. Let me just say one more thing, and then you can tell me what you think. Whether there's a top guy in the ordering, **e**, and whether there's a bottom guy in the ordering, **n**, are in principle separate issues. Some people, such as Greg Moss, want to identify these two things, but I'm not tempted to go down that path. Now, we have spent a lot of time over the last few days talking about whether there's a top guy. I know that you think there isn't, and I understand your reasons, even if I don't agree with them. I know that you think there isn't a bottom guy either, or at least you certainly suggest that in chapter 2. I don't really understand why you think that. I don't think you spell out reasons for this, so I'm curious to know why you think this.

Gabriel: Well, a lot would depend on how we motivate the confrontation with this paradoxical absence. As you say, there are various motivations – which I perfectly well understand – for speaking this way. But let me suggest the following: let's say that we have this very elementary form of intentionality: we are thinking of something. So, there's an arrow to something, as it were, an arrow which points in some direction, and **n** is just a case where there's nothing in the object slot. That would be one way of thinking about **n** without yet thinking of it in terms of a fusion of no objects. At least, that's my way of thinking about it. I don't see immediately how this is paradoxical. Sometimes, after all, your intentionality runs empty. But there is another way of thinking about nothingness. I find it hard to imagine a field of sense with nothing in it. So, it is impossible to have an absence of all things. A common way to argue that there is a nothingness is the good old abstraction argument. Reality would be there without me, without the table in front of me, etc., and, in this manner, I can apparently take everything away. At the end, what's left is nothing. That's the classical way of getting to nothingness without turning it into an object. And now the question is: is there really nothing left? Even in the case of the empty field, there may be something left. In particular, even in the case of **n**, there's going to be a field of sense for it to be an object in your sense and for it to exist in my sense. So, **n** is not **n** at all. There's too much left. When we are trying to get there, we stop before we make it there. That's my picture; we can't make it to **n**. It's just a very empty space that we wind up with – but that's not really **n**. This is roughly the position I have committed to in some side remarks in *Why the World Does Not Exist*.

Priest: OK, so there are two issues there. Let me take them in the order that you raised. For the first of them, "nothingness" is a perfectly good grammatical noun phrase in English and in German. I don't think that's contentious. You can say "I'm thinking of nothing, **n**," and that's perfectly grammatical. One of the issues that this raises – and it's a big issue – is how to understand intentionality in general. And this raises all kinds of questions about non-existent objects because, what your suggestion amounts to, if I get it, is that the grammatical noun phrase "**n**" does not refer to anything. We're thus in the territory where you say "I'm thinking of blah," and "blah" is a noun phrase that doesn't refer to anything. Some people might see talking about Sherlock Holmes like this. I find that view unsatisfactory. I find a noneist parsing of intentionality, even when it relates to non-existents – to things referred to by a name which some people think doesn't refer to anything – a much more satisfactory account of intentionality for reasons we can talk about, but I discussed them at length in *Towards Non-Being*.

Gabriel: And I agree with many of your reasons.

Priest: Yes, and I know that. You think you can think about objects like Sherlock Holmes. So that's fine. I don't really see any reason to treat nothingness as a special case. The name refers to an object. It's a paradoxical object in that it's an object and not an object. But, nonetheless, if you're thinking about **n**, it does seem to me that there's a relationship between you and something, and it has a certain kind of phenomenology. If I'm thinking of the Eiffel Tower, there's a typical phenomenology that goes with that. The same goes for when I'm thinking of Sherlock Holmes; and if I'm thinking of nothingness, again, there's a typical phenomenology. I know what it's like to be engaged with that particular object. So, it seems to me there's no particularly good reason for denying the object nothingness any more than there is to denying the object Sherlock Holmes. To be sure, it's paradoxical, it's an inconsistent object, and that's a difference, since I don't think Sherlock Holmes is inconsistent. But I don't find that a particular reason to be worried, for obvious reasons.

Gabriel: Well, a lot will depend on how we understand the statement "It's both an object and not an object." I think, though, that this captures some of the phenomenology of nothingness. I get the phenomenology as well. I've been reading many of those famous texts about *das Nichts* of various stripes. And I've experienced various things while understanding them. I found them very interesting and I thought I was engaging in a structured philosophical activity while reading them. There was nothing in the phenomenology which suggested that this is illusory in a way – that is, much more illusory than the Sherlock Holmes case or the number case or the mundane table case. So, I agree with all of that. And I also do not think that texts written about nothingness from Plotinus to Heidegger and Nishida and beyond are all subject to some weird form of illusion. I think this is an extremist view, and I wouldn't want to hold that. We agree, then, for similar reasons, and you have this very easy maneuver for saying why. "Nothing" is a perfectly good noun phrase, to summarize the whole case in your elegant way. However, I read "it's both an object and not an object" as a characterization of the matter as being something like the following: we think it's not an object, but then, as we start thinking about it, it just turns out to be an object. I read this, therefore, as meaning that it's not what you thought it was. And that would be very different of course from believing there's a true contradiction here.

Priest: Sure. If you think it's a perfectly good object in some sense, then we're at least halfway there. The other question, then, is why it's not an object. There's an informal reason – namely, that, if you think of it as what remains when you take away everything, there's nothing left. So, it can't be an object because you've removed all the objects. But there's also a formal reason – namely, that, if you define it as I did in chapter 1, then, modulo certain assumptions – and every deduction has assumptions – you can prove that it's non-self-identical, which is logically equivalent to there being nothing which is identical to it. That is, it's no thing, no object. So, there's this mereological argument for that conclusion. (I must confess that, when I discovered that, I was really surprised, just because I knew that you could have a bottom element in a mereology in a consistent way.) This argument presupposes that you can define an object as that which is something or that which is self-identical – they're much the same thing. You might well disagree with that, but if you think that's right, then the formal mereological argument, I think, is very plausible.

Gabriel: It is plausible. The question is whether there's anything which corresponds in the argument itself – or somewhere in the assumptions driving the argument – to the issue in reality: that when I'm trying to think about nothing, I think about too much, so to speak. I think about an empty field. That's part of my phenomenology. I don't think about absolutely nothing. My thought is directed. But, for one thing, there's a difference between thinking about nothing and thinking about a cat. And I think that the difference is indeed in the object. The difference between the cat and nothing is that nothing is the empty field which is not quite nothing, after all. Now, the question is whether I am succumbing to a mistake of a Berkeleyan form here. You might say, "Look, you cannot think about a tree that's not thought about, etc."

Priest: No, I don't think that's what's going on. What I think is going on is this: nothing, as I define it, namely as the fusion of no objects, is not the same as the empty field. That takes us to the second point you raised at the start, as to whether there can be a truly empty field. We can come back to that in due course. But **n**, as I defined it, and the empty field – however one is to think of this – are different things, though one can think about both. Since these things appear to have different properties, you're thinking about different things in each case. At this point, therefore, I would say that, whatever you think about the empty field, thinking about **n**, as I defined it, is thinking about something different. There's always the possibility that you're thinking about something and you mis-characterize what you're thinking about. That can happen. For example, I'm thinking of the greatest president in the history of the United States and I take it to be Donald Trump. Well, you know, I just mis-characterized the object of my thought, because Trump is not the greatest president at all. These cases do arise, but I don't see that there's much wiggle room in that direction in the case of **n**, simply because it doesn't depend on any contingent identification. The contradictory conclusion simply follows from the definition of the particular object I have specified.

Gabriel: Of course. My worry is that there is a gap between the phenomenology of nothingness and the object **n**. But my question is how your mereological exercise of defining an emptiness operation relates to the experience of nothingness. Why would I think of the phenomenology of nothingness as an encounter with **n**?

Priest: I quite like Heidegger on this. He points out that the phrase "thinking of nothing" is ambiguous, which it absolutely is. It could mean: for no x am I thinking about x; in other words, there's no target of my thinking. Or it could mean that I'm thinking of the object nothingness. The first of these – if there's no x when you're thinking about x – is what it's like when you're unconscious. The phenomenology of thinking about nothingness is certainly not like that. Maybe I am just repeating myself now, but when you're thinking about **n**, the object I have defined, you're targeting a very specific object and, moreover, one that turns out to have contradictory properties. Of course, you can think about other things, and you might choose to call these "nothingness." But that is just changing the subject. I don't know if I have much more to say about this.

Gabriel: There is a line of thought, which I find attractive in a certain context and will specify in a second. And then there's a translation of this line of thought into the context of field of sense ontology and, *mutatis mutandis*, to our discussion. Here's a little bit of background: Schelling has this notion of the non-ground (*Ungrund*). Now, translating this a little into my language, the non-ground would be the background against which everything appears. That's Schelling's idea. He fully accepts that to exist is to stand out from what he calls a ground and applies this to being itself.

Priest: So, Heidegger stole this from him?

Gabriel: Entirely. This can be proven historically. Now, the only predicate of the non-ground, according to Schelling, is what he calls the predicate of predicatelessness, *das Prädikat der Prädikatlosigkeit*. It's clearly in the nothingness area, but he then dynamized it. He doesn't leave it at the stage where you simply have a contrast between all contrasts and something that has no contrast. Instead, he now dynamizes it in something like the way in which you start establishing relationships between everything and n – that is, in terms of grounding. So, you both connect the two. But then Schelling says that once the non-ground enters the realm of reason, as a grounding relationship, it then turns into what he calls love. Love here is a new concept which, according to Schelling, is the concept of indeterministic relationships between entities. This is why he says that entities can stand in this relation, but they don't have to; they decide to be in that relation. The space of decision here is the non-ground's presence among the entities. I've written a lot about this and therefore about what it would take to dynamize nothingness or the nothing in that sense. Schelling believes that nothingness, as it were, collapses; full-blown nothingness collapses into being. That is what he began to think in 1809, and for thirty years he tried to work out the idea, how this happens, how there is this collapse, how nothing is unstable and turns into everything by way of becoming an object, etc. There's a whole story to be told here, for which I have a lot of sympathy. I always found it exciting, which is why I wrote about it. Now, I try to translate this into my terms, which is what I meant when I said in my chapter that I connect nothingness to the non-existence of the world in my sense. When you work through the ontology of fields of sense, there are all these fields of sense, and then, at some point, one feels an inclination to wonder if there is a field of sense of all fields of sense. Let's assume that I'm right for the moment. At least under certain conditions, what you experience when you try to move to the all-encompassing field is that there's nothing there. We try to grasp all these particular fields and now I want to try to grasp them together. We find, though, that there's something which constantly escapes our grasp. And at this point

I say, "well, that's because there's nothing there." In my picture, the non-existence of **e** and nothingness coincide. That's the picture with which I'm working.

Priest: Yes.

Gabriel: This is all fairly informal because I haven't thought about what this means on the technical side.

Priest: I wasn't aware of the Schelling material. But until we get to the dynamic bit, I'm pretty much on board. In fact, I say many of these things in chapter 1. I don't think I'd buy into this dynamic stuff, though, and Schelling isn't here to speak for himself. But you are, so let's talk about your Gabrielesque spin on Schelling. What you said was that you think about the ground of existence as the non-existence of **e**, did you not? A couple of thoughts here: first of all, if you identify nothingness, the ground, with the nonexistence of **e**, it does seem to me that you're taking nothingness to be a certain object. So, again, we're halfway to the contradiction. And none of this shows that there is anything wrong with the arguments for the other half. You don't get out of a contradiction just by endorsing one half of it! So that issue still remains. But, secondly, it seems to me that the non-existence of **e** is a different object from **n**, in exactly the same way that the non-existence of Sherlock Holmes is – I'm happy with the thought that this is an object. There are objects like the non-existence of Sherlock Holmes. In technical terms, it's a trope; it's the trope of non-existence that applies to Sherlock Holmes; or, in your case, the trope of non-existence which applies to **e**. How you handle that, given your view about **e**, I'm not sure, but let's put that aside. The trope of non-existence, which applies to some object or another, I take to be very different from nothingness, because for nothingness you remove everything, including all the tropes. Thus, **n** is not a trope. That's the way I'd go with respect to your suggestion.

Gabriel: Can we come back to your characterization of **n** as the fusion of no objects? You take it to characterize an object. I am more inclined to say that there is no such object. The characterization characterizes no thing.

Priest: This takes us back to the topic of a previous discussion, as to when a bunch of things has a fusion. Now, you might say, "Well, the empty set of things is just one of those sets such that the things in it don't have a fusion." That's a possible line. But it is not going to work in standard mereology for the following reason: at least in standard mereology, the guys that don't have a fusion are the guys that don't cohere with each other. They are a gerrymandered bunch.

Gabriel: Exactly, that doesn't apply here at all.
Priest: It doesn't, because there aren't any things. So, there aren't any things that are gerrymandered.
Gabriel: Right, that's the advantage of **n** over **e**.
Priest: So that argument won't do. And, at the moment, I'm at a loss to see any other argument that'll do it. This is quite distinct from the worry about whether the totality of all objects is a gerrymandered totality, which we've discussed; and I just don't see any argument that I find plausible for the claim that the totality of no things does not have a fusion.
Gabriel: I need to think about what kind of operation fusion is. This might be unclear to me because there are some demands on fusion, such as don't gerrymander, etc. And the fact that there are debates about this seems to betray an unclarity about the operation of fusion itself. There might be different operations of fusion.
Priest: Perhaps. I am assuming that fusion, whatever it is in the case at issue, behaves in a certain way, though that is pretty standard in mereology. There is an issue about when a bunch of things has such a fusion. I'm happy to go with the thought that they do as long as the collection is not gerrymandered. I don't know how to define that notion in a way that I find fully satisfactory. But I think that, however you do it, **e** and **n** are perfectly kosher objects.
Gabriel: I would tend to read this as more grist to my mill. Given that field of sense ontology predicts that there's no overall structure to the fields, it's not surprising that we won't find an answer to what the operation of fusion is for all part–whole relations. You would say the nature of it is clear. But then I could say the nature of existence is also clear. Then, the question is what falls under it, and I advocate a radical pluralism just below existence itself.
Priest: It's perfectly possible that there's no neat answer to the question of when a fusion exists or when some things have a fusion. Maybe it's just a very untidy matter. If it were like that, I guess it wouldn't surprise me. But perhaps it's time to turn to the other point you raised initially about whether there could be a truly empty field of sense: a field of sense with absolutely nothing in it. Of course, that is not the same as the question of whether there is a field of sense with **n** in it. But it's an interesting question. I can't say that I have thought much about it before. Offhand, I don't see why there couldn't be such a field. I'll ask you to explain your thinking in a minute, but let's suppose you're right for the moment. It doesn't follow that there's no such thing as nothingness, because when I'm talking about nothingness, I'm not talking about the field of sense with nothing in it. After all, **n** is an object, and, if every object is

in a field of sense, the field of sense of **n** is not empty. Though, of course, it's not an object as well, so matters are a bit tricky, since we are in contradictory territory here. At any rate, if there's always got to be something in a field of sense, one of the things in the field of sense could be nothingness – maybe it's not in all fields of sense, maybe it's not in the field of sense of quantum physics, maybe not in the field of sense of mathematics, but certainly in some fields of sense, such as the field of sense of some of the books that I write! So, all this is compatible with the view that every field of sense has some objects in it. But let's explore the question of whether or not every field of sense must have something in it. What's your reason for supposing that?

Gabriel: Well, my reason for supposing this is that, if you have a field of sense, you have a sense or many senses constituting the field, and that means that you have what I call the furnishing function, which corresponds on the ontological level to intentionality. What we know as intentionality from our mental lives is the sense in fields of sense, it being just one form, that one shape, that sense can take: human thinking. Then take away the human and the thinking from it, and then you have the shape of sense itself. Now, could there be a sense such that it has its field but doesn't map any objects onto the field? I don't see why not.

Priest: Onto the field or from it? Does the mapping go from the field to the objects or the objects to the field? I would have thought it went from the field to the objects.

Gabriel: Yes, from the field to the object.

Priest: If there were no objects in the field, it would be the function that has the field as input, but no output. It would just be the totally undefined function. This makes perfectly good mathematical sense. That doesn't mean that it makes philosophical sense. But do you think there's a reason why such a thing wouldn't make philosophical sense?

Gabriel: Well, I do think it might make philosophical sense, but I don't see why I should advocate it. I see there is an ontological possibility, which corresponds to something like 1 divided by 0, or whatever; "1 divided by x" not being defined for 0, etc. So indeed, it makes perfectly good mathematical sense. But why would it make ontological sense? Currently I just don't think it does. So, there could be an empty field. I just don't see why I would think there is one. Which kind of sense or sense-making practice would motivate me to think that this is the case of the empty field? I don't think that I have reasons to rule this out, though. Here's another question associated with this issue, which got me puzzled yesterday when I was writing. Could there be the following scenario: a field of sense just containing itself. Do I have reasons for believing that there's no such field? In the text I'm writing at the moment, I've called such a field a "monad." So let a monad be a field of sense with contains just itself.

Priest: I don't see why there couldn't be such a field. I think we agreed the other day that, if you've got a text of some kind, whether it's philosophical or fictional or whatever, then it constitutes a field of sense for the objects that occur in it. Now, a question: Could you have a text that refers to no objects. Let me write a story for you. This is going to be a very short story (and an exceptionally boring one). Let's give this story a name. Let's call it "Gabriel!" This is it:

Gabriel!

Gabriel: I'm happy with that.
Priest: OK. Then, it would seem that this field of sense has no objects in it. But even that is not nothingness, **n**; it's a field with nothing in it.
Gabriel: Yes, exactly. I'm happy with that.
Priest: Now let's make the story a little less boring:

Gabriel!

Gabriel!

Gabriel: That shouldn't be a problem; that would be a monad.
Priest: Yes, that will be a monad in your sense.
Gabriel: Thanks to our conversation, I am clearer about how a field of sense can appear in itself. And then I say that there are some loops in the realm of sense. I have just committed to the realm of

senses being at least in part non-wellfounded. This opens up the possibility that there might be a singular field of sense, where a singular field of sense would contain one object, which is a certain way. So, in that field of sense, o is f, and that's all that's the case. Let's change the story a little:

Gabriel!

> Gabriel! = Gabriel!

Priest: That makes perfectly good sense. We're in the realm of self-reference, and so the realm of non-wellfoundedness here.

Gabriel: Indeed. That's all I wanted to say at this point, because I was wondering if there might be a way of translating what I do into a monadology – perhaps a non-wellfounded one – whereby you can reduce all the other fields to monads by thinking of them as being composed of such fields. But it would require a long story to get there. Well, I think that we can close the case here, but I want to say that you're right: I'm happy to say that, given these considerations, I have many fewer problems with **n** being an object and not an object in the mereology that you formulate. There's nothing which leads me to reject this immediately. The unresolved issues have to do with what it is to constitute a fusion and maybe not with the operation of fusion itself. That's an unresolved philosophical issue. And, who knows, for some reason it might just be untidy. But that does not affect **n**, so I'm much more inclined to accept **n** than **e**.

Priest: If you do go that way, then you're going dialetheic. But you said that you were currently undecided about that, so you might not be unhappy to go that way.

Gabriel: That might just be an interesting issue. I have no general objection to it. Therefore, this would be a case for thinking that dialetheism is true, would it not? It might be very local, confined just to **n**, but dialetheism would still be the correct view there.

Priest: Sure. One thing we've learned from paraconsistent logic is that you can localize contradictions. If you couldn't, then dialetheism wouldn't really be very plausible. Modern logical technology has its uses.

Gabriel: Yes, though the technology, on its own, can never solve philosophical problems.
Priest: Indeed. It is at the service of thoughtful philosophical inquiry.
Gabriel: Of the kind we have been having this week.
Priest: Agreed.

Part III
Postscript

10

Transcending Everything

Gregory S. Moss

10.1 Introduction

To the unattuned reader, the dialogue between Priest and Gabriel may seem to be a parochial dispute. However, it represents a significant moment in the history of philosophy, not least of all because both philosophers have completely abandoned the classical view that there cannot be true contradictions. The deep disagreements presuppose a common set of assumptions, one of which is the truth of *dialetheism*.[1] The question is not whether there are true contradictions but *what those true contradictions are*. Second, it cannot go unnoticed that both have deeply generous ontologies that set language free to speak about what is in a way that transcends nature and the philistine naturalism that has long had a stranglehold on philosophy. Their dialogue assumes a Meinongian spirit and seeks to discover its limits, or whether there are any of which to speak. Gabriel and Priest have let Plato's beard grow long. Finally, both are properly global thinkers who look to Madhyamaka for inspiration. We can only hope that the generous spirit of thinking and reading that pervades their dialogue will not be an aberration – a sunspot – in the decades to come.

I analyze the dialogue between Priest and Gabriel with any eye to unveiling their main point of disagreement. While Priest holds that **everything** is an *inconsistent* being, Gabriel denies that **everything** is a being that has any properties whatever. While Gabriel is happy to acknowledge that the concept of **everything** is contradictory, for him it is not a true contradiction. For Gabriel, **everything** is not a being. In the course of the analysis, I offer my own set of reflections, and I ask the reader to consider whether each philosopher does not provide the premises necessary for inferring that **everything** and **nothing** – in the final analysis – are indeed *absolutely* contradictory beings.

---

[1] See p. 172 below for my defense of this interpretation of Gabriel's position.

10.2 Graham Priest and the Dialetheic Structure of Nothing

10.2.1 The Gluon of Everything

As Plato teaches us, whenever we speak, we speak about something that is – even when we say that something is not. "Non-being is ... being something that is not, – if it's going not to be."[2]

Whenever we proclaim that something *is not* (μὴ ὄν), we affirm that *something which is* "is not." Let us consider Plato's example from the fifth hypothesis of the *Parmenides*: "The One is not." What *is* the One that is not? Among other things, the One *is* "that which is devoid of parts." Accordingly, the One that *is not* also is: it *is* that which *is* devoid of parts. If the One had *no* being at all, it could not even be the subject of a proposition. When we say "The One is not," we do not mean "*nothing* is not" – we mean something – the One – is *not*. Even more paradoxically, as Plato's *Sophist* long anticipated, by articulating the predicate "is not," we inevitably speak about *the being* of that which *is* not – we cannot speak about non-being without invoking "to be" – without acknowledging the being of that which is not.[3]

Priest follows in Plato's footsteps[4] and affirms the general principle that something is a being if we can speak about it. In Priest's language, however, "being" means nothing other than "being an object."[5] Because something must be a being (or an object) if we can speak about it, and we can speak about **everything**, Priest infers that **everything** is a being – **everything** is an object.[6] It is of paramount importance to note that both Priest and Gabriel endorse a *version* of the *major premise* of the argument. For both Priest and Gabriel, one cannot deny the being of something without thereby committing oneself to its being.[7]

Gabriel asks whether **everything** can be characterized.[8] Priest answers in the affirmative: all objects "share the most fundamental property of being an object."[9] Even if we cannot access **everything** *de re*, we can access it by the power of thought, *de dicto*, with the

---

[2] Plato (1997), 162a; Plato (1996), p. 81.
[3] It has long been noted that Parmenides' argument against the possibility of thinking or speaking about nothingness *negates itself*. See Plato (1997), *Sophist*, 238d–239a.
[4] For Priest's refutation of Quine's attempt to shave Plato's beard in "On What There Is," see Priest (2016), ch. 5.
[5] See Priest (2014b), pp. 49–50. Also, see ch. 1, p. 35.
[6] Ch 1, p. 19. Note that, although "being" is identified with "object" here, "being" signifies *sosein* or the "is of predication," not the "is of existence."
[7] Gabriel (2015a), p. 180.
[8] See Gabriel, ch. 2, §2.3: FOS and (neo-)Meinongian object-theory.
[9] Priest, ch. 3, p. 72.

name "**everything**".¹⁰ Indeed, because **everything** is the mereological unity of all objects, the predicate "is an object" applies to all of them. The predicate "is an object" is a unifying predicate of the totality of objects. Since "to be an object" is synonymous with "to be" (in the sense of *sosein*), **everything** can be further characterized by the predicate "is a being."

Because the world is a unity, there ought to be some principle in virtue of which the parts of the world are *unified* into one whole. Priest calls this principle of the unity of objects "the gluon."¹¹ Because Priest identifies being with unity, and the gluon is the principle of unity, it follows that the being of something is its gluon.¹² Because **everything** is a mereological fusion of all beings, there must be a principle of unity in virtue of which all beings are unified into **everything**. Thus, **everything** – like all objects – has a gluon.¹³

In *One*, Priest argues that we should *expect* everything to be contradictory. He writes:

> Indeed, we should expect everything to be contradictory. Any gluon is an object, and so a part of everything. Any gluon is an object, and so is part of everything. But any proper gluon is not an object, and so is not part of it.¹⁴

As it is expressed here, the fact that the gluon both is and is not an object constitutes the contradiction. Because we can meaningfully speak about being an object, the gluon of everything must be an object. The gluon, however, is also *not* an object:

> ... It is and it is not an entity. It is because we have spoken about it. But it is not, for if it were, it would be another object, and we would need a new gluon to unify the original plurality.¹⁵

Priest's reasoning here is classical and well grounded.¹⁶ If the gluon were itself an object, the gluon would be a separate being in addition

---

[10] Ibid., p. 76.
[11] Priest (2014b), p. 48.
[12] Ibid., p. 51.
[13] In Priest (2014b), §4.6, Priest draws upon the symmetrical relation of **everything** to all objects in order to argue that the gluon of everything is every thing. As Priest says: "the gluon of everything is identical to all parts of everything." "It is every thing."
[14] Priest (2014b), p. 54. In his discussion of Nagarjuna, Priest will also conclude that "the contradiction is that the nature of everything – that is, emptiness – both is and is not empty." He also notes that, more generally, "Gluon theory entails that everything has contradictory properties." See Priest (2014b), §4.6.
[15] Priest (2014b), p. 9.
[16] In many ways the reasoning here is analogous to the problem of participation in Plato's (1997), *Parmenides*, 132a-b, and Aristotle's solution in Aristotle (2002), 1045b8–25.

to the other objects which it unifies. Consider a syllable "ab." If the gluon of "ab" were itself an object, in addition to the objects "a" and "b," *the gluon* of "a" and "b" would be a third object, "x." With the addition of "x," a *new* plurality is formed – instead of "a" and "b" there is "a," "b," and "x." Since the gluon is what unifies the plurality, there must be a gluon that would unify the gluon "x" with the other objects, "a" and "b." If we assume anti-symmetry, whereby the principle of unity of the whole *cannot be identical* to the objects (the parts) that it unifies, then another gluon, "x^2," must be introduced in order to account for the mereological unity of the new plurality. However, this gluon, x^2, cannot be an object, for, if it were, the same problem would arise, and a new gluon, x^3, would be posited to account for the unity of the objects. Thus, in order to account for the unity of the whole, the gluon that fuses the objects together cannot be an object.

If the gluon or the being of everything is not an object, then it is *not* a being. What is more, note that the assumption of the non-identity of the gluon and object that it unifies is the same as the assumption invoked by Gabriel in his argument against the existence of the world. Gabriel claims at the outset of his argument against the world that "this unified totality differs from each and every thing that is unified by it, and accordingly becomes an additional field of sense, the field of all fields."[17] In short, if this premise holds, and the being of **everything** is not a being, then Gabriel's argument that **everything** is not a being would be well motivated.

If this reasoning is applied to **everything**, then **everything** would result in contradiction, as Priest indicates. On the one hand, the gluon of everything is an object, and must be one object in the fusion of all objects. On the other hand, the gluon of **everything** is not an object, and is therefore *not* one of the objects in the fusion of all objects. As a result, **everything** would be contradictory, for it would both include its gluon and exclude it. However, given these arguments in *One*, we seem to come to an impasse. We know from Priest's essay "Everything and Nothing"[18] that **everything**, considered from the viewpoint of non-standard mereology, is *not* an inconsistent object, as *One* suggests.

In chapter 1 Priest acknowledges that, in standard mereology, anti-symmetry is the salient axiom in operation. Under the axiom of

---

[17] Gabriel (2015a), p. 189.
[18] Note that there is a subsection in *One* entitled "Everything and Nothing." Unless otherwise indicated, "Everything and Nothing" refers to the first chapter of this book, not *One*.

anti-symmetry, the whole cannot be a proper part of itself. In *One*, anti-symmetry appears to be the key assumption by which the contradictory identity of the being of **everything** is established. If the gluon cannot be a part of itself, then the gluon cannot be an object and must *transcend* the totality that it unifies. In short, if we adopt a standard mereological approach to **everything**, and **everything** is the mereological fusion of all beings, then **everything** must be dialetheic. However, innovations in formal mereology which reject the anti-symmetry axiom have demonstrated that a consistent concept of **everything** is possible.[19] By dropping the anti-symmetry axiom,[20] the whole can be a part of itself without contradiction, and **everything** would not be dialetheic on *a priori* grounds alone.

By denying the anti-symmetry axiom, one undermines the argument by which **everything** is not an object. Naturally, this poses a challenge to Gabriel, who denies that **everything** is an object. According to non-standard mereology, **everything** is not inconsistent *a priori*. As a result, Priest argues that Gabriel cannot deny the existence of the world on *a priori* grounds alone. Priest gives examples of wholes that are parts of themselves: the aleph and propositions.[21] As Priest notes, these examples have the function of exemplifying the coherence of dropping the anti-symmetry axiom.[22]

As we know, Gabriel will answer Priest's challenge by simply accepting that it is *logically possible* that **everything** is a being.[23] Gabriel will insist that his argument against the being of the world is a *defeasible* and *ontological* one – not an argument from logical impossibility.[24] Because Gabriel grants it to be logically possible for wholes to be their own parts, and fields of sense can appear in themselves as objects, Gabriel grants not only that it is logically possible for objects to be in themselves, but it is even an *ontological fact* that some objects are parts of themselves. Although Priest and Gabriel may dispute the meaning and function of Borges', aleph, Gabriel's FOS ontology can accommodate mereology that drops the anti-symmetry axiom.

Given this wide-ranging agreement on what is logically possible, the main point of the disagreement is whether the world (**everything**)

---

[19] Priest cites Cotnoir and Bacon (2015).
[20] Note that Hegel also denies anti-symmetry in his logic of the concept, whereby the whole is a part of itself. See Hegel (2001), pp. 117, 160.
[21] Priest, ch.1, p. 28.
[22] Priest, ch. 3, p. 71.
[23] Gabriel, ch. 2, p. 56.
[24] For more on Gabriel's treatment of possibility, actuality, contingency, and necessity, see Gabriel (2015a), chs 10 and 11, pp. 263–317.

is a being.[25] Given that it is logically possible for the world to exist, Gabriel and Priest demand arguments from each other that transcend the domain of what is logically possible. In order for the dialogue to progress further, logical possibility must be set aside, and the ontological question must be met directly.

10.2.2 *The Inclosure Schema*

Independently of whether we take a standard or non-standard mereological approach to the world, the fact that we *can* meaningfully speak about it implies that it must be a being in either system. On Priest's own terms, the main question of interest is whether the object, **everything**, is dialetheic. As a principle, Priest suggests that we should accept dialetheia only when it appears that there is no better way to go.[26] In the following I draw upon Priest's metaphysics of nothingness in order to demonstrate that, on his own terms, **everything** is characterized by the inclosure schema.

Priest argues that **nothing** is the ground of reality, a thesis he has already extensively developed in *One*.[27] The term "nothing," like everything, can be read as a quantifier or as a noun phrase. **Nothing** signifies "a noun phrase with the widest scope."[28] As Priest writes: "An object, x, cannot be an object, be something, unless x is not nothing. That is, for something, x, to be an object, it must be distinct from **n**."[29] Given that **nothing** signifies the absence of all objects,[30] **nothing** is not an object. If the object were identical to **nothing**, then the object would not be an object. Thus, in order to be a *determinate* object, the object must be distinct from **nothing**. Because all beings must be distinct from **nothing** in order to be objects, to be an object means to "stand out against the background of nothingness."[31] All things depend upon **nothing** as the background of being.[32]

However, because we can meaningfully speak about **nothing**, **nothing** is also an object.[33] It is that which is the absence of all objects. Thus, **nothing** is dialetheic: it is both an object and not an object. Because **nothing** is not an object, there is nothing that one

---

[25] Priest, ch. 3, p. 69.
[26] Priest (1998), p. 424.
[27] See ch. 1, p. 34. As he puts it in Priest (2014b), p. 180: "nothing is the ontological backdrop for anything."
[28] Ch. 1, p. 25.
[29] Priest (2014b), p. 18. Also see Ch. 1, p. 35.
[30] Ibid., p. 15.
[31] Ibid., p. 18.
[32] **Nothing** like **everything** has a gluon. In the case of **nothing**, it is its own gluon.
[33] Ch. 1, p. 31.

can speak about. Thus, **nothing** is ineffable.³⁴ But it is an object, and we have described it as ineffable. Thus, it is both ineffable and not ineffable. In sum, Priest identifies two inevitable contradictions that arise upon speaking about **nothing**: it is and is not an object; it is and is not ineffable.³⁵ Finally, Priest draws the dialectical inference that follows from these reflections. Since **nothing** is an object, and all objects are grounded on **nothing**, **nothing** is the ground of itself. And finally, since **nothing** is not an object, it is not the ground of itself.³⁶

Having briefly reconstructed Priest's position, I will now reconsider the concept of **everything** in light of these considerations. What is **everything**? It is the mereological fusion of all objects. Since **nothing** is an object, it follows that **everything** must include **nothing**. Thus, **everything** can be the fusion of all objects only if it is the fusion of *both* **everything** and **nothing**. **Everything** is always already the fusion of **everything** and **nothing**. Now, because **nothing** is dialetheic, and **everything** includes both **everything** and **nothing**, **everything** must ultimately be dialetheic as well. Indeed, Gabriel asks a fitting question: "how can the operation of a mereological fusion of all objects escape the fate of inclosure?"³⁷

As is already evident, **everything** is dialetheic in virtue of **nothing**. Note, the important caveat, however, that here the contradiction follows not from the fact that **everything** both is and is not an object but from the fact that **nothing** itself both is and is not an object. Priest continues to hold the thesis from *One* that "Everything and nothing then interpenetrate."³⁸ Priest still holds that **everything** is contradictory, but he holds this view on account of the dialetheic character of **nothing**.

However, let us consider the idea that, apart from **nothing**, **everything** is not dialetheic. If **everything** is not dialetheic and **nothing** is, then **everything** excludes **nothing**. If **everything** excluded **nothing**, then it would not be **everything**. Thus, the **everything** that excludes **nothing** is not **everything**. There is no way to truly consider **everything** in such a way that it excludes **nothing**. The concept of **everything** that excludes **nothing** would fail to correspond with what **everything** is: all objects. Thus, it would be a *false* **everything**. Considered independently of **nothing**, **everything** may be consistent, but that does not

---

³⁴ Priest (2014b).
³⁵ Ibid., p. 17.
³⁶ Ibid., p. 20. "What we have seen, then, is, as promised, that in the sense explained, n is the ground of reality (all objects), including being and not being a ground of itself."
³⁷ Gabriel, ch. 2, p. 52.
³⁸ Priest (2014b), p. 181.

mean that **everything** is consistent. Instead, it would follow only that a false **everything** would be consistent. As the fusion of *all* objects, **everything** must be the synthesis of **everything** and **nothing**. Because **everything**, in virtue of what it is, engenders the fusion of **everything** and **nothing**, **everything** appears to be dialetheic in virtue of itself. We miss the dialetheic character of **everything** when we abstract from *meontology*.

Everything is the fusion of all objects, including **everything** (itself) and **nothing**. Because **nothing** is an object, it must fall within the totality. This is the element of *closure*. However, no object can be an object unless it stands out against the **nothing** which grounds it. Because **everything** is *an* object that includes all objects, it can only be what it is if it stands out against **nothing**. Since **nothing** is the ground (and background) of **everything**, **nothing** must be beyond **everything**. This is the element of *transcendence*. Of course, the **nothing** that stands beyond **everything** both is and is not an object – for we are indeed *speaking* about the absence of the object beyond **everything**. Here it appears that **everything**, when conceived as *truly* **everything**, namely as the fusion of **everything** and **nothing**, does in fact instantiate the inclosure schema.[39]

The resulting contradiction is the following: **nothing** must be both within **everything** and beyond **everything**. What is more, it is the very nature of **everything** (*qua* **everything** and **nothing**) that engenders the contradiction. This is related to the dialetheic character of **nothing** but it is not (strictly speaking) identical to it. On the one hand, it is in virtue of the fact that **everything** is the fusion of *all* objects that **nothing** must fall within **everything**. On the other hand, it is in virtue of the fact that **everything** is an object, and objects are impossible unless they stand out against **nothing**, that **nothing** (even **nothing** *qua* object) falls outside of **everything**. Accordingly, by my lights, **nothing** and **everything** instantiate the inclosure schema.[40] Here note that the application of the inclosure schema to **everything** operates *without* the problematic assumption that an object cannot be its own gluon that Priest has already rejected in chapter 1.

To further elucidate this contradiction, consider the fact that **everything** is all-inclusive. As all-inclusive, every object is within it, and it is thereby infinite and Absolute. Thus, on the one hand,

---

[39] Priest (1995), pp. 3–4. For another brief and concise definition of the inclosure schema, see ibid, p. 233.

[40] Priest notes that (at the very least) nothing instantiates the inclosure schema. See ibid., p. 18.

everything is unbound. On the other hand, **everything** is bound, for **nothing** falls outside of it. **Everything** is bound and unbound by **nothing** – the true **everything**, the true infinite – is infinite and finite. What Priest writes about Hegel's true infinity applies in this case to **everything**.[41]

Everything can be *conceived* as an *infinite* object only if it is bounded (for all conception is a kind of binding). But it is infinite, and so it is not bound by **nothing**. Thus, **everything** is the bounded-unbounded. In sum: by my lights, if **everything** really is an object, and **nothing** is the ground of reality, then **everything** is dialetheic. As Priest writes: "I think there is a great deal to be said for the thought that the world is indeed a contradictory object – and none the worse for that."[42] In my own parlance, I call the view that **everything** is dialetheic "Absolute Dialetheism." Absolute Dialetheism affirms the proposition that "**everything** is a being" to be a true contradiction.[43] I have given a number of arguments for this thesis elsewhere.[44] For now it is sufficient to indicate why Priest's own meontological concept of reality can be enlisted to motivate a dialetheic concept of **everything**.

10.2.3 From *Ground to* Ungrund: *Nothingness and Self-Referential Predication*

Is **everything** a being? As noted, this is the main point of disagreement between Priest and Gabriel. But we should not overlook an equally important disagreement that reflects their differences on the first question. While Priest recognizes absolute **nothingness** as a *dialetheic* object, Gabriel flat out denies that this is an ontological possibility.[45] Given these differences, it should be of some help briefly to distinguish two senses of nothingness at work here: relative and absolute **nothing**.

---

[41] Ibid., p. 105. As Priest states: "However, Hegel does have a point here: if an object is infinite it falls in the category of the infinite, and this is to set a bound on it. In this sense, to conceive an object as infinite is a contradiction in terms. We are, here, on familiar ground. To be bounded and to be truly conceived are, in a sense, the same thing. For if something is bounded it can be conceived as that which lies within the boundary; and if something is conceived it is bounded by the terms of the conception. Hence, an unbounded object is essentially the same as an inconceivable object. And we are back with the contradiction at the limit of the conceivable."

[42] Priest, ch. 3, p. 79, footnote 21.

[43] As Priest points out, with paraconsistent logic in hand, the fact that the object everything is contradictory would not impose any spurious contradiction on more ordinary objects such as "New York." See Priest (1995), p. 55.

[44] See Moss (2020) and Moss (forthcoming).

[45] See Gabriel, ch. 4 p. 95: "There is no such object as **nothing**."

Priest argues that **nothing** is the ground of objects. On the one hand, the proposition "the absence of objects is the ground of objects" attributes the predicate "is the ground" to **nothing**. On the other hand, *all* objects are *grounded* by **nothing**. Accordingly, in Priest's analysis the relation between **nothing** and objects is defined by the relation of ground to grounded. In order for objects to be objects, they must be *distinct* from **nothing** – their ground. Because the ground is *not* identical to all the objects which it grounds, the ground of objects, **nothing**, is *not* all-encompassing. As the ground, **nothing** is one object – the ground – that makes objects possible. Thus, the concept of **nothing** as ground is not absolutely **nothing**. It is a relative nothingness – it is *in relation to* the grounded.

Priest claims that the dependence is not reversable.[46] However, there is an unusual *dialectical* sense in which the ground depends upon the grounded. If there were no objects, then there would be no-thing for **nothing** to ground. If there were no-thing to ground, then **nothing** would not be the ground of anything. But to be a ground is to be the ground of something. Thus, if no object had being, then **nothing** would not justifiably have the predicate "is the ground." The predicate "is a ground" can be attributed to the ground only *retroactively*. On the one hand, the **nothing** would still be the **nothing** even if there were no objects, while, on the other hand, **nothing** would not *be* "the ground" of objects if objects never had any being.[47]

Because **nothing** is an object, and **nothing** grounds objects, **nothing** grounds itself. So, in the special case of **nothing**, there is no difference between ground and grounded. However, since objects must be distinct from **nothing** to be objects, even **nothing** *qua* object must be distinct from **nothing**. In the special case of **nothing**, the object is both distinct and not distinct from **nothing**. However, on Priest's account this identity of ground and grounded appears to be a special case and does not hold absolutely. For example, it does not appear to hold for the object "Sai Kung Town," a village in Hong Kong, which is one object among others and is not the ground of all objects. Naturally, since objects are not **nothing**, and **nothing** is an object, **nothing** is that object whose being consists in not being an object. **Nothing** *qua* ground is not the void of being – it is the being or the object that is constituted by not being an object.

---

[46] Ch. 1, p. 35. "The dependence does not go the other way."
[47] See Ibn Al Arabi (1980), p. 54. Also both Schelling, in his *Investigations into the Essence of Human Freedom*, and Hegel's logic of reflection, in his *Science of Logic*, develop this kind of dialectical argument.

In addition to relative nothingness, Priest appeals to a concept of *absolute* **nothingness**. Priest appeals to *absolute* **nothing** in his argument for the ineffability of **nothing**. **Nothing** is ineffable because it is *absolutely* devoid of all being. Because there is no being there – *not even a ground* – about which to speak, **nothing** is ineffable. Thus, in order to infer the ineffability of **nothing, nothing** must be *absolutely* **nothing** – it must transcend the ground and all ground–grounded relations. Because it has no being, it cannot even be the object (being) that is not an object (a being). The difference between "relative" and "absolute" consists in whether one predicates "is an object" to "the absence of all objects."

Now, as Priest notes, we do in fact describe absolute **nothing** as the absence of all beings, and we thereby render it a being. Because relative **nothing** is a being, in order to speak about the absolute **nothing** we cannot help but identify it with the relative **nothing**. Thus, the contradiction constitutive of **nothing** is the contradictory identity of absolute and relative **nothing**. Indeed, the term "nothing" in both "relative" and "absolute" nothing have the same fundamental meaning: *the absence of all objects*.

For Gabriel no object corresponds to absolute **nothingness**. Because there are no conditions under which absolute **nothingness** could be true, Gabriel must hold absolute **nothingness** to be meaningless. Given Gabriel's commitment to formal Meinongianism, by which "we cannot claim that something does not exist without thereby committing to its existence,"[48] one might expect Gabriel to infer that absolute **nothing** has being. However, we will see that independent ontological considerations motivate Gabriel's view that *absolute* **nothingness** is a meaningless term – a view that is of paramount importance for his defence of the non-existence of the world.

To make any progress on the question of the being of **everything** and **nothing**, it is of paramount importance to gain a clear sense of the *methodological* principles that are operating in conceiving **everything** and **nothing**. Indeed, the function of *self-referential* predication is one essential methodological consideration that is employed in the dialogue but not thematically engaged. Priest praises the method of self-reference in *Beyond the Limits of Thought*.[49]

Let us first consider how the concept of *absolute* **nothingness** exhibits *self-referential* predication – the methodological principle guiding my own Absolute Dialetheism. Since **nothing** *qua* absolute is the absence of all objects, and **nothing** is the object that is

---

[48] Gabriel (2015a), p. 180.
[49] Priest (1995), pp. 3–4.

the "absence of all objects," **nothing** must lack itself – it must be devoid of its own being – the absence of objects.[50] Thus, **nothing**, the absence of all objects, is not **nothing**, the absence of all objects. To put it otherwise, if **nothing** were the absence of all objects, then it would not be **nothing**. It can be **nothing** only if it is *not* "the absence of all objects." But **nothing** is the absence of all objects. Thus, **nothing** can *be* **nothing** only if it is *not* **nothing**. The concept of **nothing** is *self-predicative*, and it is in virtue of that self-predication that **nothing** is *self-negating*.

To put it simply: **nothing** is self-predicative: **nothing** is **nothing** at all. This may appear as a simple tautology, but it is more than this – it is *dialectical*. This identity statement is indeed informative but at the cost of consistency. Because the absence of all objects is the absence of all objects, the absence of all objects is *not* the absence of all objects. Methodologically, we discover that the self-referential application of the concept of **nothing** results in the *self-negation* of the concept. Indeed, Priest's inference that **nothing** is ineffable follows directly from the self-referential predication of **nothing** to itself. Just as emptiness itself is empty in Madhyamaka,[51] itself a source of wellspring of inspiration to Priest and Gabriel, so must **nothing** be **nothing** in Priest's meontological account of beings.

The self-negation of **nothing** is *infinite*. Because **nothing** is the absence of the absence of all beings, it must also be the absence of the absence of the absence of all beings. However, as the absence of all beings, it must be the absence of the absence of absence, *ad infinitum*. **Nothing** refuses to be identified with anything. **Nothing** appears to exhibit the structure of ἄπειρων. With **nothing** there is always a remainder.

Although Priest acknowledges that **nothing** is dialetheic, the contradiction at which we have arrived is only the threshold for another – indeed more significant – contradiction. In what follows I will take Priest's position on **nothing** as premises to push towards an identity of **everything** and **nothing** – an identity Priest does not endorse. Hegel famously proclaims that the dialectical self-negation of **nothing** engenders the identity of **nothing** with being.[52] Priest denies this

---

[50] Note that, from this, it follows that, if **nothing** is absolute, it cannot be a relative **nothing** (since the latter is an object). Thus, the dialetheic character of **nothing** is such that absolute **nothing** both is and is not relative **nothing**.

[51] See Nagarjuna (1995), ch. 13, "Examination of Compounded Phenomena," p. 36. See Priest, ch. 3, p. 81, where he explicitly endorses the view that "all objects are empty," and Gabriel, ch. 4, p. 94, where he indicates that Madhyamaka is a motivating force in his critique of metaphysics.

[52] See Hegel (2015), p. 45. For the sake of parsimony, I will forsake any historical exegesis

identity, an identity accepted (albeit for very different reasons) by a variety of thinkers within various traditions, e.g. German Idealism, Existentialism, and Neo-Platonism.[53]

In order to see why **nothing** cannot be other than **being**, we must consider only that **nothing** is the absence of all objects. Insofar as it is the absence of all objects, it has *no* determinations and is completely *indeterminate*. Because it is indeterminate and the absence of all objects, **nothing** cannot have *any* properties whereby it would be distinguished from anything else. To put it otherwise: if **nothing** were different from *any* object, it would not be absolutely **nothing** – the absence of all objects. Thus, **nothing** cannot be different from any object. Thus, **nothing** is completely *indistinct*.

Note that the indistinguishability of **nothing** from being neither requires a classical view of the principle of non-contradiction nor does it follow from the principle of explosion. Rather, it follows from the same assumption about **nothing** that generates ineffability: that **nothing** is the absence of all objects. Because **nothing** is totally *indistinct*, **nothing** can be distinct neither from any object nor from any distinction, or from an object and its properties. Since relative **nothing**, **everything**, and being are all objects, **nothing** cannot be different from relative **nothing**, **everything**, or being. Thus, **nothing** is indistinct from **everything**.

In short, because **nothing** is **nothing** at all, **nothing** is not the object "**nothing**." Because **nothing** is not **nothing**, it is devoid of any separable determination and must thereby be indistinct from **everything**. Thus, **nothing** is **everything**. Given that **nothing** is totally indistinct, **nothing** cannot be distinct from the gluon of **everything**.[54] Thus, the gluon of **everything** is **nothing**,[55] and all objects are unified

---

of Hegel's text and will instead focus on the systematic reason for identifying nothing with being.

[53] See Priest (2014b), p. 54, footnote 17. In the Western tradition, this identity of being and nothing does not originate with Heidegger or Hegel but is already present in the work of Meister Eckhart and Pseudo-Dionysius. See Meister Eckhart (1981), p. 287, and Pseudo-Dionysius (1987), p. 98. In each case the identity means something different – my argument tracks Hegel's thinking more closely, since it is the simplest and (by my lights) follows from one of Priest's assumptions.

[54] It is important to note that the identity of **nothing** and **everything** does not follow from the contradictory character of the gluon of everything. It is true that the gluon of **everything**, g, has the properties of every thing, and is every thing, such that it must be true that $g = e$ and $g = n$. However, for Priest, identity is not transitive. Accordingly, for Priest it does not follow from this that **everything** is **nothing** ($e = n$). My claim is that the identity of **everything** and **nothing** follows from the absolute indistinctness of **nothing**, not from the properties of the gluon of **everything**.

[55] Again, it is my view, not Priest's, that the gluon of **everything** is **nothing**.

by **nothing**. Absolute **nothing** is **everything**, and the gluon of **everything**. In sum, **nothing**, construed as the absence of all objects, must be the mereological fusion of all objects – **everything** – and their gluon.

What is more, since **nothing** is totally indistinct, it cannot be distinct from the predicate "is an object." We know, however, that to be an object (to be a being) is *not* to be **nothing**. Thus, the very concept of an object is inherently dialetheic: to be an object is to be **nothing** and not **nothing**.[56]

Here Gabriel's critique of Priest's definition of the object, namely his question about how identity statements can be both informative and non-contradictory, takes center stage.[57] When one states of each object in the mereological fusion of **everything** "that it is an object," one does not distinguish one object from another. Rather, each is unified by the same "object" or "being." According to Gabriel, the term "proper property" is that which "puts one into the position of distinguishing one object from another in a domain."[58] As is evident, since being or "being an object" does not distinguish any object from another object, "being" or "object" is not a proper property in Gabriel's sense.[59] What is the principle by which one can *differentiate* being an object (being) from **nothing** (the absence of all objects)? Simply put: what is *the principle* by which being (or being-an-object) can be differentiated from **nothing**? This is what I call the problem of the missing difference.[60]

Because the property of being, or "being an object," is only a principle of unity of objects, it does not differentiate objects. Indeed, as a principle of unity among objects, "being an object" can only provide a principle that unifies **everything** and **nothing**. Thus, "being" cannot draw the difference between being and non-being. Nothing, however, is equally impotent to draw the difference between being and **nothing**, exactly because there is nothing there.

---

[56] I note in passing that this formulation comes very *close* to Priest's formulation of the Nagarjuna paradox. See Priest (2014b), p. 18: "The contradiction is that the nature of everything – that is – emptiness both is and is not empty." To be empty is to lack *independent* being. Certainly, the concepts of nothing and emptiness are interrelated: one cannot elucidate what emptiness is without appealing to non-being. To translate the paradox in terms of our analysis, in order to be an object, the object is *independent* of nothing, and is thereby not empty. However, since the object *in itself* is indistinguishable from nothing, it lacks independence and is thereby empty.

[57] Gabriel, ch. 2, p. 60.

[58] Gabriel (2015a), p. 49.

[59] In Gabriel's terms, "Existence is never a proper property." Gabriel (2015a), p. 55.

[60] For a lengthy discussion of this problem, see Moss (2020), pp. 159–89.

It appears that neither being[61] nor **nothing** can differentiate being from **nothing**.

Because the absence of all objects is indistinct, **nothing** has no limits. Accordingly, **nothing** is *all-encompassing*. As all-encompassing, it is *absolute*. With **nothing**, therefore, there is *no* remainder. However, **nothing** has a remainder, as we indicated earlier. **Nothing** both is with and without remainder. In addition to the true contradiction that "nothing is and is not an object," there is another *absolute* dialetheia: **nothing** *is no being and every being*. **Nothing** cannot be identified with any being, for it is **nothing**, but it is for this very reason that it is indistinguishable from them all. Priest's invocation of the net of Indra[62] beautifully illustrates this result. **Nothing** is the whole net, for it *unites* them all. Further, because it is indistinguishable from each node of the net, we can affirm with Priest that "All the jewels in the net encode each other. Each one, as it were, contains the whole."[63]

Nonetheless, because we can meaningfully speak about **nothing**, it must also be one object among others. Accordingly, it is one of the nodes, one of the jewels, in the whole network. Thus, we would agree with Fazang that the whole net is a member of itself.[64] However, because we have raised the **nothing** to unity with **everything**, the net represents a *dialetheic* view of **everything**, which is thoroughly emptied of its independence from **nothing**.

Finally, this contradiction has significant implications regarding our conception of **nothing** as the ground of objects. As we noted earlier, the ground of objects, **nothing**, is not absolute. However, **nothing** is all-encompassing and absolute. Thus, **nothing** transcends the ground–grounded distinction altogether. **Nothing**, to borrow a term from Schelling and Boehme, is the *Ungrund*.[65] Instead of

---

[61] One recourse might be to suppose that some particular being (some *particular object*) in the mereological fusion of everything differentiates being from nothing. But since this being would already be an object, and as such would by definition not be nothing, it would *already presuppose the distinction* rather than account for it.

[62] See Priest (2014b), ch. 11, p. 180. Also consider the following metaphor from Fazang, which fits this picture well: "If we take ten coins as symbolizing the totality of existence, and examine the relationship of existence amongst them, then, according to Huayang teaching, coin one will be seen as identical with the other nine coins." See Priest (2018a), p. 115. If the coins are metaphors for the elements of reality, then **nothing** would be one distinct coin and each of the others as well.

[63] Priest (2014b), p. 180.

[64] Priest, ch. 3, p. 82.

[65] I note in passing that the concept of the *Ungrund* is of great importance to Gabriel's FOS. See Gabriel (2015a), p. 168. This Schellingian heritage of the FOS is originally indebted to Jakob Boehme, from whom Schelling borrows the term. See Boehme (2010), p. 41.

occupying one side of an opposition, it is all-encompassing and thereby transcends all oppositions.[66] Because it is indistinguishable from **everything**, it is *"gleichgültig"* – i.e., indifferent, or equally distributed throughout **everything**. Because I hold that **nothing** is the gluon of **everything**, it is the gluon of **nothing** *qua* ground and is just as much the "original ground"[67] as it is the non-ground. **Nothing**, as we might expect, is both the ground and the non-ground – it is both the object constituting the ground and the *absolute* transcending and negating the ground. In short, the very same principle in virtue of which Priest affirms the **nothing** to be ineffable also "grounds" the **nothing** as an *absolutely dialetheic Ungrund*.

Once **nothing** is acknowledged as the ground of **everything**, I would contend that it cannot remain in the background alone but spreads out everywhere – into the foreground too. Although, *qua* absolute, there may be nothing other to the **nothing** against which it may stand out, the dialetheic character of **nothing** ensures that it *stands out against itself*. The dialetheic Absolute calls for a "logic of paradox" in the spirit of the philosopher and founder of the Kyoto School, Nishida Kitarō, for whom the absolute is a contradictory identity that expresses itself in all things in virtue of its perpetual self-negation.[68]

10.3 Markus Gabriel and the Meaninglessness of Everything

We formulated the main dispute between Priest and Gabriel in terms of *being*: is **everything** a being? Because our main focus now turns to Gabriel's Field of Sense ontology, we ought to reformulate the question in terms of Gabriel's terminology. First, instead of everything, we will speak of the "world," since (similarly to Priest's definition of **everything**) the "world" connotes a *unified totality* that metaphysics

---

[66] See Schelling (2006), p. 68. By no means do I mean to imply that Schelling's philosophy in his *Freedom Essay* is fully compatible with the arguments laid out here. I mean to borrow the concept of the *Ungrund* only to illuminate a structural feature of **nothing**.

[67] Schelling (2006), p. 68.

[68] As Nishida writes: "the world of the absolute, through its own absolute self-negation and absolute nothingness, determines itself and expresses itself within itself," and "a true logic must adequately exhibit the self-expression of the absolute. Therefore it must be paradoxical. True facts which bear existential testimony of themselves are always paradoxical" Nishida (1993), p. 29. To further adjudicate this dispute between Gabriel and Priest about the putative being of **nothing**, it would be advisable to consult the Kyoto School, in particular the thought of Nishida, Tanabe, and Nishitani, since it is in their philosophical works where one discovers the most extensive discussion of these senses of nothingness and their relationship to one another.

aims to know.⁶⁹ Unlike Priest, Gabriel does not technically differentiate "being" from "existence."⁷⁰ For Priest, "existence" means the capacity to enter into causal relations, while "being" requires only that something can be *named*. Accordingly, on his definition, anything which exists has being, but many things can be without existing, such as Zeus. On Priest's account, since the world can be named, it is a being. However, he remains *un*decided about whether the world possesses any causal powers.⁷¹ Thus, on Priest's account, the world is a being but may or may not exist.

Priest admits that any definition of existence is probably circular.⁷² Indeed, it is difficult to see how one can define existence without already appealing to what exists. If this is the case, Priest's own criterion would be circular too. Although the causality criterion gives us a measure by which to decide what exists, the defence of the position is too thin to grant much confidence. In order to determine whether the world exists, the dialogical exchange ought to consider both the meaning of existence and to what extent it is itself amenable to philosophical speculation. Whether existence is "appearance in a field of sense" or "the potential to act causally" is no trifling matter, and it has immense consequences for our ontology. Indeed, the existence of the world hangs in the balance.

Prima facie, their views appear quite close, since neither is committed to the existence of the world. Gabriel argues that the world does not exist. But this proximity is illusory, since Gabriel never links existence with causal powers. Indeed, some entities with causal powers exist, and would not exist without them, but things (in general) do not exist in virtue of having causal powers. Because Gabriel does not distinguish between "being" and "existence," we can reformulate the question "is everything a being?" into Gabriel's language: *does the world exist*? In what follows we will use the term "existence" in a way that is freed from any necessary connection to "causality."

Priest and Gabriel both share the view that one cannot deny

---

⁶⁹ Gabriel, ch. 2, p. 55.
⁷⁰ Note, however, that when Gabriel uses the term "being" he is not using it in the same way Priest does.
⁷¹ Priest, ch. 3, p. x77 footnote 4.
⁷² Priest (1995), p. xvii. Priest quotes Plato's *Sophist* (1997, 247e). However, the citation by no means justifies the view that what exists is spatio-temporal, since this is not the sense of Plato's δύναμις, which in the dialogue concerns categories. If no non-circular definition of existence can be given, then one feature of existence would be the fact that it transcends definition. For a discussion of existence as trans-definitional, see Moss (forthcoming).

the being of something without thereby committing oneself to its being. On Gabriel's account, this means that "we cannot claim that something does not exist without thereby committing to its existence." Priest uncovers a conflict between this principle and Gabriel's no-world view: if this principle had *un*restricted application, then Gabriel's denial of the existence of the world would commit him to its existence. Likewise, if to deny the existence of something necessarily commits one to its existence, would it not follow that denying the existence of the **nothing** would commit Gabriel to its existence? Simply put: on Gabriel's own FOS ontology, Priest argues that Gabriel should abandon the no-world view and acknowledge the existence of the world.

What justifies Gabriel's denial of the existence of the world? What justifies Gabriel's refusal of being to absolute nothing? If Priest's argument is right, Gabriel must both deny and accept the existence of the world. Thus, Priest suggests that Gabriel ought to endorse my own position, namely *Absolute Dialetheism*, whereby it is true that the world both exists and does not exist.[73] After a brief recapitulation of Gabriel's FOS ontology, I demonstrate that Gabriel can successfully respond to Priest's objections and avoid appealing to Absolute Dialetheism. In order to respond successfully, Gabriel must restrict the Meinongian principle by appealing to *independent* ontological considerations. However, Gabriel's defense can succeed only if he abandons every sound argument against the existence of the world.

10.3.1 Field of Sense Ontology

A significant disagreement underlying the question of the metaphysical application of formal mereology is whether existence can be a proper property. "Being" does not differentiate among the various beings – it does not contain any differentiating feature by which it would be distinguished as "this" in contrast to "that" being. According to Gabriel, the term "proper property" is that which "puts one into the position of distinguishing one object from another in a domain."[74] As is evident, since being does not distinguish any individuals from one another, being is not a proper property in Gabriel's sense.[75] Gabriel rejects the idea that being is a metaphysical property whereby being would be universally instantiated in all entities.[76] By

---

[73] Priest, ch. 3, p. 80.
[74] Gabriel (2015a), p. 49.
[75] Gabriel is clear that "Existence is never a proper property." Ibid., p. 55.
[76] See ibid., pp. 69 and 55.

denying that being is a proper property, Gabriel avoids the problem of the missing difference discussed in §10.2.3.[77]

If existence is not a proper property, what is it? In the simplest formulation, "appearing in a field of sense" means that beings exist only "in a context." Ultimately, existence is a *property* of fields of sense, a kind of *relation* between an object and the field of sense in which it exists:

> objects could not exist alone; they are not absolutes, but only exist as *relata*. Objects only exist relatively to their domain, as existence is the property of their domain to contain exactly them.[78]

For Gabriel, terms have meaning if they have truth conditions, and only terms that refer to objects can have truth conditions. Accordingly, for him, a term can be meaningfully employed (or conceived) only if it *actually refers to an object*. Thus, Gabriel affirms a kind of Meinongianism:

> absolute non-existence is impossible. Everything exists, but in different fields of sense. It does not co-exist. There is no all-encompassing field in which surprisingly there somehow are unicorns and there are no unicorns. There are unicorns (for instance, in *The Last Unicorn*), and there are no unicorns (for instance, in Milwaukee).[79]

As we already know, Gabriel's "formal Meinongianism" means that "we cannot claim that something does not exist without thereby committing to its existence."[80] Gabriel also formulates this to mean that *conceivability implies actuality*. Because he has contextualized (or, what is the same, *relativized*) all existence claims, Gabriel endorses an *ontological relativism*, whereby things do not exist or not-exist absolutely, but each thing exists only *in relation to some field of sense*.

Although zombies do not exist in Hong Kong, they do exist in *The Walking Dead*. To claim that "zombies do not exist" is only a half-truth, for they do not exist in Hong Kong. But they certainly do exist in other fields of sense, such as *The Walking Dead*. As is evident, Gabriel's ontological relativism commits him to a *relative* concept of non-being. Zombies have non-being, but only *relative* non-being. They are not absolutely nothing. Although they are non-beings *relative to* the field of sense of Hong Kong, they do have being in relation to the television series.

---

[77] See this chapter §3.2.
[78] Gabriel (2015a), p. 140.
[79] Gabriel (2015a), p. 178. Gabriel puts it more speculatively here: "if there is anything whatsoever, there has to be some object that does not exist." Ibid., p. 60.
[80] Gabriel, ch. 2, p. 58.

Although Gabriel and Priest are both dialetheists, between them there is a significant disagreement about what true contradictions there are. Gabriel's claim that "everything exists, but in different fields of sense" commits him to dialetheism, the view that *some* contradictions are true.[81] Although Gabriel argues that his concept of imaginary objects commits him to dialetheism, his dialetheism does not seem restricted to what is imaginary.

If everything exists, so must contradictions. Indeed, Gabriel's concept of existence is such that "absolute non-existence is impossible."[82] Since absolute non-existence is impossible, it is impossible for contradictions, or the objects and states of affairs they describe, to be absolutely non-existent. These contradictions do not absolutely exist, but they certainly exist *relative* to some field of sense. The "round square" certainly does not exist in the field of sense investigated by geometry, but it certainly can exist in *the domain of contradictory objects*. "The round square" cannot be imagined, yet it still refers to an object in this domain and successfully instantiates the form of the contradiction: "both A and not A." Even if we deny that it is true that round squares exist in the field of sense studied by geometry, we know what people *mean* when they claim that "the square is round." Since for Gabriel *conceivability* implies (some form of) actuality, the "round square" must exist, but obviously in a field different from that studied by geometry. Simply put: *contradictions can be conceived, so they exist*. This means that *every* contradiction is true and corresponds with an object that exists, *except* for the contradiction articulated in the claim that "the world exists" or "the world does not exist." Without understanding why these contradictions cannot be true, we cannot understand Gabriel's no-world view.

10.3.2 Why the World Does Not Exist

One of Priest's objections is that Gabriel's argument against the existence of the world begs the question.[83] Priest notes that Gabriel accepts that objects can (and in fact do) exist in fields of sense to which they are identical. Objects can exist "in themselves." Since Gabriel does not deny all cases of self-containment, he must give an independent reason for denying it in the case of the world. However, Gabriel claims that the world is *not* one of these objects. Gabriel's argument against the existence of the world assumes that "this unified

---

[81] See ibid., pp. 53–4, and Moss (2020), ch. 9.
[82] Gabriel (2015a), p. 178.
[83] Priest, ch.1, p. 29, footnote 22.

totality differs from each and every thing that is unified by it."[84] This assumption, however, is tantamount to the denial of the existence of the world as such an object. Thus, Gabriel's argument against the existence of the world begs the question.[85]

Unlike anything else, Gabriel's dialogue with Priest has done great work to clarify the status of Gabriel's argument against the existence of the world. In *Fields of Sense*, Gabriel's argument *deduces* the non-existence of the world from his definition of existence. His definition of existence, or "appearance in a field of sense," is defined as local or relative such that that for every domain there must be something that does *not* appear in it, but appears in *another* field. The world, defined as the unified totality, is an all-inclusive object, such that there is nothing that does not appear in it. But such an object simply violates the definition of existence. Thus, the world does not exist. Note that Gabriel does not conclude that existence is relative but assumes it from the outset. Most simply, the deduction proceeds as follows: Only relative objects exist. The world is a non-relative or absolute object. Thus, the world does not exist.

Consider Gabriel's more thorough version: since to exist is to appear in a field of sense, the world must appear in a field of sense in order to exist. Given that it must exist in a field of sense in order to exist, the world can *either* appear in *another* field or it can appear in *itself*. Since the world can exist neither in another field nor in itself, the world cannot exist in any fields of sense. Thus, the world does not exist at all.[86]

For the argument to succeed, Gabriel must demonstrate why the world cannot exist in *another field* of sense or in itself. If the world existed in another field, this field in which the world exists would encompass the world. Because Gabriel's definition of existence entails that existence is *locative*[87] – namely, that "for every domain there is something *not* [my emphasis] appearing in it"[88] – the world would necessarily appear as *one field alongside other fields*, which would contain other objects. Since the field in which the world exists would "encompass more than the world," the field in which the world exists would contain *more objects than exist in the world*. In this case, the world would not be the totality of all things, which is absurd, since it is by definition the unified totality of all things. Thus, the world, as

[84] Gabriel (2015a), p. 189. As we noted earlier, in §2.1, this same assumption is invoked in Priest (1995) to infer that the gluon of everything is not an object.
[85] Also see Priest, ch. 3, p. 71. For a full explication of this critique, see Moss (2020), ch. 9.
[86] Gabriel (2015a), p. 189.
[87] Ibid., 61. "There is no bare existence, only existence as this or that."
[88] Ibid., p. 60.

the field of all fields, could exist only if it exists *in itself*. The world (as the object) must appear in the world (as the field of sense).

According to Gabriel, it is *also* impossible for the world to appear in itself.[89] Since Gabriel does *not* posit a universal rule precluding self-containment, his argument is only that *totality cannot contain itself*.[90] Just as Gabriel never posits a universal rule for individuating fields of sense, there is no abstract rule for what exists in them *a priori*, such that there is *no a priori principle* excluding the possibility of self-containment. Likewise, Gabriel's argument against the world does not proceed from the assumption that the principle of non-contradiction is an absolute principle of all being, by which one could determine what absolutely does not exist, for he denies any absolute principle by which one would determine what can and what cannot exist in fields of sense.

If we read this passage carefully, we see that Gabriel invokes the *same assumption* as in the first disjunct. If the world exists within itself (rather than in another), Gabriel claims that it will still appear alongside other fields. The reason is the same: Gabriel's definition of existence, "appearance in a field of sense," entails that for every domain there must be something that does *not* appear in it, but appears in *another* field. For this reason, if the world appears in any field of sense at all, it will appear *alongside other fields* in which other objects appear that do *not* appear in it. Thus, since the world can exist only by excluding some objects from itself, it can exist only if it is *not the world*.

Is Gabriel's argument question begging? Decidedly it is *not*. The common assumption in both disjuncts is that existence is relative, or local. This definition allows self-containment in the case of relative beings, such as propositions. For example: when I say "this proposition is true," the proposition appears in itself, but it also appears in another field of sense, namely my chapter "Transcending Everything." Thus, Gabriel's definition of existence is specifically designed to accommodate symmetrical wholes and, more generally, objects that exist "in themselves" under the condition that there are some objects that exist outside of them in other fields. In the case of my chapter, all the other sentences in this text exist beyond the field of sense-object "this proposition is true." If we interpret the aleph as a [relative] point of all points (which in any case Gabriel is not inclined to do), Gabriel's definition of existence would happily accommodate this as well. Because the putative object "the world" is *all-inclusive* by

[89] Ibid., p. 189.
[90] Ibid., p. 188.

definition, it violates the existence condition in a way that "this proposition is true" does not. Thus, in Gabriel's FOS ontology, existence *itself* must be the criterion by which one determines the acceptability of self-containment in any case.

Given these independent ontological considerations, Gabriel must deny that his formal Meinongian principle that "we cannot claim that something does not exist without thereby committing to its existence" has *un*restricted application. Rather, the principle must be significantly *qualified*. We will discuss the conditions that restrict the application of this principle in §3.4.

Given that Gabriel's argument against the existence of the world is deduced from the definition of existence, the disagreement between Priest and Gabriel about whether the world is a being depends upon the *definition of existence*. Why should we accept that existence is relative to a particular domain? For Gabriel, because existence cannot be an *absolute* property that all things share in common, existence is *bound* to relative fields. However, Gabriel's concept of the proper property (as well as the concept of the genus and the set) assumes *the duality* of principles of identity and difference. As Gabriel states, "this unified totality differs from each and every thing that is unified by it, and accordingly becomes an additional field of sense, the field of all fields."[91] The assumption is that the principle that *unifies* all fields is fundamentally different from the fields that are *unified* by it. Gabriel's argument against conceiving of existence as a proper property assumes the impossibility of *absolute self-differentiation* from the very beginning.

However, this assumption is not self-evident. I note in passing that Hegel argues that the concept is the absolute self-differentiating being:

> The concept of God realizes itself most fully as this universal that determines and particularizes itself – it is this activity of dividing, of particularizing and determining itself, or positing a finitude, negating this – its own finitude and being identical with itself through its negation of this finitude. This is the concept as such, the concept of God.[92]

In Gabriel's terms, although "being" cannot be a proper or (metaphysical) property if the principles of identity and difference are assumed to be separate, in his seminal *Science of Logic*, Hegel argues that being (and indeed every category of the logic) is self-differentiating. Although space constraints do not allow me to give the argument

---

[91] Ibid., p. 189.
[92] Hegel (1984), p. 324. Naturally, if we adopt Hegel's vision of the self-dividing totality, we would be forced to reject Gabriel's "ontological realism" whereby being and thought come apart. Gabriel, ch. 2, p. 62.

here, in "Absolute Dialetheism" I advance the view that the concept of being is *self-differentiating* and can thereby successfully be conceived as a special kind of proper (and metaphysical) property.[93] Here it is sufficient to note that, if one follows Hegel and conceives of being as self-differentiating, being would no longer preclude the existence of the world as Gabriel maintains.

10.3.3 The Inductive Ground of Existence

Let us now turn to Gabriel's justification for his concept of existence. If existence is appearing in a field of sense such that, given any field, φ, there must be something that does *not* appear in it, ε, then the world cannot exist, since it is the field φ that includes ε, which by definition cannot appear in it. What is the status of this definition of existence? First, consider that Gabriel's definition of existence is not the only logically possible definition. Other definitions of existence are logically possible, such as the definition of existence I developed in §3.2. The world does not exist according to Gabriel's definition, but it can exist according to other definitions. Thus, the world is a logically possible entity. As Gabriel states: "FOS does not provide any purely logical reasons against the existence of the world."[94] Because the world may exist on other definitions of existence, Gabriel is happy to admit that his definition is *defeasible*.[95]

If the world is logically possible, what is the status of Gabriel's claim that the world cannot exist? The impossibility of the existence of the world is *ontological*.[96] For Gabriel, ontology is concerned with the meaning of existence. If it is true that existence is appearing in a field of sense, then the world cannot exist. Thus, according to Gabriel's ontology, the world is *ontologically* impossible. However, this is consistent with the view that it is still logically possible that the world exists, since it is logically possible that Gabriel's definition of existence is false. Given that there are alternative ways of conceiving existence (such as that given in §3.2), to what independent ontological evidence can one appeal in order to defend this definition?

Gabriel argues that the relativity of existence can be attained by generalizing from the insights from mathematics, the empirical and theoretical sciences, and our pre-ontological experience:

---

[93] What is more, in Moss (2020), I systematically explicate how any attempt to impose an absolute separation of the principles of identity and difference in epistemological and metaphysical reflection leads to numerous paradoxes.
[94] Gabriel, ch. 2, p. 55.
[95] Personal Conversation, Summer 2019.
[96] Gabriel, ch. 2, p. 63.

> The no-world-view generalizes these insights beyond the frame of natural science and metamathematics by introducing a notion of relative existence, i.e. of appearance in a fos that differs from the notion that there is such a property of existence *tout court*.[97]

Neither our best mathematics nor our best sciences require the existence of the world. What is more, our pre-ontological experience is saturated with relative existence. Consider perceptual and imaginative consciousness, none of which, it seems, can have the world as its object. My perception of the tree and its horizon is never a perception of the horizon of all horizons. Just as I am impotent to imagine a 10,000-sided figure, I am even less able to imagine the totality of all totalities. In sum, Gabriel's argument for restricting existence to relative being is an *inductive* generalization from the relative fields of being – from beings given to us.[98] Most simply: we define existence by generalizing from what exists.

I would like to consider Gabriel's generalization first from the side of *form* and then from the side of *content*. Regarding the form of Gabriel's inductive argument, is the inductive inference about the meaning of existence from some to *all* or from some to *others*? In either case, the inference is inductive and seems to appeal to an *implicit* assumption that there is a *uniformity* among the cases considered that enables the extension from some known case to other *unknown* cases.[99] We should carefully consider this question in light of Gabriel's own reflections on the limits of quantification. If Gabriel's conclusion that "existence is appearance in a field of sense" applied to everything, then Gabriel would quantify over everything. Indeed, this would commit him to proclaiming some truth about all objects: for any object, π, π exists only if it appears in a *non-absolute* field of sense.

Because Gabriel is committed to the view that conceivability implies actuality, if there were a *meaningful* proposition that could be stated about all objects, then there would be an object to correspond with that proposition. However, given the no-world view, there is no true proposition that can be stated about all things.

---

[97] Ibid., p. 57.

[98] Also consider Kant, who argued that the world is not something one can experience. Rather, it is an *Idea* of reason. See Kant (1998), A644/B67.

[99] Hume (1999), pp. 114–15. What justifies this uniformity principle? If the uniformity assumption is justified by appealing to an inductive argument, and inductive arguments must assume the uniformity principle, then the argument would beg the question. Naturally, the problem of induction is not a problem particular to Gabriel's ontology – but it certainly cannot be ignored either – especially since the definition of existence itself hangs in the balance.

Because Gabriel *denies* that he quantifies over everything,[100] his claim that "existence is appearance in a field of sense" cannot be a claim about the existence condition of anything. If he (meaningfully) quantified over everything, he would commit himself to the existence of the world. Thus, his generalization cannot be from some to all.

In order to avoid quantifying over every being, Gabriel's inductive inference about the relativity of existence can only be from some to *others*. Gabriel's restriction on universal quantification is consistent with the claim that our knowledge is *fragmentary* – a fragmentation that corresponds with the non-absolute character of reality itself.[101] Because of the restriction on universal quantification, the uniformity principle that enables the inference from some to *others* cannot have an absolute scope. Instead, whatever uniformity we assert to be true can only be a *local* uniformity. What is more, such limitations are also consistent with the defeasible character of Gabriel's claims concerning the meaning of existence. Because our knowledge is limited, it is possible that our ontological claims will be defeated by further experience.

Exactly because Gabriel is committed only to speaking *meaningfully* about *some* beings – not all – his own knowledge of existence is itself fragmentary. Hence, strictly speaking, the definition of existence as "appearance in a field of sense" is true about *some* objects. The definition "existence is appearance in a field of sense" should always be *implicitly* qualified with "as far as we know." "Appearance in a field of sense" may itself be only a very *local* existence condition, one among others. Thus, ontology cannot be about what existence is if this means "what it is for *any* object to exist."[102]

If we apply this quantification restriction back to Gabriel's argument against the existence of the world, the first premise of the argument that "for every domain there must be something that does *not* appear in it, but appears in *another* field" cannot be an existence condition for *all* objects – only some. Since the world is the field of sense in which nothing appears outside of it, it cannot exist *under this local existence condition*. However, we absolutely cannot conclude that the world cannot exist, since the definition of existence cannot be meaningfully applied to every possible object. If we infer that "the world cannot exist under any condition," then we would be quantifying over everything without restriction. The world's impossibility

---

[100] Gabriel, ch. 2, p. 64.
[101] Gabriel, ch. 2, p. 57. Also see Gabriel (2020a).
[102] Gabriel acknowledges that, once we apply the existence condition back onto existence itself, we must acknowledge that "existence exists" and that it is relative.

must be a *relative* impossibility – i.e., an impossibility that is relative to the local existence condition "for every domain there must be something that does not appear in it, but appears in *another* field." At best we can infer that, *as far as we know*, the world, which is a logically possible object, does not exist according to the local existence condition "appearing in a field of sense."[103]

Given the local character of Gabriel's definition of existence, it is worth considering the philosophical and religious experience that attests to the existence of the world. Regarding the *content* of the generalization, Priest raises an important objection to this argument by arguing that much of our knowledge transcends what we know from the mathematical and empirical sciences. What is more, philosophy can surprise us at times exactly because it challenges our pre-ontological experience of the world.[104] Often the meaning of pre-ontological experience is not transparent, as the history of religious experience can attest.

Because Gabriel's definition is grounded inductively, it is a *defeasible* definition. Just like any inductive generalization, it is vulnerable to refutation by counterexample. Mystical experiences seem to offer such a counterexample, since they are often explicitly interpreted by those who claim to undergo them as experiences of the world-whole. For example, consider Schleiermacher's claim that religious experience is the *intuition of the universe*:

> Religion's essence is neither thinking nor acting, but intuition and feeling. It wishes to intuit the universe, wishes devoutly to overhear the universe's own manifestations and actions, longs to be grasped and filled by the universe's immediate influences in childlike passivity...[105]

Although Schleiermacher was a theologian, the history of religious consciousness is rife with such reports of ineffable experiences of totality by ordinary subjects with no philosophical training.[106] While

---

[103] Just as existence is relative, so must possibility be conceived in a relative way. See Gabriel (2015a), chs 10–11, for more on Gabriel's concept of possibility.

[104] See Priest, ch. 3, p. 72.

[105] I take "universe" here to mean something more than "nature" as one object among others, and to mean something closer to "totality" or "world." Schleiermacher (1996), p. 22. For Gabriel's use of Schleiermacher, see Gabriel (2015c), pp. 146–84. Also consider Al Ghazali, a proponent of Sufi, who holds that *only God is*: "So there remained nothing with them save ALLAH. They became drunken with a drunkenness wherein the sway of their own intelligence disappeared; so that one [1] exclaimed, 'I am The ONE REAL!' and another, 'Glory be to ME! How great is MY glory!' [2] and another, 'Within this robe is nought but ALLAH.'" Al Ghazali (1924), Part I, p. 106.

[106] The classical study of such experiences is William James's *The Varieties of Religious Experience*.

the no-world view can plausibly explain *away* mystical experiences of the unity of all things and can plausibly interpret the phenomena of the "oceanic feeling" without appealing to the concept of the world,[107] the meaning of such experience is neither univocal nor by any means obvious – Gabriel can always deny that they exist. However, such experiences can equally be marshalled in an inductive argument for the existence of the world, and it is not a trite or irrelevant matter that Gabriel asks Priest if he has had a mystical experience that would (ironically) justify his speech about the world.[108]

Naturally, we should be wary about naively employing our pre-ontological experience as a criterion for the truth of philosophical claims, especially when philosophical experience challenges those preconceptions. Whatever definition of existence we provide, it should not only attend to our pre-ontological experience, but it should also attend to our *philosophical* experience. More specifically, the *phenomenology* of the *philosophical* experience of raising the question "what is being?" or "what is **nothing**?" muddies the water. My own philosophical experience in thinking about **nothing**, as I have articulated it in §2.3, demands that **nothing** be conceived as **everything**, the unified totality, and something unified by the totality. Such philosophical experience calls us to question the truth of Gabriel's premise that the "unified totality differs from each and every thing that is unified by it." In short, religious and philosophical experience alike – each a form of *Weltgeist* – attest to the existence of the absolute and will not go quietly into the night.

10.3.4 Mysticism and the Meaninglessness of Everything and Nothing

Although Gabriel's denial of universal quantification should restrict his propositions about the world to *local* fields of sense, Gabriel does not appear to limit his claim that the world does not exist to some fields.

According to Gabriel, the world does not exist at all: "let my mantra be repeated – that it does not even exist."[109] Here Gabriel

---

[107] Gabriel, ch. 2, p. 27. Just as Gabriel argues that people do not understand their own experiences when they believe that they are thinking about the world so he can also argue that people mis-understand their own mystical experiences when they believe they have experienced unity with the world. However, some evidence cannot be simply explained away, such as the non-duality of subjectivity, which Gabriel accepts. Gabriel, ch. 4, p. 94.
[108] See ibid., p. 90.
[109] Ibid., p. 95.

appears to speak *in his own voice* when he proclaims that "it does not even exist" without further qualification. Since we can translate this to mean that, for *any* field of sense, π, it is not identical to the world, φ, Gabriel appears to quantify over everything. Thus, it appears that he has violated the limits of what his ontology allows one to express. Priest raises the objection that Gabriel's ontology falls victim to the paradox of expressibility.[110]

Gabriel acknowledges that a problem arises whenever one asserts anything about the world. Moreover, he recognizes that his theory does not allow him to *assert* it to be true that the world does not exist. Instead, he holds that "the world does not exist" is itself completely *meaningless*. Because the world does not exist, Gabriel further infers that the non-existence of the world is not a truth about any object.[111] For Gabriel, a concept can be meaningful only if it has truth conditions. Since claims about the world cannot refer to anything, and a claim can have truth conditions only if it refers to something, Gabriel infers that claims about the world do not have truth conditions.[112] Given that a statement can be meaningful only if it has truth conditions, Gabriel infers that claims about the world are meaningless: "For me, saying anything about the world is plain nonsense, like saying the following: XCEANNR$_{s12*}$."[113] For Gabriel, terms have meaning if they have truth conditions, and only terms that refer to objects can have truth conditions. Accordingly, for him a term can be meaningfully employed (or conceived) only if it *actually refers to an object*. This undergirds his *Noneism* and his Meinongianism,[114] whereby *conceivability implies actuality*.[115] Gabriel remarks that, because the world is meaningless, speaking about the world means nothing different from "XCEANNR$_{s12*}$."[116]

Having demonstrated both that Gabriel can accommodate Priest's counterexamples and that his argument for the no-world view does not fall victim to any vicious circularity, we must now tackle Priest's

---

[110] See Priest (1995), p. 124. The very same critique Priest raises against Russell's theory of orders can apply, *mutatis mutandis*, to Gabriel's ontology. Just as Russell cannot explain his theory of orders without quantifying over all functions, Gabriel cannot explain his no-world view without quantifying over everything that exists.

[111] Gabriel (2015a), p. 174. For a brief look at the history of the problem of onto-theology in respect to the indeterminacy of the concept of the Absolute, see "The Emerging Philosophical Recognition of the Significance of Indeterminacy," in *The Significance of Indeterminacy*, ed. Robert H. Scott and Gregory S. Moss.

[112] Gabriel (2015a), p. 203.

[113] Ibid., p. 200. See Gabriel's longer discussion of this issue, pp. 200–5.

[114] Ibid., p. 180.

[115] Ibid., p, 185.

[116] Ibid., p. 200.

most powerful objection. Since Gabriel writes about the world in *Fields of Sense*, Priest draws the inference that Gabriel's own claim that the world does not exist is meaningless.[117] When Gabriel argues that the world does not exist, either he is saying something meaningful or he is not. Given that the noun phrase "the world" is meaningless, it follows that his claim that "the world does not exist" says nothing meaningful. Saying "the world does not exist" is like saying "'XCEANNR$_{s12*}$' does not exist." Since this is meaningless, and has no truth conditions, Gabriel cannot claim *that it is true* that the world does not exist." Accordingly, we have uncovered another (perhaps surprising) point of agreement between Priest and Gabriel: *neither* commits to asserting the truth of the proposition "the world does not exist." A certain tension arises: at times Gabriel will assert, in his *own voice*, that the world does not exist (which implies that he is asserting this to be true), yet he must also deny that one can assert any truths about the world. How can this tension be reconciled? We will put this question to rest only once we have addressed the *positive* role of self-refutation in Gabriel's thought.

Naturally, Gabriel does not acquiesce to Priest's objection but uses it to illuminate his own view. Because Gabriel recognizes that all claims about the world are meaningless, he neither asserts it to be true that the world exists nor asserts that it does not exist. Because Gabriel is not committed to *asserting* the truth of the claim "the world does not exist," his utterance "the world does not exist" can be meaningless without that meaninglessness compromising his position. In place of asserting the claim "the world does not exist," Gabriel adopts *metametaphysical nihilism* whereby claims about the world are nonsense: "My central claim is metametaphysical: it is the claim that we get mired in plain nonsense when we assume that the world exists."[118]

Gabriel's metametaphysical nihilism is well motivated by his other philosophical commitments. If we consider the point about negative existentials, we will remember that Gabriel endorses a view under which conceivability *implies* actuality. If the word "world" were meaningful, then it would have truth conditions. For Gabriel, this is possible only if we acknowledge that there is some being to which we are referring when we speak about the world. Thus, if we can speak meaningfully about the world, then the world must exist. Since the world cannot exist, Gabriel must proclaim "the world" to be a completely meaningless phrase.

[117] See ch. 1, p. 29.
[118] Gabriel, ch. 4, p. 93.

Either the claim that "the world does not exist" is meaningless, and its truth-value cannot be evaluated, or "the world does not exist" *is* meaningful and must be false, since conceivability implies actuality. No matter how we read the proclamation that "the world does not exist," the proclamation is either meaningless or false. Therefore, Gabriel is exactly right to distance himself from the claim "the world does not exist" is true.

Although Gabriel does not give much attention to this concept in the dialogue with Priest, absolute **nothing** must be just as meaningless as **everything**. If we could meaningfully conceive of absolute **nothing**, then it would be actual – it would exist in a field of sense. However, Gabriel claims that absolute **nothing** does not exist.[119] According to Gabriel: "Nothingness is what you experience when you begin to realize that metaphysics is impossible due to the absence of its alleged object."[120] Absolute **nothingness** is a *non-objective* absence to be confronted:

> Once we realize that it [the world] simply does not exist, we face nothingness. But *pace* Priest what we thus face is not an object, but rather the fact that there is nothing to be thought about . . .[121]

"Absolute **nothingness**" here signifies the non-being of the world. Because the world is meaningless, so must the *negation* of the world be equally meaningless. Both **everything** and (absolute) **nothing** are meaningless – they can neither exist nor be *meaningfully* conceived.

Given that the term "world" is meaningless, we are now in possession of the *qualifying* condition that restricts Gabriel's formal Meinongianism. The principle must be qualified to read as follows: "as concerns that about which one can speak *meaningfully*, we cannot claim that something does not exist without thereby committing to its existence." If the principle is restricted in this way, then Gabriel would no longer be beholden to the world's existence. By invoking the meaninglessness of the world, Gabriel's no-world view no longer stands at odds with his Meinongianism. This qualification is already implied in his principle that conceivability implies actuality. If it is true that if something is conceivable, then it is actual, and, since the world is not actual, then the world is *in*conceivable.[122]

Because the ontological investigation into existence motivates this qualification, Gabriel can successfully respond to Priest's critique

---

[119] "There is no such object as nothing." Gabriel, ch. 4, p. 95.
[120] Gabriel, ch. 2, p. 65.
[121] Ibid.
[122] Note that, as a result, Gabriel must simultaneously hold the world to be logically possible and inconceivable. The latter is the result of his ontological investigation.

that he makes an ad hoc exception for the world. However, it leaves his argument vulnerable to Priest's critique that *absolutely none* of Gabriel's claims about the world can be true.

Consider Gabriel's argument that the world does not exist from §3.2 above. The term "the world" appears in the premises of that argument – e.g., "either the world appears in another field of sense or it appears in itself." Since the "world" is meaningless, no premise containing the world can be true. Since an argument is sound if it is valid and all the premises are true, and the premises of Gabriel's argument cannot be true, his argument against the existence of the world cannot be sound. As a consequence, Gabriel cannot claim that any of his arguments succeed in demonstrating the non-existence of the world. He cannot hold the no-world view to be true, and he cannot hold that any of his arguments for the no-world view are sound arguments. They either commit him to the world's existence or they mean nothing. Although in §3.3 we discovered that Gabriel could assert the non-existence of the world only according to a *local* existence condition, the thesis on meaninglessness also undermines even the truth of this local assertion of the non-existence of the world.

More significantly, the meaninglessness of the world undermines even the meaningfulness of his *metametaphysical* nihilism. If "world" is meaningfully articulated in the claim that "the world is meaningless," and conceivability implies actuality, a world must exist that has the *sense* of being meaningless, which Gabriel denies. However, if "the world" is meaningless, then "the world is meaningless" has no truth conditions whatsoever, and there are no conditions under which it would be true.

As I have argued in *Hegel's Foundation Free Metaphysics* (FFM), the no-world view can succeed only by drawing upon a strategy employed by the mystical tradition.[123] As I noted there, in *Fields of Sense* Gabriel shows no sympathy with mysticism, and even seems hostile to the position.[124] In *FFM*, I suggest that Gabriel can employ a strategy from the mystical tradition to motivate the no-world view.[125] The type of mysticism I mean to invoke in this discussion is the thesis that the world transcends conceptual determination and is accessible only through non-conceptual or immediate means. Rather than attempt to grasp the world via concepts, judgments or propositions, mysticism employs the argument to transcend the argument and thereby *experience* existence in a non-conceptual way. Although

---

[123] Gabriel, ch. 4, p. 67.
[124] See Gabriel (2015a), p. 201.
[125] Moss (2020), p. 295.

there are various types of mysticism, some do take the world as the object of mystical intuition.[126] Although Gabriel does not invoke anything like this definition of mysticism, his defense of the no-world view certainly depends upon employing a similar, dialectical strategy employed by various mystical traditions.

Given the mystical view that no speech about the world is meaningful, *the mystic's own speech about the world cannot be meaningful*. If the mystic's speech were meaningful, then it would be false. Thus, the only way for the mystic to succeed in the argument is to *speak meaninglessly*. By speaking meaninglessly, the mystic presents a coherent view, for they speak in a way that *is consistent with their thesis*. The mystic cannot meaningfully say what they mean. Instead, all they can do is point to, or show, the meaninglessness of what they are saying by speaking meaninglessly themselves and by drawing all claims about the world into meaninglessness.[127] Only by drawing all claims about the world into meaninglessness can the mystic *show* the truth of what they are saying, since they cannot say it meaningfully. In his response to Priest's objections, Gabriel seems to have endorsed this suggestion by pointing to the *dialectical* character of "world" and by explicitly drawing himself closer to the mystical position of Neo-Platonism that posits the One as the *non-being* that is beyond being.[128]

Similar to this mystical approach, Gabriel can only *point to*, or *show*, the truth of the non-existence of the world (and his metametaphysical nihilism) *through an act of meaningless speech* and by

---

[126] Wittgenstein (1999) and Nishida (1993) are paradigmatic examples. Although Schleiermacher takes God to be the object of mystical feeling, his God is all-inclusive and thus does not exclude the world.

[127] Wittgenstein (1999) and Nagarjuna (1995) employ this strategy, albeit to establish very different positions. See Garfield's comparison of each of these strategies in his commentary on Nagarjuna's *The Fundamental Wisdom of the Middle Way*. Nagarjuna (1995), p. 213.

[128] Gabriel, ch. 2, p. 67. Being appears to be beyond being. See Plato (1997), *Republic*, Book 6, 509b, where we discover the principle of all existence, the Good, is ἐπέκεινα τῆς οὐσίας or "beyond being," or Pseudo-Dionysius (1987), p. 49 [585–8], where the principle of unity of all things is the "being beyond being" or ὑπερουσία οὐσία. In the *Divine Names*, Pseudo-Dionysius further identifies the One beyond being as non-being: Pseudo-Dionysius (1987), p. 85. I note in passing that, although Gabriel is right that for Neo-Platonism the one is beyond being, and indeed beyond everything, the tradition usually conceives of the one as simultaneously indistinguishable from everything, a view which is closer to Absolute Dialetheism than Gabriel's no-world view. Consider both Pseudo-Dionysius and Meister Eckhart, both of whom make this claim. See Pseudo-Dionysius (1987), p. 98: "He is being for whatever is" and "He is the being immanent in and underlying the things which are, however they are," and Meister Eckhart (1981), p. 201, who asserts that "Therefore God is free of all things, and therefore he is all things."

drawing all claims about the world into meaninglessness. Only by *consistently* drawing all claims about the world into meaninglessness can he *show* the truth of what he is saying, since he cannot *say* it meaningfully or truthfully. As Gabriel puts it, his claim that "the world does not exist" is "dialectical":

> The use of an apparently meaningful noun phrase "the world" in "the world is not my left hand" is purely dialectical. i.e. it takes place on a lower rung of the ladder, designed to lure in the metaphysician who believes herself to be in a cognitive, epistemic, or at least, semantic touch with the world as an object.[129]

Once one *sees* that no claim about the world could be said in a meaningful way, then Gabriel must admit that his own claims about the world are meaningless. Although his claims about the world cannot be true, the act of speaking meaninglessly about the world can still *show* the reader there is no world about which anyone can meaningfully speak. Or, to put it ironically, the truth of Gabriel's proclamation that "the world does not exist" cannot be meaningfully said, but it can be *shown* in virtue of his own *performance of meaningless speech*. Because Gabriel must resort to this distinction between saying and showing in order to defend *the truth* that the world does not exist, Wittgenstein's *Tractatus* and Gabriel's proximity to Wittgenstein's views on nonsense take center-stage in Priest and Gabriel's dialogue.[130]

Gabriel means to lure Priest into uttering meaningless propositions about the world.[131] By attempting to lure him into uttering something meaningless, Gabriel means to show Priest that he cannot say anything meaningful about the world and thereby *show* him the truth of its non-existence without thereby asserting the non-existence of the world himself. Accordingly, the optimal method for Gabriel to demonstrate the non-existence of the world would be a *dialogical* one. Because the world is meaningless, and Priest and Gabriel's main point of disagreement concerns the existence of the world (in Gabriel's terms), or the *being* of the world (on Priest's terms), Gabriel must hold his debate with Priest to be fundamentally meaningless. While Priest holds that they are arguing about something, for Gabriel

---

[129] Gabriel, ch. 2, p. 66.

[130] See Priest, ch. 3, p. 80, and Gabriel, ch. 4, p. 92. Priest argues that Gabriel falls victim to the same critiques raised by Priest (1995), ch.12. Gabriel retorts that his ladder is different from Wittgenstein's, whereby "the world does not exist" is not the first rung of the ladder.

[131] In the Buddhist tradition this is called "skillful means." Thanks to Dennis Prooi for pointing to this connection.

the argument is really about nothing. Thus, much of the dialogue is really concerned about whether their conversation has any meaning whatsoever.

On this point of meaninglessness, Gabriel also draws close to Nagarjuna, whose philosophy is a point of inspiration. Nagarjuna famously writes that "I prostrate to Gautama who through compassion taught the true doctrine, which leads to the relinquishing of all views."[132] Since the Buddha teaches the relinquishing of all views, Nagarjuna must relinquish his own view – such as those views about the emptiness of all things – as well. Similarly, once we recognize the meaninglessness of all views of the world, Gabriel must relinquish his own view of the world, namely his view that "it does not exist." Although Gabriel does not endorse the relinquishing of all assertions, he does endorse relinquishing all assertions about the world, and, in this way, he draws close to the spirit of Madhyamaka.[133] When Gabriel speaks about the world in his *own* voice, which he is apt to do, then he must advocate the relinquishing of his own assertions about the world. Whereas Priest takes Madhyamaka as a metaphysical inspiration, Gabriel follows the skeptical and anti-metaphysical impulses of that tradition.

Without endorsing the self-refutation of his own "mantra," Gabriel's own assertion becomes a *Stolperstein* to revealing the nothingness at the bottom of things. Ironically, any critique of metaphysics that does not refute itself cannot succeed. Gabriel can reveal the nothingness of the world by denying the truth of his claim that the world does not exist. He can successfully deny that all assertions about the world fail to express meaning by recognizing the meaninglessness of his own propositions about the world.

Because Gabriel cannot assert anything true about the world, the truth that "the world does not exist" must simply be *ineffable*. When we see that the world does not exist, we *confront* the nothingness of the world. This *mystical* confrontation with the nothingness of the world arises only once we recognize that all speech about the world falls into falsehood or meaninglessness. For this reason, the sense of truth that applies to the insight that the world does not exist cannot have any discursive sense. The "truth" of the non-existence of the world must be something akin to Heidegger's sense of truth as unconcealment.

The truth of the no-world view demands a new concept of the fact. Concerning facts, Gabriel writes: "There are facts only if some-

---

[132] Nagarjuna (1995), 27.30.
[133] Gabriel, ch. 4, p. 94.

thing or other is true of an object."[134] However, if there is no object "world," there cannot be any facts about it. Thus, there cannot be any fact that the world does not exist. If it is a fact that the world does not exist, then it is only a fact on a different definition, namely one that is freed from the condition that the fact be true of an object.

However, this "unconcealment" must be ineffable – otherwise the *nothing would vanish* into a thing, and the world would reappear. Whatever truth there may be in the non-existence of the world, it is an ineffable truth that transcends all language, even the proposition "the non-existence of the world is ineffable." While Wittgenstein asserted that "*Nicht wie die Welt ist, ist das Mystische, sondern dass sie ist*," Gabriel must invert Wittgenstein: *dass die Welt nicht existiert – das ist das Mystische*. Without a *mystical* concept of truth (and facts), Gabriel must abandon the no-world view. In a word, Gabriel's ontology must invoke an inverted mysticism, whereby *the nothingness of the world* (rather than its existence) transcends conceptual determination and is accessible through non-conceptual means.

Indeed, Gabriel says that "nothing is an experience," but he cannot say that "nothing is an experience" and that be true. As Gabriel points out, nothing is no object at all – it cannot even be an experience, otherwise it would not be absolutely nothing. Like Priest, Gabriel must hold that nothingness is ineffable, but in Gabriel's case that nothingness is the non-existence of the world. Whereas Priest can say that nothing is ineffable and this truth be *discursive*, Gabriel cannot assert that nothing is ineffable and this be discursively true, since this would commit him to the existence of the object, absolute **nothingness**, which he has denied.

On the point of meaninglessness, the dialogue with Priest has opened Gabriel to carefully reconsider his position on the meaninglessness of totality.[135] If Gabriel abandons the thesis on meaninglessness, then he would be forced to accept a form of Absolute Dialetheism. As we know, Gabriel cannot hold the "no-world view" to be true, since it is a meaningless position. On Gabriel's terms, who can hold the "no-world view" *to be true*? Only the Absolute Dialetheist can hold the no-world view to be true. Since conceivability implies actuality, if we conceive the "world" then it must exist. Thus, if we meaningfully conceive and assert the term "world" in "the no-world view is true," then the world exists. But the "no-world view" asserts that the world does not exist. Thus, if the no-world view is true, then *the world exists and does not exist*. For this reason, if the no-world view

[134] Gabriel (2015a), p. 46.
[135] Gabriel, ch. 4, p. 94.

is true, then the world must exist, but only as a *true* contradiction. Thus, the *truth* of the no-world view engenders the truth of Absolute Dialetheism.[136]

What *is* the world? We Absolute Dialetheists proudly assert that "*the world* is nothing," and we invite Gabriel to join us in the chorus. By asserting the truth of Gabriel's view – by asserting the truth of the no-world view, we acknowledge the truth of the world and raise Dialetheism to the throne of the Absolute.[137]

---

[136] Absolute Dialetheism is not a univocal view. On the one hand, one can hold the thesis that the Absolute is a true contradiction and hold that the Absolute is rationally conceivable. On the other hand, one can hold the view that the truth of the Absolute contradiction transcends conceptual comprehension. For a tentative typology of Absolute Dialetheism, see Moss (2020), pp. 239–47.

[137] Thanks to Dennis Prooi for his helpful comments on the early drafts of this contribution.

References and Bibliography

Al Ghazali (1924) *The Niche for Lights*, trans. W. H. T. Gairdner. London: Royal Asiatic Society.
Aristotle (2002) *Metaphysics*, trans. J. Sachs. Santa Fe, NM: Green Lion Press.
Badiou, A. (2005) *Being and Event*, trans. O. Feltham. New York: Continuum.
Balderston, D. (1993) *Out of Context: Historical Reference and the Representation of Reality in Borges*. Durham, NC: Duke University Press.
Barwise, J., and Etchemendy, J. (1987) *The Liar*. Oxford: Oxford University Press.
Benoist, J. (2017) *L'Adresse du réel*. Paris: Vrin.
Berto, F. (2013) *Existence as a Real Property*. Dordrecht: Springer.
Berto, F., and Jago, M. (2019) *Impossible Worlds*. Oxford: Oxford University Press.
Berto, F., French, R., Priest, G., and Ripley, D. (2018) "Williamson on Counterpossibles," *Journal of Philosophical Logic* 47: 693–713.
Blatti, S., and Lapointe, S. (eds) (2016) *Ontology after Carnap*. Oxford: Oxford University Press.
Bliss, R., and Priest, G. (2017) "Metaphysical Grounding, East and West," in S. Emmanuel (ed.), *Buddhist Philosophy: A Comparative Approach*. Hoboken, NJ: Wiley Blackwell, pp. 63–85.
Bliss, R. L., and Trogdon, K. (2014) "Metaphysical Grounding," in E. Zalta (ed.), *Stanford Encyclopedia of Philosophy*, http://plato.stanford.edu/entries/grounding/.
Boehme, J. (2010) "Life Beyond the Senses," in *Genius of the Transcendent*, trans. M. L. Birkel and J. Bach. Boulder, CO: Shambhala.
Borges, J. L. (1964) *Labyrinths: Selected Stories and Other Writings*, ed. D. A. Yates and J. E. Irby. New York: New Directions.
Borges, J. L. (1970) *Dreamtigers*, trans. M. Boyer and H. Morland. New York: Dutton.

Borges, J. L. (1971) *The Aleph and Other Stories*, ed. and trans. N. T. di Giovanni. New York: Bantam.
Brandom, R. (2015) *From Empiricism to Expressivism: Brandom Reads Sellars*. Cambridge, MA: Harvard University Press.
Brassier, R. (2013) "Nominalism, Naturalism and Materialism: Sellars's Critical Ontology," in B. Bashour and H. D. Muller (eds), *Contemporary Philosophical Naturalism and its Implications*. London: Routledge, pp. 101–14.
Buchheim, T. (ed.) (2018) *Jahrbuch-Kontroversen 3: Nicholas Rescher: Why is There Anything at All?*. Freiburg: Alber.
Bunt, H. C. (1985) *Mass Terms and Model Theoretic Semantics*. Cambridge: Cambridge University Press.
Carnap, R. (1950) "Empiricism, Semantics, and Ontology," *Revue Internationale de Philosophie* 4/11: 20–40.
Carnap, R. ([1932] 1959) "The Elimination of Metaphysics through Logical Analysis of Language," trans. A. Pap, in A. J. Ayer (ed.), *Logical Positivism*. New York: Free Press, pp. 60–81.
Casati, F., and Priest, G. (2019) "Heidegger and Dōgen on the Ineffable," in H. Scott and G. S. Moss (eds), *The Significance of Indeterminacy: Perspectives from Asian and Continental Philosophy*. New York: Routledge, ch. 14.
Chalmers, D. J. (2009) "Ontological Antirealism," in D. J. Chalmers et al. (eds), *Metametaphysics: New Essays on the Foundations of Ontology*. Oxford: Clarendon Press, pp. 77–129.
Chisholm, R. M. (1973) "Parts as Essential to Their Wholes," *Review of Metaphysics* 26/4: 581–603.
Chisholm, R. M. (1975) "Mereological Essentialism: Some Further Considerations," *Review of Metaphysics* 28/3: 477–84.
Cook, F. H. (1977) *Hua-yen Buddhism: The Jewel Net of Indra*. University Park, PA: Pennsylvania State University Press.
Cotnoir, A., and Bacon, A. (2012) "Non-Well-Founded Mereology," *Review of Symbolic Logic* 5: 187–204.
Cotnoir, A., and Varzi, A. (2021) *Mereology*. Oxford: Oxford University Press.
DeLanda, M. (2006) *A New Philosophy of Society: Assemblage Theory and Social Complexity*. New York: Continuum.
Ennis, P. (2011) *Continental Realism*. London: Zero Books.
Ferraris, M. (2016) "A Brief History of New Realism," *Filozofija i Društvo* 27/3: 591–609.
Frank, M. (2004) *Philosophical Foundations of German Romanticism*, trans. E. M. Zaibert. Albany, NY: SUNY.
Gabriel, M. (2009) *Skeptizismus und Idealismus in der Antike*. Frankfurt am Main: Suhrkamp.

Gabriel, M. (2014a) "Die Ontologie der Prädikation in Schellings *Die Weltalter*," *Schelling-Studien: Internationale Zeitschrift zur klassischen deutschen Philosophie* 2: 3–20.
Gabriel, M. (2014b) "Existenz, realistisch gedacht," in Gabriel (ed.), *Der Neue Realismus*. Berlin: Suhrkamp, pp. 171–99.
Gabriel, M. (2015a) *Fields of Sense: A New Realist Ontology*. Edinburgh: Edinburgh University Press.
Gabriel, M. (2015b) "Neutral Realism," *The Monist* 98/2: 181–96.
Gabriel, M. ([2013] 2015c) *Why the World does not Exist*, trans. G. Moss. Cambridge: Polity.
Gabriel, M. (2016a) *Sinn und Existenz: Eine realistische Ontologie*. Berlin: Suhrkamp.
Gabriel, M. (2016b) "Metaphysik oder Ontologie?," *Perspektiven der Philosophie: Neues Jahrbuch* 42: 73–93.
Gabriel, M. (2018a) *Neo-Existentialism: How to Conceive of the Human Mind after Naturalism's Failure*, with contributions by J. Maclure, J. Benoist, A. Kern, and C. Taylor. Cambridge: Polity.
Gabriel, M. (2018b) "Grenzen des Realismus? Neuere sprachphilosophische Einwände gegen den semantischen Realismus," in E. Felder and A. Gardt (eds), *Wirklichkeit oder Konstruktion: Sprachtheoretische und interdisziplinäre Aspekte einer brisanten Alternative*. Berlin: DeGruyter, pp. 45–64.
Gabriel, M. (2018c) "Être vrai," *Philosophiques* 45/1: 239–47.
Gabriel, M. (2020a) *The Limits of Epistemology*, trans. A. Englander. Cambridge: Polity.
Gabriel, M. (2020b) *The Meaning of Thought*. Cambridge: Polity.
Gabriel, M. (2020c) *The Power of Art*. Cambridge: Polity.
Gabriel, M. (2020d) *Fiktionen*. Berlin: Suhrkamp.
Gabriel, M. (2020e) "Saying What is Not," in D. Finkelde and P. M. Livingston (eds), *Idealism, Relativism, and Realism: New Essays on Objectivity Beyond the Analytic–Continental Divide*. Boston: DeGruyter, pp. 217–32.
Gabriel, M. (forthcoming a) "Cosmological Idealism," in J. R. Farris and B. P. Göcke (eds), *Rethinking Idealism and Immaterialism*. London: Routledge.
Gabriel, M. (forthcoming b) "Die Metaphysik als Denken des Ungegenständlichen," in M. Gabriel and T. Dangel (eds), *Metaphysik und Religion: Festschrift für Jens Halfwassen zum 60. Geburtstag*. Tübingen: Mohr Siebeck.
Gabriel, M. (forthcoming c) "Gadamer and New Realism," in T. George and G.-J. van der Heiden (eds), *The Gadamerian Mind*. London: Routledge.

Gabriel, M., and Krüger, M. D. (2018) *Was ist die Wirklichkeit? Neuer Realismus und hermeneutische Theologie*. Tübingen: Mohr Siebeck.
Gaitsch, P., Lehmann, S., and Schmidt, P. (eds) (2017) *Eine Diskussion mit Markus Gabriel: Phänomenologische Positionen zum Neuen Realismus*. Vienna: Turia + Kant.
Gironi, F. (2018) "Introduction," in F. Gironi (ed.), *The Legacy of Kant in Sellars and Meillassoux*. London: Routledge, pp. 1–20.
Gödel, K. (1995) "The Modern Development of the Foundations of Mathematics in the Light of Philosophy," in K. Gödel, *Collected Works*, vol. III: *Unpublished Essays and Lectures*, ed. S. Fefermann et al. Oxford: Oxford University Press, pp. 374–87.
Grim, P. (1991) *The Incomplete Universe: Totality, Knowledge, and Truth*. Cambridge, MA: MIT Press.
Halfwassen, J. (2005) *Hegel und der spätantike Neuplatonismus: Untersuchungen zur Metaphysik des Einen und des Nous in Hegels spekulativer und geschichtlicher Deutung*. 2nd edn, Hamburg: Meiner.
Heath, P. (1967) "Nothing," in P. Edwards (ed.), *Encyclopedia of Philosophy*. London: Macmillan, vol. 5, pp. 524–5.
Hegel, G. W. F. (1984) *Lectures on the Philosophy of Religion*, trans. R. F. Brown, P. C. Hodgson, and J. M. Stewart. Berkeley: University of California Press.
Hegel, G. W. F. (2001) "Vorlesung 10," in *Vorlesungen Ueber die Logik: Berlin 1831*. Hamburg: Meiner.
Hegel, G. W. F. (2015) *Science of Logic*, trans. G. Di Giovanni. Cambridge: Cambridge University Press.
Heidegger, M. (1962) *Being and Time*, trans. J. Macquarrie and E. Robinson. Oxford: Blackwell.
Heidegger, M. (1977) *Martin Heidegger: Basic Writings*, ed. D. F. Krell. New York: Harper & Row.
Heidegger, M. (1992) *The Metaphysical Foundations of Logic*, trans. M. Heim. Bloomington: Indiana University Press.
Heidegger, M. (2000) *Introduction to Metaphysics*, trans. G. Fried and R. Polt. New Haven, CT: Yale University Press.
Hill, J. (2017) "Markus Gabriel Against the World," *Sophia* 56/3: 471–81.
Holmes, M. R. (2017) "Alternative Axiomatic Set Theories," in E. Zalta (ed.), *Stanford Encyclopedia of Philosophy*, https://plato.stanford.edu/entries/settheory-alternative/.
Hume, David (1999) *An Enquiry Concerning Human Understanding*, ed. Tom L. Beauchamp. Oxford: Oxford University Press.
Hurley, A. (ed.) (2000) *The Aleph*. London: Penguin Books.

Ibn Al Arabi (1980) "The Wisdom of Divinity in the Word of Adam," in *The Bezels of Wisdom*, trans. R. W. J. Austin. Mahwah, NJ: Paulus Press.

James, William (1982) *The Varieties of Religious Experience*. London: Penguin.

Kant, I. (1998) *Critique of Pure Reason*, ed. and trans. P. Guyer and A. Wood. Cambridge: Cambridge University Press.

Koch, A. F. (2016) *Hermeneutischer Realismus*. Tübingen: Mohr Siebeck.

Kreis, G. (2015) *Negative Dialektik des Unendlichen: Kant, Hegel, Cantor*. Berlin: Suhrkamp.

Maudlin, T. (1998) "Part and Whole in Quantum Mechanics," in E. Castellani (ed.), *Interpreting Bodies*. Princeton, NJ: Princeton University Press, pp. 46–60.

McDaniel, K. (2017) *The Fragmentation of Being*. Oxford: Oxford University Press.

Meillassoux, Q. (2008) *After Finitude: An Essay on the Necessity of Contingency*. London: Continuum.

Meinong, A. (1960) "The Theory of Objects," in R. M. Chisholm (ed.), *Realism and the Background of Phenomenology*. Glencoe, IL: Free Press, pp. 76–117.

Meister Eckhart (1981) "Sermon 52" and "On Detachment," in *The Essential Sermons, Commentaries, Treatises, and Defense*, trans. E. Colledge and B. McGinn. Mahwah, NJ: Paulist Press, pp. 199–203.

Moss, G. S. (2018) "The Emerging Philosophical Recognition of the Significance of Indeterminacy," in R. Scott and G. S. Moss (eds), *The Significance of Indeterminacy*. New York: Routledge, pp. 1–38.

Moss, G. S. (2020) *Hegel's Foundation Free Metaphysics: The Logic of Singularity*. New York: Routledge.

Moss, G. S. (2021) "Negative Realism," in J. Rasmussen and C. Asmuth (eds), *Das Problem des Anfangs*. Königshausen & Neumann.

Moss, G. S. (forthcoming) "Absolute Dialetheism," in O. Bueno and J. Voosholz (eds), *On Markus Gabriel's New Realism*. New York: Springer.

Nagarjuna (1995) *The Fundamental Wisdom of the Middle Way*, trans. J. Garfield. Oxford: Oxford University Press.

Nishida, K. (1993) *Last Writings: Nothingness and the Religious Worldview*, trans. D. L. Dilworth. Honolulu: Hawaii University Press.

Noys, B. (2010) *The Persistence of the Negative*. Edinburgh: Edinburgh University Press.

Núñez-Faraco, H. (1997) "In Search of *The Aleph*: Memory, Truth, and Falsehood in Borges's Poetics," *Modern Language Review* 92/3: 613–29.

Parsons, T. (1980) *Nonexistent Objects*. New Haven, CT: Yale University Press.
Penrose, R. (1989) *The Emperor's New Mind: Concerning Computers, Minds, and the Laws of Physics*. Oxford: Oxford University Press.
Plato (1996) *Parmenides*, trans. Albert Keith Whitaker. Newburyport, MA: Focus Philosophical Library.
Plato (1997) *Complete Works*, ed. J. M. Cooper. Indianapolis: Hackett.
Priest, G. (1995) *Beyond the Limits of Thought*. Oxford: Oxford University Press.
Priest, G. (1997) "Sylvan's Box," *Notre Dame Journal of Formal Logic* 38: 573–582; repr. as §6.6 of Priest (2016).
Priest, G. (1998) "What is So Bad about Contradictions?," *Journal of Philosophy* 95/ 8: 410–26.
Priest, G. (2002) *Beyond the Limits of Thought*. 2nd edn, Oxford: Oxford University Press.
Priest, G. (2006a) *In Contradiction*. 2nd edn, Oxford: Oxford University Press.
Priest, G. (2006b) *Doubt Truth to be a Liar*. Oxford: Oxford University Press.
Priest, G. (2007) Review of A. Rayo and G. Uzquiano (eds), *Absolute Generality* (2006), *Notre Dame Philosophical Reviews* 2007.09.17, https://ndpr.nd.edu/reviews/absolute-generality/.
Priest, G. (2008) *Introduction to Non-Classical Logic: From If to Is*. Cambridge: Cambridge University Press.
Priest, G. (2014a) "Much Ado about Nothing," *Australasian Journal of Logic* 11, Article 4, http://ojs.victoria.ac.nz/ajl/issue/view/209.
Priest, G. (2014b) *One: Being an Investigation into the Unity of Reality and of its Parts, including the Singular Object which is Nothingness*. Oxford: Oxford University Press.
Priest, G. (2014c) "Sein Language," *The Monist* 97/4: 430–42.
Priest, G. (2016) *Towards Non-Being: The Logic and Metaphysics of Intentionality*. 2nd edn, Oxford: Oxford University Press.
Priest, G. (2018a) *The Fifth Corner of Four: An Essay on Buddhist Metaphysics and the Catuskoti*. Oxford: Oxford University Press.
Priest, G. (2018b) "Some New Thoughts on Conditionals," *Topoi* 27: 369–77.
Priest, G. (2019) "Objects that are Not Objects," in M. Szatkowski (ed.), *Quo Vadis Metaphysics? Essays in Honor of Peter van Inwagen*. Berlin: De Gruyter, pp. 217–29.
Priest, G. (2020) "Imagination, Non-Existence, Impossibility," in S. N. Mousavian and J. Fink (eds), *The Internal Senses in the Aristotelian Tradition*. New York: Springer, pp. 157–65.
Pseudo-Dionysius (1987) "The Divine Names," in *The Complete Works*

of *Pseudo-Dionysius*, trans. C. Luibheid. Mahwah, NJ: Paulist Press, pp. 47–133.

Quine, W. V. O. (1948) "On What There Is," *Review of Metaphysics* 2/5: 21–38.

Rayo, A., and Uzquiano, G. (eds) (2006) *Absolute Generality*. Oxford: Oxford University Press.

Redding, P. (2007) *Analytic Philosophy and the Return of Hegelian Thought*. Cambridge: Cambridge University Press.

Rödl, S. (2018) *Self-Consciousness and Objectivity: An Introduction to Absolute Idealism*. Cambridge, MA: Harvard University Press.

Rorty, R. (1997) "Introduction," in W. Sellars, *Empiricism and the Philosophy of Mind*. Cambridge, MA: Harvard University Press, pp. 1–12.

Routley, R. (2018) *Exploring Meinong's Jungle and Beyond: The Sylvan Jungle*, vol. 1, ed. M. Eckert. Cham: Springer Nature Switzerland.

Sachs, C. (2018) "Speculative Materialism or Pragmatic Naturalism," in F. Gironi (ed.), *The Legacy of Kant in Sellars and Meillassoux*. New York: Routledge, pp. 85–106.

Schelling, F. W. J. (2006) *Investigations into the Essence of Human Freedom*, trans. J. Love and J. Schmidt. Albany: SUNY.

Schleiermacher, F. (1996) *On Religion: Speeches to its Cultured Despisers*, trans. Richard Crouter. Cambridge: Cambridge University Press.

Sellars, W. S. (1963) *Science, Perception and Reality*. London: Routledge & Kegan Paul.

Tahko, T. E., and Lowe, E. J. (2015) "Ontological Dependence," in E. Zalta (ed.), *Stanford Encyclopedia of Philosophy*, http://plato.stanford.edu/entries/dependence-ontological/.

Thiem, J. (1988) "Borges, Dante, and the Poetics of Total Vision," *Comparative Literature* 40/2: 97–121.

Thomasson, A. L. (2014) *Ontology Made Easy*. Oxford: Oxford University Press.

Vaihinger, H. (1922) *The Philosophy of the "As If": A System of the Theoretical, Practical and Religious Fictions of Mankind*. London: Routledge.

Varzi, A. (2009) "Mereology," in E. Zalta (ed.), *Stanford Encyclopedia of Philosophy*, http://plato.stanford.edu/entries/mereology.

Wagner, R. (2003) *A Chinese Reading of the Daodejing: Wang Bi's Commentary on the Laozi with Critical Text and Translation*. Albany: SUNY Press.

Wigglesworth, J. (2013) *Metaphysical Dependence and Set Theory*, PhD thesis, CUNY Graduate Center.

Wigglesworth, J. (2015) "Set-Theoretic Dependence," *Australasian*

Journal of Logic 12/3, https://ojs.victoria.ac.nz/ajl/article/view/2131/3276.

Williamson, T. (2003) "Everything," *Philosophical Perspectives* 17: 415–65.

Wittgenstein, L. (1999) *Tractatus*, trans. C. K. Ogden. Mineola, NY: Dover.

Wolfendale, P. (2014) *Object-Oriented Philosophy: The Noumenon's New Clothes*. Falmouth: Urbanomic.

Zalta, E. N. (1983) *Abstract Objects: An Introduction to Axiomatic Metaphysics*. Dordrecht: D. Reidel.

Zalta, E. N. (1988) *Intensional Logic and the Metaphysics of Intentionality*. Cambridge, MA: MIT Press.

Zipfel, F. (2001) *Fiktion, Fiktivität, Fiktionalität: Analysen zur Fiktion in der Literatur und zum Fiktionsbegriff in der Literaturwissenschaft*. Berlin: Schmidt.

Žižek, S. (2016) "Afterword: Objects, Objects Everywhere," in A. Hamza and F. Ruda (eds), *Slavoj Žižek and Dialectical Materialism*. New York: Palgrave, pp. 177–92.

Index

Abhidharma tradition 123
absence of objects 138, 139
   and nothing(ness) 158, 159, 160,
      162, 163, 164–5, 166, 167,
      183
   Absolute Dialetheism 54, 170, 189
absolutism, ontological 64
actuality, implied, and conceivability
      171, 172, 177, 181, 182–3,
      184, 188
"The Aleph" 41, 42–54
   Borges' character 27, 51–2, 70–1,
      83–5
   characterization 41, 46, 61
   Daneri 44–6, 51n39, 52
   "false Aleph" 51, 84
   and field of sense (FOS/fos) 51,
      174–5
   fiction 41, 42–3, 45, 47, 51
   incoherency 46–7, 53, 71, 84
   and world 41–2, 43, 70, 84
Alexander's dictum 99
all-inclusivity 161, 173, 185n128
anti-symmetry 85, 120
   and gluons 156, 157–8
   and parts 27, 70, 71, 108, 121,
      157n21
   and set theory 47–8, 133
apple example 76, 90
Aristotle 115, 124
arithmetic, axiomatic theory of 72, 87
art example 107–8, 122
Atlantis example 136–7

Australia example 19–20, 22, 59

Bacon, A. 27
Badiou, Alain 26, 49
becoming 2
Beethoven's 9th Symphony example
   22
being
   definition 169
   and everything 153, 156, 158, 168,
      169
   and Gabriel 156, 169
   and Heidegger 34, 37n50
   and identity 157, 165, 175–6
   and nothing(ness) 37n50, 143, 165,
      170, 183
   and objects 34, 41, 61, 62–3,
      154–5, 166–7
   and the One 154, 185
   world as 158, 169
Boehme, Jakob 167
Boolean Algebra 27, 138
Borges, J. L. 28, 41–3, 47, 51–2,
   70–1, 83–5
   Borges character 44, 84
   see also "The Aleph"
Bradley regress 119
Brandom, Robert 5
Brassier, Ray 7–8
Buddhism 5, 68, 123, 187
   Abhidharma tradition 123
   Huayan philosophy 6, 28n19, 82,
      94

Madhyamaka thought 81–2, 94, 153, 187
Buenos Aires 45, 46
bundle theory 88, 118–19

Cantor, Georg 89
Carnap, Rudolf 24, 40
Carroll, Lewis, example 25
causality 99, 100, 102–3, 137, 169
Chalmers, David 102, 114
characterization
 "The Aleph" 41, 46, 61
 and everything 154–5, 158
 and field of sense 60, 61, 72, 85, 103–4, 123
 and nothing(ness) 31, 141, 142, 144–5
 and objects 22, 23, 76, 90–1, 144
Characterization Principle (CP) 60–1
Chinese philosophy 5, 68, 82, 94, 105
Christianity 33, 100
closure 160
cognitive state 30
conceivability and implied actuality 171, 172, 177, 181, 182–3, 184, 188
conditionals 32–3, 34
consciousness 11, 12, 14, 113, 117
context 23, 25, 105–6
contextualism, object theoretical 61
contradiction 1–3
 contradictory entities/objects 1–3, 79n21, 136, 138, 161, 172
 and everything 153, 155, 156–7, 159–61
 Gabriel 141, 153, 172–3
 and nothing(ness) 31–3, 141, 142, 144, 159–65
 and objects 1–3, 138, 162–3
 see also dialetheism
Copernican revolution (Kant) 13, 14
correlationism 5
Cotnoir, A. 27
counterfactuals 34–5, 77, 117

Daneri, Carlos (character in "The Aleph") 44–6, 51n39, 52
Davidson, Donald Herbert 117
DeLanda, Manuel 10
descriptions 116, 117, 122
dialecticality 93, 162, 164, 185, 186
dialetheism 153
 Absolute Dialetheism 167
  Gabriel 53, 170, 188, 189
  Moss 53–4, 79, 161, 169, 170, 176, 185n130, 188–9
 and everything 157, 158, 159–60
 Gabriel 53–4, 79n21, 101, 148, 170, 172, 188, 189
 Priest 154–68, 172
 see also contradiction
differentiation 166–7, 175–6
domains 42, 77–8, 91, 103
 domain of quantification 77–8, 131
Doyle, Arthur Conan 77–8, 117
 see also Holmes, Sherlock, example
dualism 6, 137

Eleatic riddle 59
electrons example 27
emptiness 81–2, 94–5, 145–7, 166n57
 empty field 139, 141, 142, 145, 146
essentialism, mereological 49, 73–4, 91
everything (e) 19–38, 39–68, 69–82, 83–95, 153–89
 absolutely everything 13, 78, 128–9
 Gabriel 40, 41, 47, 52–3, 60, 68, 86, 93
 and being 153, 156, 158, 168, 169
 and characterization 154–5, 158
 and contradiction 153, 155, 156–7, 159–61
 and dialetheism 157, 158, 159–60
 and existence 136–7, 144, 180–1
 and field of sense 27–9, 132–3
 and anti-symmetry 156, 157–8
 fusion of objects 26, 40, 69, 76, 80, 123, 156, 159–61, 166
 and gluons 154–8, 161, 165–6, 168

everything (e) (*cont.*)
   and loops 47–8, 54, 55, 113
   and objects 68, 70, 88–9, 120–1, 122
   and parts (of a whole) 71, 73, 93, 106, 121, 157–8
   and wholes 86, 106, 136–7, 157
   and intentionality 29–31, 92–4
   and meaninglessness 133, 134–5, 168–89
   mega-object everything 6, 10
   and nothing(ness) 144, 159–61, 165–6, 168
   and objects 136–7
     and field of sense 68, 70, 88–9, 120–1, 122
     fusion of objects 26, 40, 69, 76, 80, 123, 156, 159–61, 166
     and gluons 155–7, 161
     as ideal or real object 62–3, 77, 91
     and set theory 47–8, 87
     and totality 156–7, 168–9, 180
     and unity/unification 155, 167
     and Wittgenstein 133, 134–5
     and world 29–31, 66, 90–2, 122, 168, 181–8
   see also being; world
existence 20–1, 99–109, 170–9
   definition 105, 169, 175, 176
   and everything 136–7, 144, 180–1
   and field of sense 12–13, 61, 101, 170–9
   and objects 83, 99, 105–6, 130, 171
   and quantification 130, 180–1
   and world 72, 184
   and grounding 143, 144, 176–80
   and identity 115, 175–6
   and nothing(ness) 35–6, 61, 144, 170, 183
   and objects 99–100, 117, 136–7, 172–3
     and field of sense 83, 99, 105–6, 130, 171
     non-existing objects 20, 137, 175
   and proper properties 170–1, 175–6
   and Sherlock Holmes 101, 102–3, 144
   and totality 56, 172–3, 174, 177
     and world 56, 173, 174, 177
   and truth 105–6, 181, 182
   and wholes 136–7, 174
   and world 43, 78–80, 91, 169–70, 172–3, 182
     and dialecticality 93, 162, 164, 185, 186
     and field of sense 72, 184
     and totality 56, 173, 174, 177
   see also objects, non-existing
expressibility "objection" 66
exteriority, relations of 10

falsity 115
Faust example 53
Fazang 82, 167
Ferraris, Maurizio 4
fiction 70
   fictional objects 43–6, 53, 117
     and field of sense 83–4, 101–3
fiction, instructive 58, 62
fictionalism, metametaphysical 43, 58, 62
field, empty 139, 141, 142, 145, 146
field of sense (FOS/fos) 11–12, 29n22, 50n35, 83, 88–9, 101–9
   and characterization 60, 61, 72, 85, 103–4, 123
   definition 103–7
   and emptiness 139, 141, 142, 145–7
   and everything 27–9, 132–3
     and anti-symmetry 156, 157–8
     fusion of objects 26, 40, 69, 76, 80, 123, 156, 159–61, 166
     and gluons 154–8, 161, 165–6, 168
     and loops 47–8, 54, 55, 113
     and objects 68, 70, 88–9, 120–1, 122
     and parts (of a whole) 71, 73, 93, 106, 121, 157–8

and wholes 86, 106, 136–7, 157
and existence 12–13, 61, 101, 170–9
and objects 83, 99, 105–6, 130, 171
and quantification 130, 180–1
and fiction 70
and "The Aleph" 41, 42–3, 45, 47, 51, 174–5
fictional objects 83–4, 101–3
and intension 48–9, 73, 85, 88, 104, 106
and mereological loops 27–8, 47–8, 54, 55, 113, 147–8
and nihilism 64, 65, 68
and nothing(ness) 95, 139, 143–4, 147–8
fusion of objects 31, 138, 144–5, 148, 160–1
and gluons 165–6, 168
and wholes 65, 81, 95, 167
and object theory 57–64
set theory 63, 82, 103–4, 133
and objects 14, 99, 114–18
and everything 68, 70, 88–9, 120–1
and existence 83, 99, 105–6, 130, 171
fictional objects 47–9, 70, 83–4, 101–3
and neo-Meinongian theory 61, 63
and parts (of a whole) 48, 157–8
and world 61, 70, 76
and self-containment 54, 71–2, 174–5
and totality 123–4, 156, 176
and world 55, 69, 122
and "The Aleph" 41–2, 43
and existence 72, 184
and objects 57, 61, 70, 76
world field 55, 56, 86, 87, 89, 90, 122
see also fusion of objects, mereological; gluons; parts (of a whole); wholes, mereological

field of sense, global 82
financial assistance 75
Frankel, Zermelo 77
Frege, Gottlob 90, 105, 112, 116, 118
furnishing function 42, 114, 123, 146
fusion of objects, mereological 52, 73
and everything 26, 40, 69, 76, 80, 123, 156, 159–61, 166
and nothing(ness) 31, 138, 144–5, 148, 160–1

Gabriel, Markus *see* everything (e); existence; field of sense (FOS/fos); no-world-view; nothing(ness) (n); world
"Gabriel!" story 147
Gibson, J. J. 4
gluons 12–13, 118
and everything 154–8
and anti-symmetry 156, 157–8
and nothing(ness) 165–6, 168
and objects 155–6, 161
God 99–100, 175–6, 185n128
Gödel's theorem 72, 87
God's-eye view 85, 126
grass 28, 54
Greece example 136–7
Greek philosophy 105–6
Grim, P. 89
grounding 45
and existence 143, 144, 176–80
ground of reality 3, 14, 34–7, 158, 161
non-ground 143, 168
and nothing(ness) 3, 14, 34–7, 158, 161, 162–3
and objects 160, 162–3, 167–8
gunk 27

Harman, Graham 4, 10, 11, 13
Hegel, Georg Wilhelm Friedrich 5, 40, 161, 175–6, 184
and nothing(ness) 8, 165
Heidegger, Martin 8, 36, 40, 187
and being 34, 37n50

Heidegger, Martin (cont.)
  and nothing(ness) 24–5, 31–2, 33,
    34, 36, 37n50, 142, 143
  and objects 36, 37n50
  and Priest 9, 33, 34, 36, 37n50
hill example 35–6
Hofstadter, Douglas 113
Holmes, Sherlock, example
  and existence 101, 102–3, 144
  as object 77–8, 82, 117, 144
  and intentionality 112, 140
Huayan philosophy 6, 28n19, 82, 94
Husserl, Edmund 21, 50n35, 105

Ibn Al Arabi 162n47
idealism, absolute 62
identity 86, 88, 107–9, 164–5
  and being 157, 165, 175–6
  and existence 115, 175–6
  and intentionality 112, 113, 115
  and objects 21, 59–60, 75, 82,
    85–6, 115
  and self-identity 31, 33, 60, 76,
    109, 141
identity conditions 49, 85, 91, 107
identity statements 59, 75, 90, 164,
  166
illusion 92–3, 141
imagination 43, 45, 46–7, 53
impressionist painting example 107
in-between 6, 8, 12
Inclosure Scheme 74–5, 89, 156–7,
  158–61
incoherency 65, 69
"The Aleph" 46–7, 53, 71, 84
India example 110
Indra, net of, example 82, 167
inductiveness 176–80
ineffability of nothing(ness) (n) 33–4,
  159, 163, 164, 187, 188
infinity 161, 164
intension 42, 48–9, 73, 85, 88, 104,
  106
intentionality 48–9, 73, 110–19, 124
  and everything 29–31, 92–4
  and identity 112, 113, 115

and nothing(ness) 139, 140, 146
and objects 110–12, 140
and thought 111, 113–14
isolationism, me-ontological 101

Kant, Immanuel 5, 8–9, 20, 67
  Copernican revolution 13, 14
  and objects 13, 14, 109
Kyoto School 168

ladders example 66, 80, 93, 134,
  186
Leśnewski, Stanisław 21
Lewis, David 123
Liebnizianism 109
limit concepts 3, 10, 14
logic, applied 87
loops, mereological 27–8, 47–8, 54,
  55, 113
love 143

Madam Butterfly opera example 27,
  82
Madhyamaka thought 81–2, 94, 153,
  187
mathematics 56, 72, 107
meaning 181–2, 187
meaninglessness
  and everything 168–89
  and Wittgenstein 133, 134–5
  and world 181–4, 185–8
  and nothing(ness) 65–6, 180–9
  noun phrases 29, 65–6
  "XCEANNR$_{s12*}$" example 66, 80,
    134, 181, 182
mega-object everything 6, 10
Mehlich–Koch objection 42, 70, 83,
  84
Meillassoux, Quentin 1–2, 3
Meinong, Alexius 57, 62
Meinongianism 75, 92, 153, 171,
  182–3
  neo-Meinongian theory 55, 57–64,
    83
  see also noneism
mental state 59, 62, 113–14, 124

mereology 21–3, 73–5, 88–9
  see also field of sense (FOS/fos); fusion of objects, mereological; loops, mereological; parts (of a whole); pluralism; wholes, mereological
Merkel, Angela, example 110, 111, 112–13, 117, 130
mind-dependency 62, 63
Moss, Gregory S. 67, 68, 125–6, 139
  Absolute Dialetheism 53–4, 79, 161, 169, 170, 176, 185n130, 188–9
  mystical 53, 67, 134, 185
mysticism 90, 180–9

Nagarjuna paradox 166n57, 187
nature/naturalism 153
negation 9, 115, 183
  self-negation 164, 165, 168, 175
Neo-Kantian tradition 5
Neo-Platonism 67–8, 185
New Realism 3–4, 12
nihilism, metametaphysical 41, 64–8, 182, 184
Nishida Kitarō 113, 168
no-world-view 177
  Gabriel's defense 84, 85, 87, 92
  Priest's attack 40, 41–64, 65, 71–2, 79
non-existence see objects, non-existing
non-ground 143, 168
non-wellfoundedness 120–8, 133, 148
noneism 20, 23, 75–8, 83, 89–92
  see also objects, non-existing
nonsense 93–4, 186
  "XCEANNR$_{s12*}$" 66, 80, 134, 181, 182
  see also meaninglessness
nothing, table of (Kant) 8–9
nothing(ness) (n) 8–9, 31–8, 138–49, 154–68
  absolute nothing(ness) 162–6, 167, 170, 183, 188
  and being 37n50, 143, 165, 170, 183

and characterization 31, 141, 142, 144–5
and contradiction 31–3, 141, 142, 144, 159–65
  contradictory entity 2, 3
  and objects 138, 162–3
  definition 138
and emptiness 81–2, 94–5, 145–7, 166n57
  empty field 139, 141, 142, 145, 146
and everything 144, 159–61, 165–6, 168
and existence 35–6, 61, 144, 170, 183
and field of sense 95, 139, 143–4, 147–8
  fusion of objects 31, 138, 144–5, 148, 160–1
  and gluons 165–6, 168
  and wholes 65, 81, 95, 167
and grounding 3, 14, 34–7, 158, 161, 162–3
and ground of reality 3, 14, 34–7, 158, 161
and Hegel 8, 165
and Heidegger 24–5, 31–2, 33, 34, 36, 37n50, 142, 143
and ineffability 33–4, 159, 163, 164, 187, 188
and intentionality 139, 140, 146
and meaninglessness 65–6, 180–9
and nihilism 41, 64–8, 182, 184
and objects 31–2, 140–8, 158–68, 188
  and absence of objects 158, 159, 160, 162, 163, 164–5, 166, 167, 183
  and contradiction 138, 162–3
  fusion of objects 31, 81–2, 138, 144–5, 148, 160–1
  as paradoxical object 19, 138, 140
and reality 139
  ground of 3, 14, 34–7, 158, 161

nothing(ness) (**n**) (*cont.*)
   and self-negation 164, 165, 168, 175
   and world 170, 187, 188
     no-world-view 40, 41–64, 65, 71–2, 79
noun phrases 24, 29, 40, 65–6
numbers example 118

object theory 114
   bundle theory 88, 118–19
   neo-Meinongian theory 55, 57–64
   set theory 26, 31, 49
     and anti-symmetry 47–8, 133
     and everything 47–8, 87
     and field of sense 63, 82, 103–4, 133
     set of objects 61, 76–7, 91
     Zermelo–Fraenkel set theory (ZF) 26, 132–3
objectivity, unrestricted 64
objects 13–14, 19–25, 40
   absence of objects 138, 139
     and nothing(ness) 158, 159, 160, 162, 163, 164–5, 166, 167, 183
   and being 34, 41, 61, 62–3, 154–5, 166–7
   and characterization 22, 23, 76, 90–1, 144
   and contradiction
     contradictory entities/objects 2, 3, 79n21, 136, 138, 161, 172
     nothing(ness) 138, 162–3
   definition 19–20, 59, 104–5, 131
   and everything 120–1, 136–7
     and field of sense 68, 70, 88–9, 120–1, 122
     fusion of objects 26, 40, 69, 76, 80, 123, 156, 159–61, 166
     and gluons 155–7, 161
     as ideal or real object 62–3, 77, 91
   and existence 99–100, 117, 136–7, 173
     and field of sense 83, 99, 105–6, 130, 171
     non-existing objects 20, 137, 175
   and field of sense 14, 63, 114–18
     and everything 68, 70, 88–9, 120–1
     and existence 83, 99, 105–6, 130, 171
     fictional objects 70, 83–4, 101–3
   and parts (of a whole) 48, 157–8
   and world 61, 70, 76
   fusion of objects 52, 73
     and everything 26, 40, 69, 76, 80, 123, 156, 159–61, 166
     and nothing(ness) 31, 81–2, 138, 144–5, 148, 160–1
   and gluons 155–7, 161
   and grounding 160, 162–3, 167–8
   and Heidegger 36, 37n50
   and identity 21, 59–60, 75, 82, 85–6, 115
     self-identity 31, 33, 76, 109, 141
   and intentionality 110–12, 140
   and Kant 13, 14, 109
   and nothing(ness) 31–2, 140–5, 159–68, 188
     fusion of objects 31, 81–2, 138, 144–5, 148, 160–1
   and representations 13, 30, 48, 66–7, 79–80, 92
   totality of 93, 126–7, 145, 157
   unity of objects 166, 180, 185n130
   and wholes 82, 104, 106, 156
   and world 57, 78–80, 90–2, 188
     and field of sense 57, 61, 70, 76
objects, *bona fide* 9, 19
objects, contradictory 2, 3, 79n21, 136, 138, 161, 172
objects, fictional 43–6, 53, 70, 117
   and field of sense 83–4, 101–3
   see also "The Aleph"; objects, non-existing
objects, hermeneutic 46, 53
objects, ideal 62–3, 77, 91
objects, logical 56, 72
objects, marginal 9

objects, metahermeneutic 46, 53
objects, mind-dependent 62–3
objects, non-existing 20, 23, 75–8, 83, 99–100, 140
   and existence 137, 175
   in Meinongianism 59, 60, 61
   see also noneism; objects, fictional
objects, paradoxical 19, 138, 140
objects, real 62–3, 77, 91
objects, relative 173
objects, sets of 61, 76–7, 91, 115
objects, simple/saturated 112
objects, surprising 112
objects, vague 49
objects-for-themselves 11
One, the 67–8, 94
   and being 154, 185
ontology, flat 10–12, 118
ontology, negative 67
ontology, positive 67, 95
openness, hermeneutic 49n32
orders, theory of (Russell) 181n112

paradox
   and intentionality 113
   Nagarjuna paradox 166n57, 187
   paradoxical objects 19, 138, 140
Parmenides 6, 10, 154n3
parts, non-existing 137
parts (of a whole) 21–2, 29n22, 31n31
   and anti-symmetry 27, 70, 71, 108, 121, 157n21
   and everything 71, 73, 93, 106, 121, 157–8
   part–whole relations 48, 50, 74, 88–9, 121
   see also field of sense (FOS/fos); wholes, mereological
perception, philosophy of 4
philosophical experience 180
Plato 105, 153, 154
   Neo-Platonism 67–8, 185
Plotinus 67–8
pluralism 87, 88
   radical ontological 6, 68, 145

possibility 125–6
   conceptual 28, 42, 47, 52
   logical 125, 158
   ontological 125, 146, 162
predicatelessness 143
predication 19, 59, 163–4
presentation, modes of 42, 48, 103–4
presidents of the US example 142
Priest, Graham *see* anti-symmetry; being; contradiction; dialetheism; everything (e); field of sense (FOS/fos); Meinongianism; nothing(ness) (n)
Priest as a woman example 70, 84, 100
properties 23, 45–6, 76, 108–9, 114–16, 165, 166
   contradictory 46, 142
   non-determining 128, 129–30
   proper 60, 109, 166
   and existence 170–1, 175–6
propositions 28, 54–7, 85–7, 174, 177
Pseudo-Dionysius 165n53, 185n128
pseudo-objects *see* objects, fictional

quantification 23–4
   existential 59, 64
   universal 64, 91–2, 128–33, 135, 178, 180
   unrestricted 39, 52, 64, 91–2
quantum theory example 132
quantum universe 49, 103–4
Quine, W. V. O. 39n2, 115

realism 4, 62, 116–17
   New Realism 3–4, 12
reality 49, 57, 139
   ground of 3, 14, 34–7, 158, 161
regress 28, 73
   of sense 6, 14
relations/relationships 82, 143
   part–whole relations 48, 50, 74, 88–9, 121
   relative dialetheism 53–4
relativism 171

religious experience 179–80
  see also God
relinquishment 187
representations 13, 30, 48, 66–7, 79–80, 92
Rorty, Richard 7
round squares example 172

Sai Kung Town, Honk Kong, example 162
Sartre, Jean-Paul 113
satori 81, 94
Schelling, F. W. 143, 144, 167, 168n66
Schleiermacher, Friedrich 179, 185n128
Scholze, Peter 124
self-consciousness 113
self-containment 54, 71–2, 174–5
self-differentiation 175–6
self-identity 31, 33, 60, 76, 109, 141
self-negation 164, 165, 168, 175
self-reference 113, 114, 163–4
Sellars, Wilfrid S. 55
sense 5–6, 114, 184
  regress of 6, 14
sense, field of see field of sense (FOS/fos)
senses 48–9, 103–4, 108, 115–18, 123–4
sentences 21, 24, 29–30, 54, 114
  atomic 24, 79, 92
set theory 31, 49, 133
  and anti-symmetry 47–8, 133
  bundle theory 88, 118–19
  and everything 47–8, 87
  and field of sense 63, 82, 103–4
  set of objects 61, 76–7, 91, 115
  Zermelo–Fraenkel set theory (ZF) 26, 132–3
sets 115
shadows 9, 35
snow 28, 54
spouse example 35
stories see "The Aleph"; fiction; objects, fictional

subatomic particles 12
Śūnyatā 94
Sylvan, Richard 20

temporal reality 49
Thiem, Jon 51n39
things 131
  see also objects
thought 111, 113–14, 116
time/temporality 49, 88, 89, 117–18
totality 64, 179–80
  and everything 156–7, 168–9, 180
  and existence 56, 173, 174, 177
  and inclosure 74–5, 89, 157
  of objects 74–5, 78, 93, 126–7, 145, 157
  and world 54, 55, 88, 168–9, 173–4, 175, 180, 188
  and existence 56, 173, 174, 177
totality, absolute 51, 52, 54–5, 56, 72
totality, additive 54, 88, 123
totality, unified
  and everything 168–9, 180
  and field of sense 123–4, 156, 176
  and world 54, 55, 88, 168–9, 173–4, 175, 180
  and existence 56, 173, 174
tragedy, bad 124
transcendence 52, 157, 160
trees example 35
trolls example 42
true/false noun phrases 29–30
true *simpliciter* 70, 79n21, 83, 101, 102, 103
truth 102
  and existence 105–6, 181, 182
  and meaning 171, 181–2, 184, 187–8
  truth conditions 171, 181–2, 184

unconcealment 187, 188
Unger, Peter 123
Ungrund see grounding
unicorns example 64, 102
uniformity 177, 178

Index

unity/unification 48, 64, 155–6
  and everything 155, 167
  unity of objects 166, 180, 185n130
  see also gluons
univocity 50, 111, 112

vagueness 88, 89
volcano example 118

wholes, mereological 6, 21–2, 48–52, 86, 124
  and everything 86, 106, 136–7, 157
  and existence 136–7, 174
  and nothing(ness) 65, 81, 95, 167
  and objects 82, 104, 106, 156
  part–whole relations 48, 50, 74, 88–9, 121
  world as 51–2, 63, 65, 67–8, 81, 108, 155, 179
  see also parts (of a whole)
Wittgenstein, Ludwig 33–4, 80, 133–5, 136, 186, 188
world 41–64, 102, 169–75, 181–8
  and "The Aleph" 41–2, 43, 70, 84
  and being 158, 169
  and dialecticality 93, 162, 164, 185, 186
  and domains 77–8, 91
  and everything 29–31, 66, 90–2, 122, 168, 181–8
  and existence 43, 78–80, 91, 169–70, 172–3, 182
  and dialecticality 93, 162, 164, 185, 186
  and field of sense 72, 184
  and totality 56, 173, 174, 177
  and field of sense 55, 69, 122
  and "The Aleph" 41–2, 43
  and existence 72, 184
  and objects 57, 61, 70, 76
  world field 55, 86, 87, 89, 90, 122
no-world-view 177
  Gabriel's defense 84, 85, 87, 92
  Priest's attack 40, 41–64, 65, 71–2, 79
  and nothing(ness) 170, 187, 188
  no-world-view 40, 41–64, 65, 71–2, 79
  and objects 78–80, 90–2, 188
  and field of sense 57, 61, 70, 76
  and totality 54, 55, 88, 168–9, 173–4, 175, 180, 188
  and existence 56, 173, 174, 177
  and wholes 51–2, 63, 65, 67–8, 81, 108, 155, 179
  see also everything (e)

"XCEANNR$_{s12*}$," 66, 80, 134, 181, 182

"Yellow Rose" 51

Zermelo–Fraenkel set theory (ZF) 26, 132–3
zombies example 171